*To the memory of my father, James McClure*
*For things left unsaid*

*And when the stream*
*Which overflowed the soul was passed away,*
*A consciousness remained that it has left*
*Deposited upon the silent shore*
*Of memory images and precious thoughts*
*That shall not die, and cannot be destroyed.*

— William Wordsworth

AUTHOR'S NOTE

A decade has passed since I wrote *Too Close to the Falls*, my child-

hood memoir that describes my life in the 1950s in the small

town of Lewiston, New York. I couldn't have imagined when I

was writing it that it would be the first volume of my memoirs,

but I seem to have an uncontrollable desire to chronicle my time on earth. Also, readers have been extremely kind about *Too Close to the Falls*. Many have written from all over the world sending well wishes and inquiring about what happened to me after my untimely liberation from Catholic school. Those letters not only encouraged me to continue to write, but challenged me to delve into my youth, both the wonderful and the painful parts, and to understand how that little girl who was born with what the nuns called "an Irish temper" managed to make it to adulthood.

There's no doubt that I had an unusual childhood, or I was an unusual child — I have never been sure which it was. One thing I am sure about is that the idiosyncrasies that began to develop in childhood only deepened in my teenage years.

At a young age I was sent to the doctor because my behaviour had been labelled as "too busy and too bossy." The pediatrician in turn added his clinical perspective, saying that I had "a metronome that ticked much faster than other people's," and the "cure" he recommended was a job. When my mother presented the doctor's orders to my father, he pointed out that it would be rather difficult for me to get a job at the age of four. However, the doctor was sacrosanct in the fifties and so my parents embarked upon a solution. My father said I could work before and after school in his drugstore. I had to learn how to read, and it would be my job to decipher the map for Roy, the black delivery car driver, who had never learned to read. Roy and I were a match made in heaven; he would drive and I would navigate. We toured the Niagara Frontier making deliveries from dawn until the coloured lights were turned on at the Falls at night. No one on God's earth had more adventures or just plain good times than Roy and I had in those years. Only after he disappeared one day did I realize how close we'd become.

As an only child I was also lucky to have wonderful parents who accepted me as I was. Though they were certainly unconventional — we never ate a meal at home, for example — I knew they loved me no matter how much trouble I got into. When I was sent home for doing an imitation of Ed Sullivan in grade four during Religious Instruction, my mother said that Sister Agnese had no sense of humour and that God was laughing his head off at heaven's gate. Over time this unqualified belief in me gave me a springboard to become whatever I wanted to be.

In 1960 my life changed dramatically. My family moved to Buffalo, and I would never again be known by everyone in town as the "pharmacist's daughter." I'd lost my job and my identity. Having to adjust to a new school was hard enough, but my greatest battle in the sixties was with my father. We had worked together side by side for most of my childhood and now, no longer co-workers, our relationship had to change. In many ways the trajectory of my life during that time mirrored what was happening in the sixties across North America. Residual fifties conservatism evolved into riots in the streets, all in a few years — and in my own life I experienced just as radical and tumultuous a transformation.

Writing a memoir is quite a high-wire act. I had to camouflage details to protect the privacy of many of the people represented here, and some scenes and dialogue had to be recreated all these years later. But I also made every effort to be as true as possible to my memories about the personalities and the incidents that occurred. I hope that I have achieved a balance, that I have conveyed the emotional truth of my experiences.

Memory is a tricky business. No two people remember things the same way. Memory is not a recording device; it is the brain's way of allowing us to select moments in order to *interpret* our pasts. All of the images on file in our brains pass through elaborate screens of unconscious needs and emerge as memories. This book is a telling of *my* story as I remember it.

*Catherine McClure Gildiner*
*June 2009*

# after the falls

PART 1

# Exodus

*I remember my youth and the feeling that will never come back anymore — the feeling that I could last for ever, outlast the sea, the earth, and all men; the deceitful feeling that lures us on to joys, to perils, to love, to vain effort — to death.*

— Joseph Conrad, *Youth*

CHAPTER 1

# <u>expulsion</u>

As we crept up the narrow winding road that rimmed the Niagara

Escarpment in our two-toned grey Plymouth Fury with its huge

fins and new car smell, my father pressed the push-button gear,

forcing the car to leap up the steep incline and out of our old life.

The radio was playing the Ventures' hit "Walk Don't Run."

I sat in the front seat with my father while my mother sat in the back with Willie, the world's most stupid dog. We were following the orange Allied moving van, and I kept rereading the motto on the back door: LEAVE THE WORRYING TO US. Two tall steel exhaust pipes rose in the air like minarets from both sides of the truck's cabin. Each had a flap that continually flipped open, belching black smoke and then snapping shut, like the mouth of Ollie, the dragon hand-puppet on the *Kukla, Fran and Ollie* television show. The smoke mouths kept repeating the same phrase in unison: *It's all your fault . . . it's all your fault.*

I pressed my face to the window as the car crawled up the hill in first gear. Lewiston, where I'd grown up, was slowly receding. The town was nestled against the rock cliff of the huge escarpment on one side and bordered by the Niagara River on the other. St. Peter's Catholic church spire, which cast such a huge shadow when you were in the town, was barely visible from up here.

The sun was resting on the limestone cliff, setting it ablaze. I squinted at the orange embers on the rock wall, but the reflection was so glaring, I had to look away. My childhood too had gone up in flames.

—

Yesterday I'd stood for the last time in my large bedroom with its wide-plank floor and blue toile wallpaper. My bed, which had been in my family for over 150 years, was now stripped naked, dismantled and propped against the wall. It was going to be left behind in our heritage home, no longer part of my heritage. My father said that the ceilings in our new house would not be high enough for the canopy. Where were we moving — a chicken coop?

I looked out my window at our sprawling yard and counted for the last time the thirteen old oak trees my ancestors had planted to celebrate the thirteen states in the union. The dozens of peony bushes near the wraparound porch had just opened. For generations now the church had taken flowers from our expansive gardens for the altar. I loved the part of the Mass when Father Flanagan would say, "Today's altar flowers are donated to the glory of God by the McClures."

As I loaded my new popcorn bobby socks into a box with my Lollipop underpants and turtleneck dickeys, I caught an unwelcome glimpse of myself in the mirror behind my door. I was twelve and very tall for my age, with white-blonde hair. I had no curves, not even in my calves. I resembled a Q-tip. When I'd told my mother I was hideous, she insisted that the early teenage years were an "awkward stage" and that soon I would "grow into myself" — whatever that meant.

I took a gilt-framed picture of my parents off my marble-topped dresser. It was an old photo of my father in his wool three-piece suit with his broad letterman grin, his arm casually draped around my lovely tall mother with her shy smile. It was taken years before I was born. Suddenly the words I'd overheard Delores, the cleaning lady, say to someone yesterday over the phone came back to me. She claimed it was a good thing that my mother only had one child, because two like me would have put her "in an early grave." As I glanced at the picture one more time before wrapping it in my eyelet slip, I realized how much my parents, who were in their forties when they had me, had aged. They now looked more like grandparents than parents.

As the car chugged toward the top of the escarpment, I, like Lot's wife, looked back at the town below me. I had no idea then that I was leaving behind the least-troubled years of my life. Strange, since I felt there was no way I could cause more trouble than I'd caused in Lewiston.

It was 1960. We were doing what millions of other people had done: we were migrating. The Okies had left the Dust Bowl for water and we were leaving Lewiston for what my mother had mysteriously described as "opportunities." Whatever the reason, we were leaving behind the chunk of rock that was a part of us.

What would I do in Buffalo in the summer heat? When I was working at my dad's store in Niagara Falls, I would wander over to the falls and get cooled off by the spray. I couldn't imagine not being near the rising clouds of mist that parted to reveal the perpetually optimistic rainbow.

What would my life be without the falls to ground me? Losing the falls was bad enough, but how could I leave the small, idyllic town of Lewiston, where history was around every corner? General Brock had been billeted in our house during the war of 1812. Our basement had been part of the Underground Railroad that smuggled black slaves to Canada. And would I ever again live somewhere where everyone knew me — where I knew who I was? I would no longer be the little girl who worked in her dad's drugstore. Roy, the delivery driver with whom I distributed drugs all over the Niagara Frontier, used to say if someone in Lewiston didn't know us, then they were "drifters."

———

Soon the escarpment was only a line in the distance, and Lewiston had disappeared. I would always remember it frozen in time:

the uneven bricks of Center Street under my feet; the old train track up the middle, worn down after not being used for almost a century; the Frontier House, the hotel where Dickens, James Fenimore Cooper and Lafayette stayed and the word *cocktail* was invented; the maple and elm trees that arched over the roads, and the Niagara River, with its swirling blue waters that snaked along the edge of town.

As we began to head south, I thought about the tightrope walker my mother and I had seen, years ago, inching across Niagara Falls carrying a long balance pole. We stood below on the lip of the escarpment, holding our breath. My mother kept her eyes shut and made me tell her what was happening.

I felt as though now, as I headed into my teenage years, it would take all I had to maintain my balance. I knew the secret was to never look down at the whirlpools below, to focus on a fixed point at eye level and keep moving. I had no idea then how much I would teeter when the winds of change in the 1960s got blowing.

My father swung the car onto a new divided highway that looked like a construction site with mounds of dirt by the side of the road. The journey had become so boring that I actually started listening to my parents' conversation. Sometimes I forgot that they too were moving to a new city and a new home. I tuned in just as my father was saying, "I know it is far less money, but when I looked up the census, I found that the average salary for 1960 is only between four and five thousand dollars."

"No one earns the average salary," my mother said.

This comment worried me because my mother was always unfailingly supportive of my father. No matter what he did, she acted like it was a stroke of genius and she was delighted to be part of the arrangement. I had never before felt tension between them. Suddenly it was as though someone had vacuum-packed the car.

In an effort to regain some air, I blurted out, "Are we moving because of me?"

"No," my mother said.

My father remained silent and pressed in the lighter to reignite his El Producto cigar, which was starting to make me carsick. He looked in the rear-view mirror at my mother, sending her a glance with an arched eyebrow. Clearly he disagreed with her.

She said, "Well, it is true that we think you would be happier in a larger place. The world seems to be aching to change a bit . . . and Lewiston is having growing pains."

"Change? What needs to change?" I asked.

"I don't mean change exactly; I just think we all need a broader scope," she said. "Different kinds of people — looking out at the world instead of closing the world out."

My father was still looking in the rear-view mirror, and although he barely moved a muscle, I could tell he was shocked that my mother was saying such things. He had no idea what in my mother's world could possibly need broadening.

When my father had announced the move, he said we were going for "new business prospects." He said that the economy had changed and that pretty soon there wouldn't be any more small, family-run drugstores. I had never thought our drugstore was small — I thought of it as enormous. He maintained that the world was being taken over by "chain stores." I didn't know what these were; I thought at first that he meant hardware stores that sold shackles. He explained how chain stores worked out better prices from the drug companies, how they didn't make specialty unguents and didn't deliver. Most of the work was done by pharmacy assistants. He could no longer compete; it was time to get out before we were forced out.

Did he really think these chain-type-stores would catch on? Had he forgotten about loyalty? I thought of all the times Roy and I had risked our lives delivering medication on roads with blowing snow and black ice, or worked after midnight to get someone insulin. It was my father who always said that customers would appreciate the service and be loyal. But just days ago, when I'd questioned him on this, he said that people could be fickle and that their loyalty was to the almighty dollar. All the service in the world couldn't keep a customer if Aspirin is cheaper elsewhere.

When I said that was terribly unfair, he pointed out that that was just human nature. People did what was best for themselves at any given time. I'd never heard him speak so harshly. He'd usually espoused kindness and "going the extra mile." He put his arm around me and said that the world was changing and it was best to move on. You couldn't stop progress. After all, America hailed the Model T; no one cried for the blacksmith.

As we drove along the ugly, detour highway, weaving between gigantic rust-coloured generators that obscured the view of the rock cliffs and the river, I asked why, since we must be getting near the city of Niagara Falls, we didn't see the silver mist of the falls spraying in the air like a geyser. My father told me the highway we were on was being built by Robert Moses (who would coincidentally name it the Robert Moses Parkway, though I never saw a park). Moses designed it so that tourists would be diverted from the downtown core of Niagara Falls and forced to drive by his monument of progress, the Niagara Power Project. No one would drive through the heart of Niagara Falls any more, which is where our drugstore was. My father predicted, accurately as it turned out, that the downtown would soon die.

—

After about a half-hour, my father circled off the New York State Thruway onto a futuristic round basket-weave exit marked Amherst. "Wait until you see how convenient this home is for getting on the highway and travelling," he said.

I wondered where we would be going since my father said travelling spread disease.

A minute later he swung into a suburban housing development with a sign that read KINGSGATE VILLAGE, and then onto Pearce Drive. When he turned into a driveway, I was too taken aback to say anything. In front of us was a tiny green clapboard bungalow with pink trim. All around it were identical houses with slightly different frontispieces. My father had picked out this place, but I felt his mortification at having to show it to us. It started to sink in that our historical colonial home with the huge wraparound porch was now history.

Why my mother had not been included in the house hunt was a mystery to me. It wasn't like she was busy. She'd never in my memory cooked, cleaned or held a job.

She was trying to find nice things to say. "Well, this should be easy to look after. No big yard to rake."

But I could feel her slowly withering, cell by disappointed cell.

A man in the next yard, which was hard to distinguish from our toupée of green turf, was outside cutting the lawn in his tank-style undershirt. Suspenders held up his pants, forming a kind of empire waistline directly under his surprisingly large breasts. He waved and said, "Howdy."

"Who is that — Humpty Dumpty?" I asked.

My mother shot me a look that said it was best not to make fun of anyone who would be our neighbour in what was to be our neighbourhood.

We got out of the car and I stood in the driveway, peering inside through the kitchen window. The floor had linoleum with a design of faux pebbles, the kind that would surround the moat if you lived next door to Sir Lancelot. The walls were covered in fake brick contact paper with fake ivy growing up it.

The moving van pulled up. As one mover chomped on a hoagie, the other jumped down from the cab, looked at the house and said to my father, "There's no way you are ever going to fit these huge pieces of furniture into this place. What am I supposed to do with them?" The front door was obviously too narrow for the French armoires and early American dressers.

My father said nothing. I had never seen him look as though he was not in charge. He just went and sat on the porch, which was actually a cement stoop. My mother, who'd inherited these antiques and cherished them, ordered the movers to unload everything onto the driveway. Then she said to my father, "Not to worry, Jim. Some of these things have been in my family for far too long. It's progress — we'll clear out some of it — deadwood."

I braced myself and followed my parents inside. My room was tiny, and now I knew why my father had said I couldn't bring my canopy bed. A single bed could barely fit in this cubbyhole. It was the size of my walk-in closet in Lewiston. Cheap cotton curtains printed with faded red Chinese pagodas adorned two small sliding aluminum windows that were too high to see out of. Since there was nothing else to look at, I went back to the living room, where my mother stood looking lost while my father was in the bathroom. Even with the door closed we heard everything, as though we were standing next to him. I just stared at the floor and so did my mother.

During the move the men broke a silver and marble ashtray, the kind that stood by an easy chair and opened like a yawn to swallow still-smouldering butts. My father said, "You'll pay for that. I'm making out a report on it right now and I'll be sure to mention your lack of care." It was unlike my father to get rattled and speak to people in an impolite tone.

Later, in the driveway, I overheard one mover, who wore his disdain in his every gesture, say to his partner, "The guy's worried about his precious ashtray?"

The other said, "He told me this place is just a stopover till his new split-level is finished."

The movers exchanged glances.

Once the weensy rooms were filled, my father, bewildered, stared at the ocean of antiques in the driveway. He said to my mother, "When I saw this place it was empty. I don't remember it being so small."

My mother refused to watch as the movers hoisted the furniture into the attic of the garage. Marble tabletops were removed with crowbars and stored in pieces. Most of the pieces would eventually warp from freezing temperatures and moisture. My parents would never sell them or look at them again.

———

My mother had inherited a large collection of historical lithographs of Niagara Falls that she had enhanced with her own acquisitions. She had spent much of my childhood going to auctions and purchasing lithographs from all over the world. In one antique lithograph journal her collection had been described as "stellar." She loved the scenes with Indians, as well as eighteenth-century ones in which European illustrators depicted their versions of explorers discovering Niagara Falls. About once a month she would get them all out and look at them. After we moved, knowing that these were relics from better times, I suggested she hang them up. She looked at me and said, "Where?"

Every once in a while there would be a flurry of activity as my father did some repulsive decorating. The basement had a rec room that the former owners had drywalled. As far as I could see the central feature was a dehumidifier. (The room always smelled of mould, so my mother called it the "reek room.") The first month we were there my father decided to build a bar, which was strange because neither he nor my mother ever drank. He used his old sliding glass pharmacy cabinets, which he dragged in from the garage, and decorated the bar with mortars and pestles left over from the drugstore. Since he didn't have any alcohol, he filled apothecary jars with coloured water and put them in the cabinets. He must have found a tavern that was going out of business, because he brought home signs like the one that said PINK LADY and had a picture of a pink cocktail with an olive in it perched at a rakish angle. He placed a dozen of these signs, with drink prices, in the display cases. I found the whole thing profoundly embarrassing — although how could it have been embarrassing when no one knew me yet? I guess it was just quietly humiliating. Back in Lewiston my parents had hosted an annual catered Christmas party, but I don't remember them having even one party in the reek room.

My father was always affable with the neighbours, talking over identical chain-link fences in the summer about chlorine tablets for above-ground pools and lawn mowers. Although my father was always friendly, most of the people on the street were younger. Our house was, as they say in the real estate world, "a starter home." Though for my parents it would be a finishing home — hardly bigger than the wooden caskets they would be carried out in.

In Lewiston my father had been used to giving out advice. People had come to him because he was the town pharmacist; he had a position in the church and community and he knew things. Here in Buffalo, people got advice from "Dear Abby." They weren't going to go to some washed-up old pharmacist. I noticed that he now exaggerated. I heard him telling a neighbour that I was New York State's high jumping champion, when in fact my title was only for *western* New York and my record was beaten before I even had a chance to get new track shoes.

My parents adapted to their new circumstances in their own way. My father bought a recliner in leatherette, smoked and watched television. He went to work for a large drug company. He described his research team as though it were the Manhattan Project; however, when I went to his building, which took up nearly a city block, people seemed to hardly know him.

My mother didn't do a thing with the house — she never even changed the carpets. She always acted like she was staying in a déclassé hotel. The only problem was that there was no room service. If she ever wondered how a college educated woman who was also a master bridge player wound up on Pearce Drive, she never once asked me.

Their new church was huge and they went unnoticed there. People didn't walk to church in Buffalo as they had in Lewiston. And no one waited around after church to go out together for brunch. Everyone drove to church and then, after Mass, they got in their cars and, with an altar boy directing traffic, filed out of the parking lot as though they were in a funeral procession.

—

Within the first few weeks of our arrival my mother and I began to venture out in our Plymouth Fury on reconnaissance missions. We decided to spread our wings a few blocks at a time. We needed to know exactly how bad it was. There were no sidewalks on the major streets, so we never saw people out strolling. The stores all had names that were so unoriginal as to be almost laughable. The convenience store was a chain called Your Convenience. The florist was called Flowers 'n' Things. Most of the stores were chains and seemed to be full of minimum-wage employees.

Once we ventured out of our cloned subdivision, which my mother and I clandestinely referred to as Tiny Town, I noticed that there was a positive correlation between distance away from Pearce Drive and how big the houses were. The majority were large, elegant brick homes with manicured lawns and built-in pools. Some were mansions with guest houses and elaborate gardens.

My father's decision to move to Tiny Town was slowly starting to make sense. When I was kicked out of Catholic school in Lewiston, Father Rodwick, the jejune Jesuit who had been my religious-instruction teacher, recommended the school in Amherst to my mother for its great advanced program. My father must have bought the only house he could afford in this swanky school district.

I had already missed the placement exam, which had been given before Father Rodwick spoke to my mother, so I would have to take it the following year. Father Rodwick thought he had seen an intellectual side of me. I studied philosophy like a fiend for him for three reasons: one, he was a great teacher; two, philosophy, unlike "religious instruction," was innately interesting; and, finally and most importantly, I had a crush on him and was convinced that the way to his heart was through his mind. I was, of course, wrong (this turned out to be a pattern). My best friend, Miranda, who not only didn't care about philosophy but barely knew how to read, had figured out within five minutes of meeting Father Rodwick that the best route to his heart was not through his brain. She ignored the labyrinthine road and took the direct path through his tender flesh. While I had been contemplating the mind–body problem, she'd solved it.

I felt a bit sorry for my parents. I knew I was not going to study any harder here than I had in the past. Father Rodwick thought he'd discovered someone with special intelligence. He was wrong. I was only experiencing a motivational blip. A girl will do anything to catch the eye of a handsome man. But there was no point in telling my parents about my prophecy of academic mediocrity. They would get the drift soon enough.

## CHAPTER 2

# a donnybrook

It was July and we'd been living in Tiny Town for a few weeks. I had no job or friends. As my mother said, "Nor do I."

While paging through a circular from the Amherst school system, my mother found out that there was a swimming class at the senior high school. I had never been a good swimmer. In grade three I had encouraged Trent McMaster to go down the Lewiston escarpment on his sled after an ice storm. He landed in a whirl-pool and went right under the Niagara River. He was rescued, but he got frostbite and lost some fingers. He was forever after called Stumpy McMaster. When parents in Lewiston wanted to warn their children against doing something stupid, they chided, *If Cathy McClure told you to go sledding over the escarpment, would you do it?*

I didn't much like swimming after that event. I could do it, but whenever I went underwater, I saw Trent's bloated jellyfish hand. Sometimes, when I saw seaweed, I'd imagine it was his digit turned green, swimming along on its own, looking for Stumpy, longing to reattach to him.

Although my mother never talked about it, I think she knew the origin of my fears. She suggested in an off-hand way that it would be a good idea to take swimming and diving lessons at the school in the summer, as she put it, "to be up and at 'em" for the mandatory fall swim program.

The information sheet said the school bus picked up kids at the corner of our street. It also said that in the boys' pool they wore no bathing suits. They swam in the nude. I started scream-ing, and my mother and I laughed so hard we almost fell over. She said it must be some sort of "homage to the Greeks." Girls had to wear bathing attire provided by the school. How disgusting was that? Mother tried to tell me that everyone had the same germs. I used one of my father's pharmacist lines, saying, "That sounds like a ladder to infection."

"Then stay home," she responded.

On the first morning I felt a nagging uneasiness. I realized I was going to meet kids of my own age and would be expected to make friends with them. The problem was that I hadn't had real friends in the past, other than the occasional boy on my street with whom I would play outside. I had never had a friend to my house because I was never there. I had worked since I was four years old, and my closest friends were the employees in the drugstore, mostly Roy, the driver, and my father.

My dad and I were like a well-oiled machine. We ate our meals together and shared the same concerns about the store and how to make things run smoothly. He taught me science principles and we did all kinds of experiments in the store basement, from osmosis to making motors with batteries and wires. We even made a plane fly with baking soda, water and some other chemicals. Much to my father's delight, whatever he taught me, I, in turn, taught Roy. I will never forget Roy's face when our monarch butterfly hatched from a cocoon. The customers all marvelled as I opened the jar and it flew around the store, finally landing in the Baby Needs aisle.

Once, when my father and I took a vacation (my mother was on permanent vacation), we rented a farmhouse in Ontario on Lake Erie — while it still had fish. My dad and I were at loose ends without a project. The farmer was an engineer who farmed on the side. He was convinced that his wheat responded positively to music. The three of us tried an experiment, playing music, Beethoven, at top decibel to one field and nothing to the other field. Both fields had the same soil and sunlight. We used pharmacy scales and measured the difference in the yield. The wheat grown to the music was larger, but not enough to be statistically significant. This project took us many trips to the farm and three years to complete. It was written up in the *Wainfleet Farm Council Newsletter,* which I saw as no different from *Scientific American.* I learned an enormous amount about sampling, statistics and just plain fun with experimentation.

I remember that my mother urged me to make friends with the girls down at the beach. I had no idea why she was saying this, since I already had a friend, my dad, and I was much too busy with our experiments to build sandcastles.

When I was in grade four, I stabbed a bully with a compass after Roy told me to hit him with something sharp. After what my mother referred to as "the compass conundrum," I was sent to Dr. Small, a psychiatrist. One thing Dr. Small had said many years before came back to me on this summer day as I walked to the bus. He said that I was far too close to my father and Roy and needed to have female friends or I would not be "socialized" correctly. He told my mother that if I didn't have girlfriends at a young age, as a teenager I would grow too far away from "normal female concerns." I remembered that phrase because I had no idea what he meant. My mother took all this claptrap to heart and soon after that arranged for some girls to come to my house. However, I didn't like playing with paper dolls and I got rid of the girls as fast as I could and went back to work with my dad, where I belonged.

As I walked to the bus stop, I was thinking how scary it was that I no longer had my job at the drugstore, nor did I have my father and Roy as co-workers and friends. It had all disappeared with the fifties. I was now a teenage girl who was going to have to make my life work with girls my own age. I had no idea how to do it, nor any real desire to do it. What on earth did they talk about?

What made them tick? I felt like I had landed on another planet and I had to make friends with the extraterrestrials.

I turned the corner and there at the bus stop was a gaggle of females. They were lacklustre girls clinging together like a bunch of peahens. One girl asked me in the flattest Buffalo accent, "Are you doing summer ed?"

"I'm taking swim class is all I know."

"What lifesaving badges do you have?" she asked, holding up a pile of small circles, all in different colours, with a Red Cross symbol and swimmer in a hideous bathing cap on each of them.

"I got the Esther Williams synchronized swimming look-alike award. It is sewn to my bathing suit. Too bad we have to wear the school's suits or I could have shown you."

All the girls stopped talking and looked at me curiously.

I heard a small laugh from behind me. A tall, lean guy in black peg-leg jeans and a black T-shirt with rolled-up sleeves was standing at the edge of his stoop, holding a cigarette.

One of the girls whispered in a reverential tone to the others, "Oh my God, it's Donny Burns."

A small-boned redhead rolled her eyes heavenward and said, "I'm going to pass out."

Donny Burns was clearly in senior high and dared to smoke right on his own front porch. He must have been allowed because he was so old and experienced. He stubbed out his cigarette on the column of his porch in what appeared to me to be an interesting way. He kept his cigarettes in the crevice between his muscles and his T-shirt sleeve. He looked a bit like an Irish version of Elvis Presley, and he was obviously the peacock of the group. He was wearing heavy cowboy boots with square toes. He leaned on one boot, letting the other slide to the side as though he were doing the tango with himself. As he left his porch to join the bus lineup, you could feel the still summer air swish.

The girl who was the swim-badge queen asked Donny if he was taking swimming. He laughed and said he was actually taking algebra in summer school so he could get into grade ten.

She asked, "Why didn't you do it earlier?"

He said, "Who are you — Edward R. Murrow?" Then he chuckled and added, "Let's just say I've been on an extended road trip."

After that day, I watched Donny Burns closely. Sometimes his father would pull out of the driveway, but he never waved. Donny would say, "There goes the old man."

Once, when his parents had gone away, he backed the car out of his driveway and beeped at us at the bus stop as we watched in breathless admiration. I had never known a boy who could drive. He stopped and offered us a ride to swimming. There were about nine girls, and we all squeezed in. He had a cigarette, which he called "a fag," hanging from his sultry mouth as he drove and spoke with it miraculously attached to his lower lip.

As he turned on the radio, he said he only listened to jazz. I heard the line "*Real, compared to what . . .* ?" I recognized it from my travels in the delivery car with Roy. I sang along in the staccato blast of the Les McCann and Eddie Harris rendition.

Donny was impressed, and after that day he began paying more attention to me.

A few days later, as I exited the change room after my awful swim class, I ran into him. I tried to avoid him because I had pink eyes and with my white hair I looked like an albino hamster. He grabbed my shoulder and asked if I wanted to walk home.

I nodded a terrified assent. We stopped at the drugstore for ice cream Drumsticks and he wolfed his down at an incredible rate. My ice cream began to melt, so I leaned on the wall of the building to stay out of the sun, and he stood opposite me with his arm leaning on the wall above my head. He smoked with the other hand and when he was done he flicked his cigarette butt away with his thumb and forefinger in a style that was James Dean–ish. I hadn't actually liked *Rebel without a Cause;* however, I really liked the poster that we'd had in our drugstore above the cigarette counter. I loved the red jacket Dean wore and that pristine white T-shirt with the hint of muscle shadow. The best part of the poster was the way he held his cigarette. To me it screamed *manly.* Donny had that same aura of danger that heated up when he smiled.

After a few weeks of walking me home, he asked me to come over to his house.

I was confused. I asked, "Uh, for what?"

"No one is home. In fact, they're all in Atlantic City. The old man has kids from, as he calls it, 'another lifetime.'"

I had never heard of anyone who had step-parents other than Hansel and Gretel. Frightened to my core for some reason I couldn't explain, I declined. I just shook my head. I was frozen with fear, so I couldn't even give him a reason.

He said, "Maybe some other time."

"Yeah, maybe," I grunted.

The next day he asked me if I was Catholic, saying I looked like a "Mick." I didn't know what a Mick was, but since my name was McClure I figured he must be onto something. When I acknowledged I was, he said he was as well but that "the old man" wasn't, so he usually went to Sunday Mass on his own at noon. He said his mom went early in the morning, but he was out far too late on the weekends for early morning sermons. He went at noon to get out of the house to have a coffee and stretch his legs. The whole idea of a boy who drank coffee, smoked and actually had a five o'clock shadow by 4 p.m. was about as perfect as it could get. He suggested he would "see me" at Mass. I nodded.

My mother always went to the first Mass of the day in the summer and fall. She said she "fell apart" in the heat. She would be ready an hour early and would sit with her feet up on a floor fan with Kleenexes under each armpit and her arms outstretched on the top of the couch until it was time to go. On this particular Sunday she wore an apricot linen dress with a matching sweater, because you couldn't have bare arms in church. The piping of the short-sleeved sweater was the same as the trim on the dress.

My father and I slept in and always went together to Mass at noon. I had pondered all week what Donny had meant by "see you" in church. Did he mean literally see me in a pew with my father, or did he mean something like walking home together. What was a date? Was this one? The whole thing made me really nervous and now, just to make my life more hellish, my father was thrown into the mix.

During the consecration, I looked around but didn't see Donny. The problem was there were two Masses, one downstairs and one upstairs. Christ the King Church had layers of worshippers. As the communion bells rang, I realized he must have gone downstairs. I'd missed him, and my only hope would be seeing him in the vestibule if both Masses ended at the same time.

On our way out I spotted Donny leaning on a faux marble column. He had an unlit cigarette behind his right ear. I assumed he'd waited for me. It was very crowded, and when I finally got within earshot of him, his face lit up with a gorgeous smile.

I said, "I looked for you upstairs but didn't see you."

As I stood smiling contentedly up at Donny, on my tiptoes in my white flats, blonde ponytail bobbing, my father charged between the two of us like a bull seeing red and snapped at me, "Get in the car." There was something in his tone that made me feel profound shame — as though I'd violated some taboo that I hadn't known existed.

As we walked to the car, my father stopped and lit a cigarette as he always did, but instead of flicking away the match, he threw it as if it were a lit bomb. He bit hard on the cigarette that drooped from his lip. After we got into the car, he glared at me. He looked as though he might leap across the seat and strangle me. I had never seen him truly angry before. The threat of violence lurked just beneath the surface. I was staggered. He threw the car into drive and almost hit some pedestrians crossing the street in their Sunday best. Panicked, they jumped back on the curb. He didn't yell; he just kept glancing at me as though I were a slut, like the kind I used to hear about who went to the Riverside Tavern in Lewiston and sat at the bar.

Finally he said in a voice of pure disgust, "Girls that chase boys come to a bad end. You looked like the kind of girl I don't want for my daughter."

*Don't want for a daughter?*

On the way home he turned every corner on what felt like two wheels. Some part of the car was making a dreadful screeching sound. As he sped into the driveway, he snapped the car into park almost before he'd fully stopped and we both lurched forward.

He jumped out. I must have been too much of a harlot to be near.

I went to the front door and there in the living room sat my mother, who'd viewed the whole scene out the picture window. Even Willie, the world's most stupid dog, picked up on the tension and began barking and running from the front door to the back, picking up the scatter rugs and growling and shaking them.

I tore through the house to my room, where I slammed and then locked the plywood door. I planned to stay there until the next day when my father went to work. I heard my parents have the first real disagreement they'd ever had, to my knowledge. I caught my father saying "disgusting display" and "throwing herself at every Tom, Dick and Harry."

My mother said in a serious tone minus its usual arch quality, "Jim, I wasn't there, but I think this donnybrook is uncalled for." She told him that she had never seen him this angry and he was really frightening her.

"You didn't see this good-for-nothing she was mooning over — making a fool of herself."

I could hear all this because he was still screaming at the top of his lungs. *A fool of myself.* That phrase exploded within me and has clung forever like napalm. No matter what I ever did with men, I worried about making a fool of myself. I didn't know the rules. Had I looked needy and pathetic? I must have or my father, who was the picture of reason, wouldn't have acted that way.

I heard my mother say that I wasn't going to be his little girl forever. Then he tore out the back door and slammed it shut behind him.

He didn't come back until dark. The first thing he did was storm through the house and try to unlock my door, saying that

I could not lock him out of a room in his own house.

I let him have it just as he had let me have it. The gloves had come off. "Congratulations! People from Appalachia could own this house," I said through the closed door.

He stomped to the basement, got a screwdriver and began taking my door off its hinges. I sat huddled on a corner of my single bed in bewilderment. As he did this, I heard my mother say in a detached way, as though she were watching a hokey version of *Dr. Jekyll and Mr. Hyde,* "Jim, please just sit down, have a Coke and a cigarette."

When he was done, I was left exposed to him as he walked around smoking a cigar or went back and forth to the bathroom. I had nowhere to hide.

Finally, when the house was quiet, I sat up in my bed. I had to go to the bathroom and I was hungry, but for a while I still refused to leave my room. I sat in the dark for hours, looking out my window at the swirling sky, a fluttering tent held up by star pegs. The moon shone on my new Ethan Allen veneer colonial mirror. (We'd had to get new tiny furniture to fit into the tiny house.) I could see myself reflected in the silver light. In my life I had been really bad before, but somehow those episodes hadn't felt life-altering. My parents had thought my deeds appalling, but seemed to realize they were just bumps along the road in the life of a high-spirited girl. I had always remained a good girl in their eyes. Not this time. My father was ashamed of me, and I was ashamed of myself. Shame is not like guilt. You can't say five Hail Mary's and get rid of shame. It enters all of your pores as a gas and then liquefies in each cell. It becomes part of you. For the rest of your life, whenever you want to be spontaneous and flirt, the forked tongue of shame is there to whisper all kinds of filthy epithets in your ear.

I hadn't thought that I was behaving badly with Donny. But I must have been. Otherwise, why would my normal father have reacted that way? How could I ever have said to Donny that I had been looking for him? It made me look pathetic and simultaneously trashy.

I looked in my bedroom mirror that night and decided on three drastic measures: I would never talk to a boy in a way that showed any kind of longing; I would never again humiliate myself; and I would never again allow my father to humiliate me. He didn't know it at the time, but I was far more enraged at him than he was at me. As of that day, I closed him out as I closed down a huge chunk of myself.

This was the beginning of the process of breaking away from him, and I knew it wasn't going to be easy. The more bound you are to a parent, the harder it is to cut the strings — and I had spent my entire childhood with my father. Like Siamese twins, the longer you are joined, the harder it is to separate and have both of you come out unscathed. As the years go by, you begin to grow vessels to each other's organs.

One thing I am is determined. When I decide something, no matter if it is a reasonable plan or some cockamamie scheme, I carry it out. The next morning I had to dress in the closet because I had no door. I didn't go to school but to Hector's Hardware Store. I ordered a solid oak door, not like the flimsy plywood one my father had removed. I chose the most expensive one they had, plus I paid extra to have it installed that day. I got a ride over to my house in the truck with the door and lock installers. While my mother just lay on the living room couch, reading the novel *Exodus,* I had a dead bolt installed on my side of the new door. I chose the size they used in downtown Buffalo on liquor store doors. When the men were finished, I paid them in cash from my savings. One good thing about working since the age of four is that you have some financial independence. The door was never tampered with after that, nor was it ever painted. I locked it every night from the inside. No one ever said a word about it.

I dropped out of swimming after that, mostly because I hated it, but I also didn't want to run into Donny again. I refused to take the summer school bus. In fact, I never once took the school bus for my entire junior or senior high career. I told my mother she had to drive me. She gladly complied every morning in her bathrobe and rollers, saying it got her out to get a drive-thru coffee and if need be she could do her drive-thru banking.

Donny tried to talk to me a few times and even called me. I refused to acknowledge his existence, ever. When he said hello to me in the convenience store, I simply walked by him as though he were a box of Rice Krispies that had jumped off the shelf and begun speaking.

Every family has its lore. My most outstanding misdemeanours had always been fodder for family legend and got trotted out at holidays. However, the Donny Donnybrook story got stored in a vault of shame and was never once alluded to by any member of my family.

After the church episode, I, like Martin Luther, pegged rules on my door — my own Edict of Nantes. The next week, when my father, who by then had grudgingly agreed to talk to me again, said it was time for church, I said, "Read my door." On it was a two-page statement that said I would not now nor would I ever go to Mass again.

This crushed my mother. Her eyes turned red and she was listless, which for her is barely moving, for weeks. Once she said to me, "I never knew how to be a good mother, but I'd hoped to raise a good Catholic."

I didn't answer.

My father only said, "Eternity is a long time."

One day, when I was getting ready to start school, I climbed up into the garage attic to find the antique full-length mahogany mirror that had been stored there. I figured I'd better get a full gander, assess the damage and shop accordingly. Besides, the attic was a perfect place to have a cigarette.

I had smoked with Roy since I was nine. It started because it was my job to warm up the delivery car in the morning and let out the clutch slowly. I was supposed to push in the lighter once Roy was in sight. I lit the cigarette for him and in order to keep it going I had to take a drag or two. I graduated to having a whole cigarette in the morning and by the time I was twelve I was buying my own packs. My dad bought Camel unfiltered by the crate and smoked over a pack a day, and he also smoked at least a six-pack of El Producto cigars a day. I used to take the red rings off the cigars and wear them as jewellery. My mother, on the other hand, never smoked, saying that it was for "hard women."

As I poked around the attic, I found the antiques that had adorned our home in Lewiston. The twin beds from the guest room, with carved vines growing up the bed posts, lay dismantled against the wall. I saw the mahogany dining room table with its hand-crafted inlay of carved fruit, its matching chairs sitting in an accusatory row like a jury. I wondered why my mother hadn't wrapped them up in old sheets or blankets. It was as if for her they no longer existed.

I found my grandmother's old console radio and plugged it in. As I waited for the radio to warm up, I leaned back on the needlepoint settee. I felt as close to relaxed as I'd been since I left Lewiston. I then listened to Louis and Ella singing, "Cheek to Cheek."

There in the attic, I felt the first chill of September, and tears clouded my eyes as I remembered how, in the autumn, Roy and I would listen to that song on his transistor radio as we collected chestnuts on the escarpment. He would sing like Louis Armstrong as he held up an especially beautiful mahogany chestnut. He would then carve them into necklaces for me as I read to him from some of the magazines we were delivering on our route. Our favourite was *Photoplay*.

Nothing was complicated back then. I never said things that were shameful. Every day started afresh. I felt loved by everyone and all I knew was the joy of working hard and marvelling at the beauty around us. Roy would sometimes pull into Devil's Hole Park along the Niagara Gorge for lunch. We would lean over the railing below the falls and see the deep cliffs and the whirlpools spinning below us, foaming at the mouth. But we were safe, eating our beef on kummelweck, letting the horseradish drip on the rocks.

I was so carried away with my reverie that I didn't even blink when I saw Roy sitting in the captain's chair of the Chippendale set. He was ageless, just as he had been in my childhood. Was it the music, the season or my loneliness that had made him appear? At the time I didn't ask myself. I was just happy to see him. There he sat, in the black pants with the perfect crease he once wore and his starched white tailored shirt that he always picked up from the dry cleaner's on Fridays.

Gradually, I began to tell him of all that had happened since moving. It poured out: the ugliness of the neighbourhood, the tiny house, the four-lane highways and the restaurants where the unhappy worked and the unhappier ate. I thought about whether or not I should mention the Donny Burns horror show. I decided he would be the only person I would tell. He wouldn't think I'd been bad. Roy just didn't think like that. Knowing that he wouldn't judge me freed me up to tell the story as I had really seen and felt it. When I got to the part about installing my own door, he started laughing — that infectious laugh he had that made his shoulders rise up and every part of his body shake. Suddenly I saw the humour in it too.

*The boss does not know with whom he messeth.*

*Do you believe how crazy he is? What happened to him?*

*He isn't crazy. He just had one little girl that worked by his side her whole life. You were each other's right hand. Now, when it's time to clap, you got to break away.*

After a few minutes he said, *You know, you got to place your child on the right path early. It's like them fights we used to go to down on Falls Street. Remember the old Circle in the Square Gym? You watch those guys. You got to get in there early and give the palooka the old one-two. The young one got to know the parent gives the first punch — that's the way o' the world. No one's fault — you just didn't get it. Then when you in the ring and he hits you the first time, you ain't got your dukes up. You get sucker-punched and that make anyone mad. What's worse, you don't know you got a glass jaw.*

Yeah, well, I got a rabbit punch — that's for sure, I said, folding my arms across my chest.

*That weren't no rabbit punch. That punch was strictly legal. Dads get into a rile-up when they wants to and it's the chil' who gots to take it. It ain't about being fair. You read the Bible. You think Abraham fair to Isaac?*

I looked askance at him, letting him know I wasn't buying in.

*This ain't no court. It's a family just tryin' to make it through troubled times. Besides, what don't seem fair today might ring fair down the road.*

After a few minutes I looked out the window. *I hate this house. Why are we here?*

*Life marches on. It can take you by the hand and tap you along. But sometimes it just kicks you where it hurts. Findin' someone to blame ain't goin' to change it.*

I nodded, knowing he was right.

*Remember the story of my Uncle Junior on the railroad? He be the best fireman on the railroad. Being a fireman is an art. The fire has to be even. Taking accurate readings of the water glass took skill. Also, a fireman would have to travel a stretch of track until he knew its ups and downs, levels and curves, like the back of his hand. Looking out of the train, he had to know every landmark so he could adjust the pressure to the elevation and turns. He was high on the hog — teaching for the B&R. He was even sent to Chicago. No one gave the smooth ride he gave. You can balance an egg on a curve with that fireman. Then one day, the train is electric and he is gone without a dime. Instead of fuelling that train, he's riding them rails.*

I inhaled and blew some smoke rings. *Sorry for whining. I know that was the one thing you "couldn't abide," as you used to say.*

As I began to feel better, Roy slowly disappeared. I sat there for another hour, still feeling his presence. When you grow up with someone, you know what they would say and you can forever travel with them tucked snugly in your heart, and ask them for help when you need it.

CHAPTER 3

# good friday

My mother drove me to school the first day of grade seven. When

we got there we noticed yellow buses lined up in rows like cheese

wagons waiting to unload pubescent cheddar. I said to my mother,

"God, to think I was supposed to be dumped out of that teeming

nightmare."

"Anyway, we're here," she said, sipping her takeout coffee from Carrol's drive-in.

It seemed strange not to be driven by my father. Most of my life we had gone to work together before dawn. I would work in the store, selling papers and stocking shelves, until it was time for school. We had breakfast with the Rotary Club at the Horseshoe Restaurant. The seersucker-suited Rotarians at the counter discussed politics. I had grown up with and now missed our "Breakfast Roundtables," as Abe Wallens, who owned a clothing store, called them. (As events unfolded in the early sixties, like the civil rights demonstrations, Krushchev's banging his shoe on the table at the U.N. and the Eichmann trial, I often wondered what they would have thought of it all.) Although I was a child, I had considered myself an integral part of the group. For me these had been my "family breakfasts," full of discussion, warmth and hilarity.

When I crossed the threshold into junior high that September, a lot of the kids, who swarmed in from four feeder schools, already knew one another. I was completely ignored. I walked into "homeroom," whatever that meant, and realized to my relief that the boys and girls were separated. I hoped that would be true for the rest of the classes.

It was easy to spot the popular girls, because they let out high-pitched squeals when their friends walked into the room. They all wore cotton dresses made of fabric covered in infinitesimal flowers and flat shoes that matched. These girls had such gorgeous tans that none of them even needed to wear stockings — which beat the two sticks of chalk that stuck out below my skirt. Their hairbands were made out of some weird embroidered ribbon that made them look like they had just walked out of a tulip field in Holland. I introduced myself to the girl next to me, whose name was Lissa. I said "Hi, Lisa." She corrected me by saying, "*Lissa,*" and then turned away to talk to a friend. Lissa was naturally beautiful and didn't even have to bother buying back-to-school shoes.

Aside from the pretty blonde girls in their dresses with the microscopic flowers, there was another group who wore carefully chosen poly-cotton wraparound skirts and white blouses. The skirts were plaid and the white blouses had button-down collars with the same plaid, matching their checkered skirts. The girls had dark hair and it looked like some of them had had it straightened at the hairdresser. They all huddled together, clutching orange schedule cards. The small-flower-print girls and I had pale institutional green schedule cards.

"Oh my God!" one of the dark-haired girls said to her friend when she saw her orange card. "Thank God you made it into the advanced program. New Year's is coming up in a few weeks. Are you taking off?"

I was amazed that New Year's was in September in Buffalo. It was typical of Lewiston to not even have the right day for New Year's.

Trying to weasel into their conversation, I volunteered, "*I'm* taking New Year's off."

The girl said, "Why? You're not Jewish," then turned and showed her friend her new school books, which were carefully covered with plastic-coated Amherst Junior High orange and black book covers. Who had school books before school even started?

Just then a large-framed girl burst into our room, screamed, "Hit the dirt!" and fell to the floor, her ample body splayed out on the tile in front of the entire homeroom. Her eyes rolled back in her head and she twitched, mimicking being shot in a war. The way she did it was hilarious and soon we were all in stitches. The homeroom teacher looked appalled and asked her name. Lots of girls called out, "That's Fran Stephens." I knew right then that Fran would be my salvation in grade seven.

The homeroom teacher, a young woman named Miss Fancher who wore a shirtwaist with tiny tucks in the bodice, asked in a tone that was supposed to sound nonchalant but was imbued with trilling admiration, "Are you related to Skip and Jeff?"

"Those idiots? Never heard of them," Fran said.

One of the girls whispered to her friend, "Do you know that Skip and Jeff Stephens are her brothers?" Then she added, "Do you have *any* idea who they are?"

The other girl indignantly replied, "Of course I know who they are. I don't live under a rock. Who wouldn't know the biggest football stars in the senior school?"

"I love how they have their own band and my sister says they play at assemblies and at the Y Teen dances."

The third girl got in on the conversation and said, "I have never seen anyone who looks more like Tab Hunter than Skip. He is the most dreamy guy in Amherst."

The first girl seemed outraged. "Are you kidding? *Get serious.* Take another look at Jeff. He's a dead ringer for Ricky Nelson — that dark hair and those long eyelashes."

Fran flopped down on her chair just as the loudspeaker crackled to life for the morning announcements. The soft-spoken principal, Mr. Wittinger, welcomed us. Then another Sergeant Bilko–type voice shot out. The bombastic blast identified itself as Mr.

Riley, the vice-principal, who was in charge of "vice of any kind." He told us that he had fought in two wars and that when an officer yelled *Hit the dirt,* he knew how to lie low and he hoped we did too. By this time we were all in hysterics, realizing that Fran's "hit the dirt" scenario had perfectly mimicked the vice-principal. She must have learned it from her older brothers, who had moved on to the senior high.

We were all impressed with Fran's knowledge of the extremely complicated life in junior high. The rest of us had no idea how to negotiate the huge school, with a thousand kids in each grade. The junior and senior high comprised two full city blocks. The Byzantine hallways were enough to make me feel that I was skulking through catacombs. Weeks later, when my mother went to parent–teacher night and tried to find the science wing, she said she felt like Pépé le Moko in the Casbah.

After my first day of school, I told my mother I had to find those matching outfits that the popular blonde girls wore. Some of the girls wore little ladybug pins on their collars that were the exact size of a real ladybug. I had discovered that this pin represented the Ladybug brand. I found Villager floral dresses and Ladybug blouses in a lady's golf shop. The Ladybug blouses were three times as expensive as any others in the store, but I had to have them. I figured that since my parents hadn't spent money on a home, they could certainly afford a few blouses. The cable-knit sweaters with matching knee socks were made by John Meyer of Norwich. I then found the shoes and bought them in different colours at a store called Pappagallo's. When I'd scrutinized the popular girls at their lockers, I'd observed that they wore oversize London Fog raincoats with their initials monogrammed on their collars. Each popular girl had several in different colours of khaki. So I got three of those as well. The whole exercise was incredibly expensive, but I figured it was, as my father used to say when we had to buy dumb raffle tickets from our customers, "just the price of doing business." I couldn't manufacture the tan because I had that white freckled skin that only burns and peels. However, I had the blonde hair, height and attitude.

After a week's surveillance, I got the fashion statement, which was to throw the clothes on as though the outfit was unplanned. You also had to be popular without trying. It was supposed to be genetic. My mother made idiotic suggestions like, "Why don't you join the Thespian Society?" I had to explain to her that it was crucial to look as though you didn't care about joining in or making friends. You just *had* them.

———

One day the entire clique was huddled in my homeroom as invitations were dispensed. I was thrilled to see one on my desk. It was only September and I'd made it. That didn't take long. I looked up and there were several of the Villager and Ladybug set hovering over my desk, anxious to hear my reply.

"Uh, Cathy," Lissa said, "sorry, there's been a big mistake. That invitation was for Kathy *MacQuire*." Kathy was the pretty girl who sat in front of me, the one who looked like Sandra Dee. I sat there dumbfounded until I heard giggling around me. After an interminable pause Lissa said again, "Uh, wrong desk."

Now everyone was looking at me — even those not involved in the incident. Snapping to, a bit late off the mark, I said, "Oh, that's okay. I was just looking at this invitation." Then I read it aloud: "'You're invited: Slumber party. Santora's for pizza.' That's a strange coincidence. I'll be at Santora's on Friday night anyway. I usually drive over there to get takeout." As Lissa started to walk away, I could tell she didn't get it. I had to spell it out. "Actually, I drive there on my own."

"You drive?"

"Sure. I like to get out for a cigarette."

"Right." She looked at her friends and rolled her eyes, a sign that she thought I was a pathetic liar. "Well, Cathy, maybe we'll see you at Santora's, then."

"I'm usually in a rush. But I'll see you if you're there," I added lamely.

Over the next few days I hatched the plot. Driving didn't scare me. I had driven all over the Niagara frontier with Roy when doing deliveries. Sometimes I drove if he had to push the car out of the snow, or if we were on country roads and I nagged him enough. So I wasn't exactly *lying* when I said that at twelve years old I smoked and drove a car. Now all I needed was a car, and the guts to drive on the Buffalo highways.

That Friday night I was crammed into my claustrophobic living room with my parents. My father was smoking a cigar and watching boxing while my mother read *Around the World with Auntie Mame*. I knew quite a bit about boxing, having spent time ringside with Roy, who placed bets on local matches at dive gyms around Niagara Falls. As the young American came into the ring, pulled on the ropes and smiled a cocky smile, my father sat on the edge of his chair and said, "Cathy, I'm putting my money on that young whippersnapper."

"He's got the moves," I said.

It was the first time we'd agreed about anything since we'd

moved. After the Donny Donnybrook incident, I was never kind to him. Every morning he woke up cheerful, and no matter how much I stonewalled him, he forged ahead with relentless exuberance, optimism and his cloying attempts at companionship. Usually I wore a hair dryer on my head with a plastic bonnet, the motor on my back like a meter maid, and walked around with an extension cord attached. Whenever my father talked, I turned on the dryer, inflating the hood with hot air, which drowned out all outside sound.

As the boxing match progressed, I yelled, "Look at that footwork. The Road Runner couldn't get that guy."

Even my mother stopped reading and said, "He really is surefooted and has such charisma."

A few minutes after an eighteen-year-old Cassius Clay won the match, I managed to say, "I think I'll go out and celebrate."

"Out where?" my father asked.

I was used to my mother's laissez-faire attitude. All she ever said was "Bye." But now that Dad had a nine-to-five job, and I was starting to morph into a teenage girl, he took more interest in my comings and goings.

"Just plain out" was all I said. He looked at me as though he wanted more information. My mood changed on a dime these days. "Out of this two-by-four, cigar-infested dump that an asthmatic wolf could blow over with one stinking breath," I shouted.

My words electrified the room. Even Willie growled. It was mean, I know, but I had needed my father to back off quickly so I'd gone for the burn.

Earlier in the evening, I had made sure the curtains were tightly closed. The people who had lived in the house before us had put thick rubber soundproof lining behind the curtains, presumably because the airport was nearby and planes could be heard over-head day and night. The soundproofing worked so well that, when the curtains were drawn, not even Willie could hear anyone approaching. I knew I would have no trouble starting the car and backing out of the driveway without my parents knowing.

But I had trouble figuring out how to get on and off the thruway. I missed the exit and had to go miles out of the way. Eventually I found myself in a downtown Buffalo ghetto. It was a warm night and people were on their porches and men were drinking from paper bags on park benches. I found it all fascinating and made a mental note to return. Finally I managed to get back on the thruway going in the right direction and to circle around the city on various freeways and return to Amherst. Over an hour after leaving the house, I pulled into Santora's, which was in actuality only ten minutes from my house.

There was the clique, or "the girls" as they called themselves, sitting right in the window. I beeped as I slipped the car into park, to make sure they saw me. As I strolled in, I counted nine of them around a table. They waved as I passed them and nonchalantly stood only a few feet away from them in the bomber takeout line.

"Cathy, you really drove," Lissa said. The others uttered mur-murings of approval.

"Yeah, I'm a bit late. I had to stop for cigarettes." I pulled out my Tareytons and said with the most disdain I could muster, "How did you get here? Did someone's mother drive you or something?" One thing I'd come to realize about a suburb, be it high end or low: no one went anywhere unless they drove or were driven. They had no choice but to acknowledge the truth that they had been chauffeured by one of their mothers.

"Do you always drive?" the one named Gretchen asked.

"No, sometimes when I'm in New York City, I take the subway. When I'm in Harlem, I take the A Train." I actually got that line from a song that Roy liked. Finally, the girls asked me to join them. I declined, saying I was meeting a friend out of town. I lit a cigarette, performed a French inhale and said I had to stick to my schedule, which was to arrive at my friend's loft at one in the morning. I got the word *loft* from a book my mother had borrowed from the library called *Breakfast at Tiffany's*. With that, I sauntered out, waved again, laid some rubber and sped away.

When I got home, I killed the motor and, looking through the back door, I saw that most of the lights were on. It was twelve-thirty and someone was still up. I walked in, yelled, "Hello," slammed the door and darted straight down to the reek room without having to see my parents. I went over to my new portable record player, placed my 45 adapter on the spindle and played "Smoke Gets in Your Eyes." (I'd loved the Platters ever since I'd seen them on *American Bandstand*.)

About fifteen minutes later, as I was dancing around the room by myself, I heard footsteps on the stairs. I could tell my father's even, executioner's pace. Quickly I lay down on our new hideous shiny tweed sectional couch with the white melamine tables connected to either end. I pretended I had fallen asleep.

He came over and sat on the edge of the couch and said, "Cathy, I know you are not sleeping and I also know that you took the car tonight."

I turned my body to face the back cushions and thought that if he didn't get off the sofa next to me I'd crawl out of my skin. Then he asked me why I'd done it, and when I didn't answer he asked if I had been trying to impress people with the car in order to make friends.

*Oh God, I really couldn't stand him.* He put his hand on my back and I yelled, "Don't do that!"

He repeated, "I know that you took the car."

"That makes two of us. *So?*" I screamed.

"So?" His voice rose slightly. "So! I'll tell you what. You could have had an accident and we could have been sued and lost our home."

"Who'd buy it? The Seven Dwarfs?"

"Your mother is sleeping and doesn't know about this joyride of yours, nor will she. For your information, you are not the only person who's had a hard time in this move. I am aware it has been difficult. I have never thrown your behaviour in your face."

Although his voice was calm, I could feel his agitation. Still, I didn't say a word.

He eventually broke the uncomfortable silence and said, "You know, your behaviour was part of the reason we left Lewiston." He must have been really upset about the car caper to bring that up.

"Putting vodka in the holy water font and taking advantage of Father Flanagan's weakness for spirits was low, and they were right to throw you out of Catholic school." Then he lowered his voice and asked how he thought my mother had felt as an active member of the Altar and Rosary Society — having to go to the meetings when her daughter no longer went to Catholic school. He never mentioned that he had been president of the Knights of Columbus and was probably equally humiliated.

"It was Miranda's idea," I yelled. "I had no idea that he would drink the holy water. If he was thirsty, why didn't he have a Coke?

Instead, he got drunk and hollered on the pulpit about the English in Ireland. If I got kicked out of Catholic school, why didn't Father Flanagan get kicked out of the priesthood?"

"This is about you, not an alcoholic parish priest who is fighting his own demons. You chose to be friends with Miranda, who is" — he hesitated — "heading down a treacherous road to a dead end." He then went into some long diatribe about spirited girls getting in trouble in small towns.

My friend Miranda had been all that was entertaining in Catholic school. Sure, she was a walk on the wild side, but she had been a better option than those girls from the Daughters of Mary Club who wanted to get together on the weekend and make beaded belts for the missions and who offered up their boredom for lost souls in Limbo. Hennipen Hall Catholic School *was* Limbo.

My father was a devout Catholic who prayed every night, kneeling at his bedside in his striped pyjamas. As a child he was an altar boy and as an adult in Lewiston he was always an usher and took up the collection at Mass. He worked tirelessly for Catholic charities, and even billeted priests with leprosy from Catholic missions in Africa. (My mother just put up with these visits and burned the sheets when they left.) If I had told my father that Miranda had done the big "It" with Father Rodwick, he would have been heartbroken. I decided to keep facing the back of the couch rather than look at his face.

After a long time, he patted my back. I arched away from him and, while still facing the wall, said, "When are we moving to the new split-level? Have they finished building it yet?"

That was when he dropped the bombshell. "We did not own the house in Lewiston."

*What?*

"It was owned by your mother's cousin, who was a nun, and she told your mom that she was welcome to it. She died and left it to a niece who is a Grey Nun. When we said we were moving, she said she wanted it back for the convent. We had no house to sell. And the store was sold at a loss." He let out a deep, sad breath and continued.

"Cath, it's the end of an era. The neighbourhood drugstore is over. I had one buyer, John Volpone. He was diagnosed with a brain tumour and died within a month. Of course, he never met the mortgage payments. But God doesn't give us second chances to be charitable. He left behind a wife and five children. What could I do — get blood from a stone? Sure, I could take his wife to court. But I don't think that is a Christian thing to do."

I couldn't believe I was hearing this. It was like another man had come down to the basement, wearing my father's uniform of a grey worsted wool suit and custom-made Dr. Scholl's shoes.

"I bought this house as a stop-gap until the money from the store came in. But it's not coming."

I heard his laboured smoker's lungs puffing like a bellows. Still I said nothing.

"This has been hard on your mother. She has had to start over. Your life is beginning. Mom is past mid-life. I have work; you have youth." His voice caught as he asked, "Cath . . . what does *she* have?"

He was clearly waiting for me to talk to him, which I had no intention of doing. The seconds ticked away as he continued breathing cigar breath into the silence.

Finally he let out a sigh, and, seeing he was getting nothing from me, hardened his voice. "I never want you to refer to or even allude to our diminished circumstances again — particularly in front of your mother. Your fit of bad temper earlier in the evening was unworthy of you. Stealing the car was stupid, but your words were cruel. If you are ashamed of your family, then I feel sorry for you. Dignity is not located by neighbourhood."

Even now I can feel the roughness of the couch fabric as it chafed my face and I can hear the tinny motor of the dehumidifier in the reek room as my father's leaden footsteps ascended the stairs.

——

During the night, my father must have mulled over the car theft and its possible correlation with my lack of friends. The next morning at breakfast at the Four Seasons Restaurant, my father ordered the silver dollar pancakes and then turned to me with renewed bonhomie and said, "Why don't you have a party?"

A party? Where? In the hideous reek room where the dehumidifier looked like a tin mummy? In the bar that advertised ridiculous drinks? Why didn't I just wear a clown suit to school with a red nose and carry a horn?

My mother never lifted her eyes from the menu. I knew she was thinking what I was thinking. My father sipped his coffee with the edible oil slick on the surface.

Breaking the silence, he said, "You know what Dale Carnegie said in *How to Win Friends and Influence People?* 'God only helps those that help themselves.'"

"Jim, I think Ben Franklin said that," my mother said.

Ignoring her, he went on. "Have a huge party and invite only the girls and boys you think are the movers and shakers. Cover all of your bases: pretty, smart, popular, athletic, the whole shooting match. The worst they can say is no. Order pizzas only if they show up."

Have girls *and* boys? I looked at my mother, who subtly rolled her eyes to let me know she knew this idea was close to demented.

Picking up on the lack of enthusiasm, Dad said, "Okay, so forget the boys. Have a slumber party. No matter how popular a girl is, or isn't, she doesn't like to miss a party. You don't even have to unroll your sleeping bag until they get here. When you're the new kid on the block, you need to do your own PR."

Is he like Gale Storm, the *Oh Susanna!* social director on the S.S. *Ocean Queen?* I thought. I would never, ever do something so stupid.

—

That afternoon I made out invitations and then tore them up. Way too thought-out. Written invitations formally announced, *I have planned this party and when you don't show up I'll be alone watching the candles melt.*

The following Monday after homeroom, I said to the girls in the clique, "Oh yeah, I'm having a slumber pizza thing on Friday. Come if you want — but it'll be crowded." I also gave the message to the popular girls in all my classes, the cool advanced girls who held office and the ruling athletes in the gymnastics club that my gym teacher had talked me into joining, and I told them just after the bell rang so they would have to get back to me for the details. No one said yes, nor did I give any of them a chance.

One girl looked concerned, as though she wanted to check with her friends because she barely knew me, and stammered, "Do I have to let you know now?"

"God no!" I said. "I can't even keep track of who I invited."

The Friday of the party arrived. I felt like it was Good Friday and I, like Christ, would have to suffer. I would forever after wear the crown of social estrangement and be permanently shunned. Why had I listened to my father? I hadn't mentioned the party at school again, hoping everyone would forget about it. As I ate dinner at Your Host Restaurant that evening with my parents, I could barely swallow. I could tell that my mother was appalled and had no idea how this whole fiasco had been set in motion. None of us mentioned the party, though it was just a few hours away. Though I had noticed earlier that there were bottles of Coke piled up in the reek room and mounds of chip bags.

I said, "Well, when no one comes, we can always drink the pop and feed the chips to the birds — if there are any in Buffalo."

"Exactly — nothing ventured, nothing gained," my father said in that horribly optimistic voice that made me want to puke. *Puke* was a Buffalo word I'd learned recently when a girl said of my mustard-coloured John Meyer of Norwich skirt and cable-knit sweater set, "I had no idea puke yellow was your colour. At least it matches your hair."

When my father left the table to, as he put it, "see a man about a dog," my mother said, "I have butterflies in my stomach. What are you going to do if only one or two girls come?"

I hadn't even thought of that. It was worse than no one coming. God almighty! Had my completely stupid father considered *that?*

"What time did you tell people?"

"I never gave them a time."

My mother just leaned back in her booth, closed her eyes and sighed.

By eight o'clock no one had arrived. My parents didn't say anything, and Willie, never one to miss an opportunity, stood right in front of the television and took a giant dump.

At nine o'clock, cars started pulling up. The first to arrive was one of those suburban plastic-wood-sided station wagons called Country Squires that people threw their golf clubs into. The Pappagallo-hoofed herds descended. Cadillacs and Buick Rivieras arrived, and Fran blasted into the driveway in her devastatingly handsome brother's red Corvette. Everyone came — there were more than thirty of us. A few parents came to the door to introduce themselves and check out my mom and dad. The first mother was wearing a mink coat that she held around her as though buttons hadn't been invented. My father embarrassed me by introducing himself as Jack the Ripper. My mother just shook hands quietly and smiled at my father's jokes. I made her promise she'd keep my father upstairs and not let him come down into the reek room to do party tricks, tell jokes or suggest Guy Lombardo tunes.

After tons of pop and pizza, and doing the twist to Chubby Checker's music, the girls wanted to make phone calls to boys. They didn't want to really talk to them, thank God, but to make anonymous contact and basically harass them. This was fine with me. Fran called a boy in our class and pretended she was a clerk from the men's underwear department at Sears, Roebuck. She told him she was sorry but the department didn't have underwear small enough for him, so his mother would have to order from elsewhere. We laughed so hard we cried.

We were in our sleeping bags on the reek room floor like sardines in a can, with the lights out, at 3 a.m., the witching hour when you're so overtired you can't sleep. This is the time when the talk turned to the inevitable — sex.

Fran said that her cousin's friend got pregnant while reading magazines at the bus station.

"Oh my God, I read *U.S. News and World Report*. It didn't matter when I was young, but now I'm past puberty. What if I get pregnant?" I asked. Then I added, "It'll be my father's fault. He makes me read it."

"It's not *all* magazines. It's the dirty ones at the bus station. Men have some kind of sex with them and if the sperms are still alive and you touch those pages, you can get pregnant."

"How do you have sex with a magazine?" a skeptic asked.

No one knew.

"It would be like the Immaculate Conception, but if you're not Mary, who would believe you?" I asked.

"Who do you think believed Mary?" Kathy, the girl who looked like Sandra Dee, asked, as though I had the Bible story all wrong.

"You know Lorraine Costello?" another girl whispered.

There was a chorus of *yeahs*.

"Well, her cousin's friend goes to Bennett High School. Last year, she got bigger and bigger but didn't know why. Then one day she went to the bathroom and a baby came out."

"Holy moly!" a muffled voice exclaimed from the dark.

"Yeah, well, guess what she did?"

We all gave up.

"She was all alone in the house. Her parents were at the cottage, so she went into the backyard and hit the baby with a snow shovel and killed it."

"Where did she bury it?" Gretchen asked.

"She was afraid to bury it in her yard in case her parents would plant tulip bulbs there in the fall, so she buried it under the bleachers at Bennett High School. She dug a small grave for it and put two crossed Popsicle sticks on the top, as a tombstone. She didn't want to give away that she had buried the baby there, so she wrote on the gravestone 'My Frog.'"

"Really?" someone asked.

"I swear on my mother's grave."

As we all lay cocooned in our individual sleeping bags on the floor in the dark, as if in a group confessional, one voice whispered faintly, "I really don't get how you do it. I mean, does gravity bring the sperm down the man's pipe thing? What makes a guy's thing stick up? Is there a lever?"

"I wondered that too. I mean, he can't just will it to rise," someone said.

A high-pitched squeaky voice from the far corner piped in, "It can't be gravity, because I walked in on my sister. She is married and she was — get this — on top of her husband."

We all gasped and then fell into stunned silence.

Fran chimed in. "I have brothers and you will not believe this, but sometimes men do it with — I swear, God strike me dead if this is not true" — she hesitated, a pause for effect, when all you could hear was breathing — "themselves!"

Everyone started laughing.

"I know it's ridiculous," she said, putting her hands in the air like a Baptist preacher about to share a revelation of the Lord. "But hear me out. I've walked into my brothers' bathroom to get the soap they stole from my bathroom because they're too damn lazy to go to the utility room to get their own, and I've caught them . . . in the act of shaking it and making it grow!"

No one said anything. I thought this was far-fetched, but then I had no idea what was true.

She continued, "I think it's like Jiffy Pop. You heat it up, shake the container and then it grows."

"Ugh. That's so gross. That is my last Jiffy Pop popcorn ever," someone said.

Fran, the sage on most topics, said, "It takes all kinds, honey."

CHAPTER 4

# hit the dirt

After my coming-out slumber party, I moved from "the nobody"

lunch table to "the girls" lunch table, where I remained for the rest

of my school career. By November I was running that clique with

an iron fist and Fran Stephens and I were best friends.

Fran wasn't particularly attractive. She was big boned, slightly overweight and her features were too large and seemed to be crammed on her face. The majority of her humour was physical. She could mimic and do sound effects better than anyone I've ever met. She could catch the smallest pretentious mannerism in someone and blow it up to complete absurdity. Years later, in the late 1960s, when Lily Tomlin was on *Laugh-In* as Ernestine, I thought how strikingly similar Fran had been to Tomlin in her sketches.

Although Fran had definite comedic talents, her main claim to fame was that she had two older brothers who were referred to as Adonis I and II. Skip and Jeff were known by everyone in the junior and senior high. They were spectacularly handsome and athletic. They were also funny and had a band. Sometimes at a pep rally before a football game, on the outdoor stage in front of the bleachers, they would be applauded as the highest scorers and all the girls would swoon. They never seemed to have a self-conscious moment and could be spontaneously witty at the microphone. They were three and four years older than me, so all I could do was admire them from afar in the same way I admired Charlton Heston in *Ben-Hur*. I, like most twelve-year-old girls, let myself long for men that had absolutely nothing to do with my existence. After the Donny Donnybrook episode, boys in my local vicinity shot electrical volts of loathing into my central nervous system.

Fran and I were the class cut-ups. We never competed, for her expertise was in physical comedy and mimicry, and mine was verbal — mostly abuse. I was a master at the one-line put-down. Together we, as my homeroom teacher used to say, "kept them in stitches." We started out doing our own version of the morning announcements on a pretend public address system — with a reversal of students' and teachers' roles. By grade nine we had graduated to doing these public address newscasts for the Friday assemblies. I would be the "straight man," delivering the newscasts about local school events mixed with current events. Fran would interrupt the newscasts with physical antics and gross exaggerations of certain teachers' foibles.

Although we spent a lot of time together, for the first couple of months of school we didn't go to each other's houses, but practised our routines at Frank's, the local diner where all the kids from our school and the Catholic schools congregated. We used to dry-run our routines for Timmy Russert, who was just a bit younger than we were and attended Canisius High School, the private Catholic Jesuit school for boys. He was our best critic. He loved current events and would laugh when we were right on; he would also let us know when we went over the line, like in grade ten when he suggested that Fran imitating Lee Harvey Oswald killing Vice-Principal Riley from the school tower might be in bad taste. His sagacity paid off, for little Timmy Russert, later known as Tim, went on to become a renowned journalist and moderator of *Meet the Press* until his untimely death in 2008.

—

One November afternoon in grade seven, I was invited to Fran's house to spend the night. Her parents were going to the country club for a big dance and they said Fran could have me over. My mother dropped me off in front of a gargantuan home that was covered with vines. I had never seen a more beautiful place. It was stone with a long, sloping roof. It had two wings with a triple garage across the back and a courtyard in the middle with a pergola shaded with grape vines. These were all unusual features for a 1960s Buffalo suburb, and I remember longing to live with those stone floors and cathedral ceilings.

Mr. Stephens owned several car dealerships, which he had inherited from his father. He drove a Corvette, as did his wife and two sons. Fran told me they all had the 'Vettes because her father thought it was good for business.

She had told me that she would be in the basement recreation room vacuuming when I arrived, so I should just come in. She'd said that the door often sticks, so I should pull hard.

I walked up the path and stood in front of two huge antique front doors with a large ornate doorknob plunked in the centre of each one. I pulled as hard as I could on the right-hand door but it wouldn't budge. I tried the left. Finally, I put my foot on the door near the knob to give myself some leverage and pulled with all my might. The doorknob broke off in my hand and I flew backwards through the air. I landed on the flagstone walkway and slid full speed until the thorns of a rose bush stopped me.

At that moment Fran's mother was speeding into the driveway in her red Corvette convertible. Having witnessed the event, she got out of the car and ran toward me as fast as she could in her gold wedgies. I lay crumpled and bleeding in the bushes, my plaid madras slacks shredded by the stone. Distressed, she leaned down to where my trail of blood stopped and said, "You know I bought those knobs in an antique shop in Milan." She tore away the knob that I was still clutching and cradled it. "It's broken right in half."

She didn't help me up but turned and yelled through the garage that had opened on its own (I had never seen anything like that before), "Fran, someone is at the door for you."

Skip came to the door, followed by Jeff, and they looked out and laughed. To my astonishment, they didn't help me up either. I was so brush-burned that I'd left a layer of freckles on the pavement.

"Jesus Christ! Next time use the bell," Skip said.

"What the hell is she doing?" Jeff muttered as they both walked away.

I limped to the door in time to hear Skip calling into the basement. "Fran, come on up here. Your wrecking crew has arrived." He and Jeff continued chuckling as they walked down the hall.

Fran popped up from the basement, saw me and screamed, "Oh my God! Were you hit by a car?"

"She broke my doorknob," her mother said, coming in behind me.

"Oops. I forgot to unlock the door," Fran said.

While Fran's mother sat at the kitchen table, trying to nurse her severed doorknob back to life, Fran got me some Band-Aids.

Mrs. Stephens was very beautiful, thin and stylish, and she had dyed white hair like Kim Novak's. Her features were all in perfect proportion, and her brown eyes were huge and turned up slightly at the edges like a cat's. She always wore her hair in Grecian curls on top of her head, with enough spray to make her hair as firm as a helmet. She wore spectacular outfits, the type my mother would have called "flashy." She thought nothing of going to the convenience store in pink leather with sequins, black stretch pants and gold high heels. The sons had her fabulous looks, while Fran had broad features and was short and stocky like her father.

On this particular evening, we sat having supper with Mrs. Stephens, Fran and her brothers. I could barely sit on my shredded epidermis. Fran had to lend me some clothes, because mine were in tatters. As we ate our chicken à la king, Fran said she was having seconds and asked me if I wanted any.

Skip said, "You're already a fat pig, you oinker. You don't need seconds." He then did an imitation of her waddling over to get more food. Their mother laughed along with the brothers. Mr. Stephens had wandered in and stood eating at the buffet table, ignoring all the cruelty to Fran while flipping through a file folder. Maybe I was an only child and didn't understand the rough and tumble behaviour of a larger family, but it all made me nervous.

Later, as Fran's parents were leaving for the dance, Mr. Stephens said, "Boys, I know you're having your fraternity business meeting here, but I want everyone out by ten."

The second the parents closed the door, Jeff turned to Fran and indirectly to me and said, "I want you out of here tonight. If I see you once, I'll smash your face in, Fran. I mean it, and you know what Skip will do." He put his fist up to her nose, shook it and said, "Stay away."

Fraternity meeting? I had seen handsome boys at football games from the senior high wearing green and white jackets with Greek letters on them. Skip was president of that fraternity. "What do they do at the meetings?" I asked Fran when we were alone again.

"I have no idea."

"Don't you ever listen?"

"No."

I had never seen boys in action as a group. The whole thing interested me, as long as I could remain anonymous. After checking out the rec room under my own reconnaissance — it was panelled and had a long bar with leather stools — I suggested that we hide in the double closet, which had louvred doors. We could see the boys from between the slats, but they wouldn't see us. It would be just a little livelier than a live TV show.

Fran didn't look thrilled by the idea and said, "A lot of what they do, you really don't want to know about."

Although I had wanted nothing to do with boys since the Donny incident, I was still secretly fascinated by what happened in the world of males. What did they do together? What did they talk about? They were having a fraternity "business meeting" tonight. What was the business? I was especially curious because Jeff had made such a point of telling us to stay away.

An hour before the meeting was scheduled to begin, Fran and I snuck down to the basement, piled coats on the floor of the closet for cushions and took ringside seats. We could see perfectly between the wide slats. A short time later Jeff brought down several cases of beer that he must have had in the trunk of his car. We sat and waited, almost afraid to breathe. As the minutes ticked away, I began to worry about what they would do if they caught us. When I asked Fran what she *thought* they might do, she said it was too awful to contemplate. She reminded me that whatever it was, it would be done in front of the whole fraternity.

We watched over the next three-quarters of an hour as most of the popular boys in the senior high descended the stairs in their moss green fraternity jackets. The business meeting, it turned out, was about raising money for a dance through a car wash. This only took about ten minutes. The twenty or so boys didn't focus on details that I would have thought were crucial, such as price, date, location or advertising. They just agreed to have it. I guess they knew what they were doing. I mean, they weren't popular and college-bound for nothing.

Then they moved on to what Skip referred to as "the entertainment." He went to the phone and dialled. "Hi, Veronica. It's Skip . . . That's right, Skip Stephens. I have some friends over and we would love to see you. Why not drop by for a date . . . right now."

The boys were smiling and snickering. One guy looked worried and said, "I got to go." He stood and darted up the stairs, and we heard the door slam.

Within five minutes Veronica arrived and shyly trailed Skip, who had answered the door, down the stairs. She was giggling coyly and looking at the floor. I glanced at Fran quizzically.

She whispered, "It's Veronica Nebozenko — she lives on our street a few doors away. I think she's in grade eleven."

I recognized the name because her father produced mud flaps for trucks. The name Nebozenko was on every mud flap in town. I had thought Veronica must be beautiful to catch the eye of this whole fraternity, so I was surprised by her appearance. Her face was not unattractive, but she was what my mother would have referred to as "horsey," with broad shoulders and huge, pendulous breasts. She wore her thin, dishwater-coloured hair in a pathetic teased flip. She had on a cheap white blouse, a pink cinch-belt stretched to capacity around her thick waist and a black straight skirt that rode up on her large hips. She wore black patent-leather squash heels like those Brenda Lee sported when she sang "Sweet Nothin's"; her feet were wide and bulged over the sides of her shoes. I again looked over at Fran. I was missing something and I wanted her to fill in the blanks. Fran responded with a look that said she wasn't as surprised as I was and that anything was possible.

The boys looked furtively at one another. Clearly they had

some sort of group vision. There was anticipation in the air. I held my breath in the darkness. Skip began introducing Veronica in a voice that was so falsely friendly as to be chilling. Jeff got up and helped lead her to the purple silk couch. The rest of the boys sat still. Skip sat down on the couch, put his arm around Veronica and handed her a stiff drink from his father's liquor cabinet. His hand rested on one of her breasts.

He said, "Wow, are these tits real?"

She nodded and giggled nervously again.

"How do we know it isn't a padded bra?"

She looked at him the way an adoring shaggy dog would look at its owner. It was a slightly quizzical look too. Finally she shrugged.

"Prove it," he said.

"How?" she asked in a voice that sounded as though she needed her adenoids removed.

He started unbuttoning her blouse.

"Forget about it," she tittered, holding her blouse shut.

"Hey! Take off your blouse," he said in the same tone a mother would use if someone entered her home without removing their dripping winter boots.

She sat there looking stunned and didn't move a muscle.

His face softened then, as did his voice. "You know, Elizabeth Taylor just wore a slip in that movie with Paul Newman. I swear she looked like you, Veronica."

That was the *open sesame*. She slowly began taking off her blouse. My hands were sweating and I looked over at Fran, then back at Veronica. What emerged was a giant white bra.

"Okay. Now, boys," Skip said, smirking at those seated around him, "this is my girlfriend, Veronica." Skip smiled his crowd-pleasing smile.

"Really?" Veronica said, beaming from ear to ear.

"Absolutely, I will be your real boyfriend."

"Not just on our street?"

"No way. And since you're my girlfriend now, I want you to show everyone your tits."

"They'll think I'm awful." She looked around the full room with an expression that was hard to read.

"Are you kidding? We think you're beautiful. Those other girls are runts."

Suddenly there wasn't enough air in the closet. I felt weak, like when I had been kneeling in church for too long on Good Friday. For the first time in my life, I realized handsome could be in the eye of the beholder. Skip's Pat Boone movie-star smile had transmogrified before my eyes. His chiselled features now looked angular, sharp and mean.

Veronica awkwardly took off her bra and her immense breasts were unleashed. They fell nearly to her waist. Everyone sat there stupefied. Jeff appeared to speak for everyone when he finally said, "Cowabunga."

I looked at Fran and she just shook her head, which told me all I needed to know. She had tried to warn me about her brothers. I couldn't imagine what else she'd seen over the years. It must have been frightening, having parents who couldn't or wouldn't control these boys. Skip and Jeff's behaviour seemed primitive, even brutal to me.

"What school do you go to?" Skip asked Veronica.

"*You* know. The Mount."

"Mount St. Joseph's Academy? Or is it *this* kind of mount?" he said, knocking her over on the couch and then climbing on top of her like Ken getting on his horse in *My Friend Flicka*. Both Veronica and Skip were laughing and seemed to be enjoying themselves as though they were pretend wrestling. Skip lifted her skirt and pulled down her white underpants, unzipped his pants and took out his pink penis, which resembled a giant eraser. He put it between her legs. She made a vague attempt to pull up her underpants, but then Skip said, "Veronica, we are on a date and you're my girlfriend."

After this I could no longer see her face, or any details. Skip breathed heavily for just a few seconds, arched his back and then went limp on top of her, as though someone had just cut all his tendons. The boys were drinking and getting rowdy as they formed a line behind Jeff.

Jeff was standing at the end of the couch. He playfully knocked Skip off and then he got on top of Veronica and started that same kind of movement, which was a bit like a snake stretching and then having a seizure. Neither boy kissed her. All the boys were now jostling for position. She said, "Oh," as though she were at a party and suddenly everyone had asked her to dance.

By about the eighth boy she was totally silent. As the line progressed, she was getting more and more messy, glistening like a fish that was still fighting the line. I began to feel nauseous and had goosebumps on my arms. I realized I might be sick. I covered myself with a winter coat and held it over my ears and eyes, praying for this to be over.

Now the closet must have been over a hundred degrees. I desperately needed to get out of the room, but knew I couldn't move.

I couldn't look at Fran. It was too horrible to acknowledge what we had seen. Our being there made us complicit in the act.

Finally Fran nudged me, and I uncovered my face. We heard Skip yell that the pizza had arrived and the boys thundered up the basement stairs. I looked through the slats again. Veronica lay limp and silent, facing the back of the couch. She slowly sat up. She had lipstick smeared all over her face. Her breasts looked red and swollen and her legs lay at an unnatural angle. Her wrinkled skirt lay bunched up on the floor.

Skip called down from the top of the stairs, "Veronica, uh . . . thanks for coming over. Go out the side door through the garage." He threw a facecloth down the stairs with the family monogram on it.

I will never forget what she looked like when she stood up. She was like a bewildered newborn calf on shaky legs. I felt like crying for her.

As she rubbed her face on the small hand towel, her orange makeup came off on it. I thought of St. Veronica, who attempted to be charitable to Christ during the crucifixion. She came forward from the crowd and dried the blood and sweat from his face. Miraculously, Christ's face was forever imprinted on the towel.

Veronica took off her ripped stockings and put them in her purse. She cleaned the rest of herself with her crumpled underpants. Before she left, she sat on the couch for a few minutes with her hands clutching her purse on her lap. Her expression looked perfectly blank. I wondered what she could have been thinking. Had she, at any point, thought she was Skip's girlfriend? Was it dawning on her now, as the boys laughed and hooted upstairs, that she had been used? Did she know all along what the game was? As each boy had lined up and said, "Veronica, will you be my girlfriend too?" she had grunted her acceptance as though she had to accept all of the boys and forgive them their sins. It was like she was sacrificing herself for them for some reason that only she understood.

Fran had been right. We should never have done this. She knew far more than I did about what boys in general, and her brothers in particular, were capable of getting up to. I thought of my father and what he had said about my "chasing" Donny Burns. Somehow, in some compartment of my brain, I equated witnessing these boys abusing Veronica with my own shame. I, too, had humiliated myself, and my father had had to witness it.

I vowed then that I'd rather be thought of as anything — cruel, unpopular, you name it — than be dismissed and humiliated as Veronica had been. I promised myself that I would never believe that I was anyone's girlfriend, no matter what they said. You'd have to be nuts to take the chance.

When we knew the fraternity boys had left and we heard Skip and Jeff open the garage and the car pull out, we hobbled up the basement stairs with our limbs aching from being stuffed in the closet for hours. Fran and I couldn't look at each other. I silently daubed more Mercurochrome on my scrapes. We never spoke about what had happened.

Late that night, when we were lying silently in the dark in Fran's twin beds, listening to WKBW radio, the deejay said he was going to play a new song from the Shirelles called "Will You Still Love Me Tomorrow?"

CHAPTER 5

# black lawn jockeys

My father never said a word about my dismal school record in terms of scholastics or behaviour. His line, delivered from behind the *Buffalo Evening News* on his Naugahyde reclining chair, was, "Your deportment is your department." He just reminded me that life was shorter than I thought and the world was smaller than I

imagined. He never mentioned the call from the guidance coun-
sellor, Mr. Myshenko, who'd said I was a "born leader who had
gone astray." I only found out about it when he threatened to call
Dad again. When I asked Mr. Myshenko why he had called my
father instead of my mother, he said that whenever they called my
home and asked the woman who answered if she was the mother
of Cathy McClure, she said *no*.

I really had no idea why Vice-Principal Riley had called in the .
guidance department. *I* was perfectly happy. My mother said it
was because we had made fun of Mr. Riley and questioned his war
record in several of our skits and men didn't take kindly to that
sort of ribbing. I guess I fell somewhere between a discipline problem and a psychological problem. I preferred to be a psychological
problem, because you didn't get detentions for being a nutbar.

I was still interested in athletics, and I was one of the few girls
on the ski jumping team. The school ski adviser, Mr. Clements,
said that he didn't know why Mr. Riley would say I had a screw
loose. He said I was as right as rain. I made one close friend on
the team, named Kip Rogers, who also lived in Tiny Town and
was a great skier. Girls loved Kip, but as a result of the Donny
Donnybrook and the Veronica episode, I had become immune to
that kind of thing, so we just had fun together. He was one of
those rare boys you could manage a friendship with. I loved to
make people laugh and he loved to be entertained, so we were a
match made in heaven. Kip was never mean, unlike so many boys.
No matter how bad someone was, he found something good to
say about them. We had ski races and gave each other tips. We
pretended that we were German ski instructors and were merci-
less critiquing each other's style.

My mother used to drive us out to the slopes two days a week all winter. Then she would wait in the freezing cold chalet while we had our lessons, jumped and did the slalom course until our legs gave out. Before we would leave for skiing, Kip would clean the car of snow and ice and blow out the driveway without anyone asking. He taught us camp songs in the car and had a way of cajoling my shy mother into singing the chorus of "Boom Chicka Boom." Afterwards, Kip always bought my mother chili in the ski lodge and insisted we sit with her and not the rest of the team because she had been kind enough to drive us there. When our team won a race, he picked my mother up in the air and twirled her. My mother said that Kip had "a blessed disposition" and when he was with us "mirth filled the car."

Although my father was hands-off about school, he was a big believer in following current events and discussing them. He said it was our responsibility as citizens to "be well versed," and that if I was to vote, which he thought of as a privilege, I had to be informed. If I eventually wanted to do adult things like get a driver's licence or use the car, I had to know what was going on in the world. He offered to pay me a quarter for each magazine of his choice that I read. His favourite was *U.S. News and World Report.* Every week he would quiz me on the yellow summary page in the back of the magazine. Also, I had to read *Time* and *The Economist.* If I didn't know the answers to his questions, he simply didn't pay me. He never once told me I had to do it; he said it was easy money and I could take it or leave it. I tried faking it once and said Dean Rusk was a cracker. He simply smiled and said, "No cigar." I began reading the magazines because it was a good way, as Roy used to say, to "bring home the lettuce." Television no longer interested me once we moved to Tiny Town. I would have had to sit in our small living room with my parents to watch it, and I found it embarrassing to be in the same room as my father when there was romance on the screen. Even Dick Van Dyke kissing Mary Tyler Moore goodbye was too much for me. But the news was something we all watched each night before going out to dinner.

I was enthralled by anything to do with the civil rights movement. I had gotten hooked on the movement when I was a kid in Lewiston and used to read *Ebony* magazine aloud to Roy at lunchtime. We would both cheer when there was a new advance. Last spring I'd read about the sit-in in Greensboro, North Carolina, where four black college freshmen refused to move from their seats at the segregated lunch counter of a Woolworth's. When I read about how angry people were at them, I was stunned. *Time* magazine quoted Greensboro residents as saying how much they despised the "four Negro youths" and integration in general. When I read this aloud to my mother, she stopped me and said she couldn't bear to hear one more word because it was so sad and unnecessary.

Television had brought the whole fracas into our home. I was fascinated by a special report by Edward R. Murrow. It showed a small black boy placed in a white school after the 1954 decision in *Brown vs. Board of Education of Topeka* ruled that segregation in schools violated the Fourteenth Amendment. The poor little guy looked so lost behind his huge desk. Only his frightened eyes peered out at the camera. All the desks around him were empty; the white students were sitting as far away from him as they could and still be in the room. They looked upon him with such hatred that it was frightening. As my mother said, "Make no mistake about it. All that hatred has been learned at home. It is the shame of America."

—

Soon after moving to Buffalo, having left behind her entire social life, my mother turned to something more hopeful — John F. Kennedy. I couldn't know it at the time, but it would be the last time I would see my mother actively engaging with the world. She had watched the glamorous senator's career unfold in *Life* magazine as he sailed off Cape Cod with his then fiancée, Jackie Bouvier. He was pictured playing football with his athletic brothers and frolicking like a schoolboy on the lawn of his sprawling Hyannis Port summer home. She saw in him a war hero who came back from torpedo boat *PT-109* with back pain, but suffered in silence. Most importantly, in my mother's eyes, he could be the first Irish Catholic to make it to the top with his unmistakable Boston Irish brogue intact.

Although my parents were both Republicans, as the election approached, my mother decided for the first time to support a Democrat. She, like millions of other women, was "crossing the line" for the handsome man who spoke to youth and who in January 1961 would famously say, "Ask not what your country can do for you; ask what you can do for your country." After his inauguration, she started waking me up every morning with that slogan. It sure beat "Onward Christian Soldiers," which my father used as his bugle call.

My mother volunteered to do the accounting for the local campaign office in late September. She'd been a math major, and had done the ordering and kept all the books for an airplane factory during the war — until the soldiers came home and took their jobs back and she gracefully retired to housewifery while still in her twenties. In her new role, she was forced to meet new people, and she even went to strategy lunches. She worked on that campaign day and night. My mother could be relentlessly sedentary, but once she got going, she organized the late stages of the Buffalo Kennedy Campaign with military precision, dividing up the volunteers to make sure every square inch of the city was covered. She rose through the ranks and quickly became one of the leaders of the Kennedy Campaign in Erie County.

My mother couldn't watch the first Kennedy–Nixon debate on television. She said she was too nervous. She stayed in her room, her head buried in her pillow, and my father and I yelled updates to her. We gave a blow-by-blow description as Kennedy edged ahead. From her room we heard only a muffled "Thank God."

Everyone at school watched the Kennedy–Nixon debates with bated breath. We saw in Kennedy someone fresh, someone who wanted to start the Peace Corps, change the world. His gorgeous smile warmed all of us out of the Cold War.

When Kennedy won the election on November 9, 1960, we all screamed, "All right!" My mother and father danced around the room. I wasn't sure why my father was so happy; he was a Republican and said he'd voted along party lines. I guess he was just carried away by my mother's happiness.

The following week my mother was honoured at a luncheon at the Statler Hilton for all the work she had done. My father left work early to attend, and I left school. I had never known him to leave work for anything. When they called her name to come to the stage, Dad had tears streaming down his face. I remember thinking at that moment that I hoped I married someone who loved me as much as my father loved my mother.

My mother was a great admirer of the Peace Corps that Kennedy was starting to put into place. Unlike her cronies back in Lewiston, she had always been interested in the wider world. In the 1950s, when America was worrying about creeping communism, and how to make a good casserole from cream of mushroom soup and tuna fish, her ten-year topic in study club had been "Emerging African Nations." When she'd studied the Mau Maus in the 1950s, she was considered eccentric. Now no one blinked at her interests and she could call herself an internationalist. She actually cared how America treated Third World countries before it became fashionable. She was so moved by the book *The Ugly American* that she became a staunch supporter of the Peace Corps initiative. She saw it as an extension of her Christianity — helping others to help themselves. Later she would put up maps of Africa and mark with push-pins spots where the Peace Corps volunteers were working. And she wrote letters of recommendation for some of her friends back in Lewiston who wanted their kids to be accepted into the Corps.

For the next few years she was revered in some remote political outposts, such as Buffalo, for having had "contacts in Camelot." For the first time in my life, my mother was busy. I felt relieved that I no longer had to entertain her.

—

The world was riveted by the Eichmann trial, which was on the news every night from April to August 1961. It amazed me that Eichmann had been found in Argentina after all those years in hiding and had been brought back to Israel to stand trial for Nazi war crimes. Eichmann was locked in a glass box just like the contestants on *The $64,000 Question.* He was old and spoke through a microphone. I felt a chill when Eric Sevareid said on *CBS News* that the cage was to protect him from being shot by relatives of people he had exterminated in concentration camps.

One of the reasons I remember this so vividly is that my mother and father disagreed about it. My parents rarely had, as my mother put it, "words." They disagreed about once every five years and it always sent me for a loop. Each time, I worried that they would get a divorce. My mother thought Eichmann should be tried for his war crimes and convicted and jailed. My father said he was an old man now who had had to live in hiding most of his life, and that had been enough of a punishment. Besides, he had just been following orders, however despicable. My mother stunned me and my father into silence when she said, "I think you are terribly wrong and am very surprised by your views, Jim," and left the room.

I read all about the Nuremberg trials of 1945 to 1949 and the issue of social responsibility. As a thirteen-year-old, I was amazed by the judgment at Nuremberg, which advocated civil disobedience if policy conflicted with one's moral code. Now that I was getting older, I felt this as a huge personal responsibility. Before I knew about the Nuremberg trials, I had thought all I had to do was follow the law and the Ten Commandments. Now I realized I had to follow my own conscience. The hard part was figuring out when the law was wrong and your conscience was right.

The editorials I read from around the world on Eichmann's situation helped me to think about the philosophy behind the events. While I agreed with my mother on Eichmann, my soul was not bound to that particular fight. I felt that civil rights was my fight. It wasn't just a current event to me. The United States was my country, and I burned with the inhumanity of segregation. Yet I could not go to a sit-in in the South. I couldn't even drive a car yet, legally. But one thing that really bothered me in Amherst were black lawn jockeys. These statues of black men in jockey uniforms and caps, leaning forward and usually holding a lamp, were placed on front lawns, near the front door. I was mystified as to why someone in Buffalo, New York, who had a tasteful large brick home with a beautifully landscaped lawn on a tree-lined street, would think, *Gee, our house isn't complete until we have a statue of a black slave topped with a small jockey cap on our lawn.*

One night in the fall of grade eight, Fran, my mother and I were on our way to Howard Johnson for clam rolls when I spotted a lawn jockey and became infuriated. My mother agreed that they were pathetically yesteryear at best. Dr. Anchesky, our dentist, had one. For some reason she thought he should know better.

Fran figured the idea was that the black jockey transformed your house from suburban drab to a pre–Civil War mansion of the South. The slave waited in the portico to help you out of your carriage so you too could attend the ball at Tara where Rhett Butler was waiting to sign your dance card. I couldn't come up with a better reason for why they were there. In the restaurant, she acted out this whole scene with a black lawn jockey coming to life in 1961, and having just seen the movie she could do the accents perfectly. My mother laughed so hard she choked on her clam rolls and we had to slap her back.

—

The next week I had to do a school project with Kip and another guy I skied with named Steve Bluefeld, known as Mr. Blue (after the song "Mr. Blue" by the Fleetwoods). Mrs. Bluefeld always had great food and she used garlic on meat. I had never known garlic to be used for anything other than warding off evil spirits in horror films and really liked it on the spicy meat sandwiches she made. Kip and I used to go over to Mr. Blue's house after school and eat gigantic meals before my mother picked the three of us up for skiing. Mr. Blue's mom would always pack a dinner for him to eat after being on the slopes, but he would throw it out the car window and go to a restaurant with us instead. I liked Mrs. Bluefeld except for her one major flaw — she had a black jockey on her lawn.

On our way over to Mr. Blue's that day, I told Kip I was going to talk to her about the statue. Kip said it was a bad idea and not really my business.

Mrs. Bluefeld was in the kitchen when we arrived. When I expressed my concern about the jockey, she laughed and said, "Cathy, it's just an antique."

Knowing that they were Jewish, and having just finished reading the bestseller *Exodus,* I came up with the perfect example to drive the point home. I said, "Well, what if someone had an antique replica in their front yard of a man from Auschwitz wearing a yellow star and holding a lantern?"

Mr. Blue's mother looked up from making our sandwiches. "Cathy, my family has been in this country for four generations."

Mr. Blue walked into the room at the tail end of this discussion and started yelling. When he got excited, he stammered. "Y-y-yellow stars — Cathy, you'd better watch what you're saying. No one needs the past thrown in their face like that. Cathy, I k-k-know you. You'd argue with your own shadow, but I'm t-t-telling you right now, you drag up this area and you will get labelled as an anti-Semite so fast you won't know what happened until you find yourself in a glass case in the cafeteria."

Kip looked at me and shook his head in dismay.

On the way home, I said to him, "Geesh, they got excited. But you know what? I bet they'll never look at that statue in the same way again."

"Or you," he said.

"What?"

Kip explained that when people fight wrongs, they don't do it on their friends' front lawns. Sit-ins at the University of Mississippi would make a difference, but he was doubtful that the world would change when black lawn jockeys were removed from the suburb of Amherst, New York.

He just didn't get it. Kip was a close friend, but I knew right then that he could not be enlisted in my Black Lawn Jockey Elimination Squadron.

—

About a week later I went to a party at the home of a boy, Travis, who would eventually have an illustrious football career and then make quite a name for himself in politics. His wealthy family had one of those offensive lawn jockeys, so I said to him, "What's with the statue? The Civil War is over, as far as I know."

Amiable as always, he put his arm around me, which I detested, and said, "Cathy, Cathy, you're an argument just waiting to happen. Come on in and take a load off. Take a night off." As I opened my mouth to object, he laughed and said, "Next time I'll buy a white one, as long as you promise to come in and save me a dance."

At that moment I had an inspiration. The phrase *next time I'll buy a white one* galvanized me, and I began forming a plan. I would paint the faces of the statues white! Then the owners, as well as the people passing by, would get the point. This was a new era. Painting the black jockeys' faces white would be the beginning of a real movement in Buffalo.

When I explained this idea to my mother, she said that she understood the intention, but it was unacceptable because it would involve defacing private property. She said many of those statues were antiques and worth a lot of money. And aside from the illegality of it, some of the homes had guard dogs and security systems. I had never heard of security systems. Either no one in my neighbourhood had them, or else they were the robbers.

My mother said that if I was bound and determined to encourage social change, we should send a letter to each homeowner, explaining that a black lawn jockey was an anachronism — a word I had to look up. I really liked *anachronism* and would use it regularly throughout high school to describe any passé fashion statement. My mother suggested we not even mention *integration*. She pointed out that subtlety was never my strong suit. She assured me that the recipient would get the point.

Not knowing how to type, I badgered my mother into typing the letters, but she made me buy the carbon paper. As I dictated, she said my title "Offensive Lawn Jockeys from History" was a good start. We signed thirty-nine letters as "The People's Committee Concerned about Black Lawn Jockeys." When delivering the letters in the dark of night, I skipped Mr. Blue's and Travis's houses. After this Paul Revere ride through Amherst, we waited. I had made a jockey-locator map, so my mother and I whipped around each day to see how many people had cringed in humiliation once they realized how odious their jockeys were. Out of thirty-nine homeowners, only two had removed them.

I told my mother, and Fran, who had now become involved, that we had to move on to Plan B.

My mother said, "The problem with Cathy is she *always* has a Plan B."

"We are painting the faces white," I said.

"Cathy, I already told you that all of those lawn jockeys are privately owned and on personal property. I am not going back to Dr. Small with a break-and-enter. Count me out," she said.

I could tell she was serious if she was bringing up Dr. Small, the psychiatrist I was sent to after I stabbed Anthony McDougall. I actually didn't blame my mother for being sore about that whole melee because she had had to keep seeing Dr. Small for months after I went back to school and work at the drugstore. She had to continue her appointments, she once told me in her most ironic tone, "to find out where I went wrong."

When I asked Fran if she was in on the next phase of the Black Lawn Jockey Civil Rights Project, she said, "Why not? It's too cold to pool-hop. Hey, won't we need some boys with us to carry the paint?"

I nixed that idea before it gathered any momentum, knowing that having boys along always ruined everything.

So I laid out the plans. We'd have to spend the night at Fran's. She slept in her own wing, which had a door that led out of the laundry room to the backyard. Her parents would never know if we sneaked out. I said I'd buy the paint and the brushes and hide them in Fran's garage. I'd also bring the jockey-locator map. I would draw a circle with a compass, with Fran's house as the central point. That would show the distance we could travel on foot. A one-inch diameter circle on my map included twenty-three lawn jockeys.

On a crisp October night we tiptoed out of Fran's house — two grade eight girls on a civil rights march. The moon was full and hung low in the sky. I told Fran that we would always remember this night. I finally felt part of the changes that were happening in the world.

The paint was too heavy to carry, so we put it in a red Radio Flyer wagon we found in the garage. We had our map and decided to work our way east. Most of the jobs were on Lebrun Road, which had mansions with huge gardens and lots of wooded areas between the homes. It would be easy to hide in the bushes and then dash out and paint the jockeys' faces white. As we approached the first house, I got nervous that the residents would wake up. What if they thought we were prowlers and called the police? I guessed we would have to explain that we were engaged in an act of civil disobedience. Let them put that in their pipe and smoke it. With as much stealth as two teenage girls could manage, we finished the job in less than five minutes.

The first jockey we painted white bore an unfortunate resemblance to Al Jolson in reverse. This wasn't the look I'd hoped for. Perhaps we should have painted them pink. I realized then that white people are really pinkish-greyish-tan. Anyway, it was too late for artistic considerations, so we just rolled our red wagon ahead.

At the next house we hid in the bushes again. The home had several wings and lighting that flashed on when you moved past it. It was two-thirty in the morning, but I was sure I saw two shadows on the driveway near the garage. They were about thirty feet away from where we crouched. They seemed to be male, and at least as old as senior high school. I skulked from tree to tree, getting closer, leaving Fran in the bushes, and I could see their faces as they moved into the light to have a cigarette. They were definitely greasers, or "rocks," as tough guys at our school were called. One was tall, had a black pompadour and thick lips and wore a leather jacket. He spit on the driveway and lit a cigarette as he huddled near the garage door to block out the wind. The other looked surprisingly like the jockeys we were painting, except he was white. He was short, wore a green jacket and was round-shouldered. He had blond Johnny Winters–style Brylcreem'd hair combed straight back and a colourless face. The shadow he cast on the driveway under the basketball net was long. When I was about ten feet away, I could see that his eyes had red lids like some nocturnal rodent.

Scared, I tiptoed back to Fran, who was mixing the paint with a stick, and whispered, "We'd better hide. There are some robbers here."

Fran ran to the edge of the wooded area and giggled as she jumped into the light and began waving to the boys. She said in a theatrical whisper, "You came!" Then she dashed up the driveway, gesticulating wildly. "Hi, Jitters, hi, Joe."

I raced after her. Enraged, I whispered, "Wait a minute. What the hell are these thugs doing here?"

Fran just shrugged as if to say it was too late and she could care less what I had to say about anything now that these guys were here. No one who looked that dangerous could have gone to Amherst Junior High School. Fran tried to placate me when she realized how furious I was. First she said that we needed someone to help with the paint and also to drive. Did she actually believe these cretins could be helpful? She said that no boy that went to Amherst Junior High could know, as she put it, "the workings of the night world." She'd had to cast farther afield and had come up with these guys. She said her cousin knew Joe from grade school, and Joe had brought his buddy Jitters from Industry. I pictured this tiny white maggot as a captain of industry, sitting at a desk in a Wall Street office. Maybe I'd misjudged him.

"What type of industry is he in?" I asked.

"You know, Industry is a jail for kids who are still minors," Fran said. "It isn't exactly jail. It's in between reform school and jail. It's —"

I interrupted, "Skip the distinctions. I get the drift. Here they come."

"Where the hell have you been? It's colder than a witch's tit out here," said the one named Jitters.

Joe said, "You're damn lucky we came. We had to hitch a ride out here to Richville."

"Lucky? I don't recall inviting you," I said.

Fran intervened. "When I met you at my cousin's wedding, you said you had your licence. Didn't you drive?" ·

"We hitched 'cause the car got repossessed," Joe said, laughing as though he'd never heard anything so hilarious.

"Who's the snarling bitch?" Jitters asked, nodding toward me.

"This is my friend Cathy," Fran said.

I ignored them and went to get the wagon and paint. Fran and Joe wound up making out in the woods, while Jitters followed me, making offensive remarks under his breath so that I could just catch the occasional rude or threatening word. By the time we made it to the next house, Fran and Joe had caught up with us. I didn't want help from any of them, so I ignored them.

The boys had brought flasks in their back pockets and took swigs as though they were film extras for *On the Waterfront.* Jitters, who moved from one leg to the other with alarming frequency, like he was balancing on a beam that only he could see, said as he grabbed the paint away from me, "You're takin' way too long. We aren't at some art gallery," and he threw the paint on the jockey, splashing it everywhere.

Then he opened a new can of paint and slapped SUC ME in three-foot letters on the front of the brick house. I was taken aback by the vulgarity of this and realized at that point that civil rights had been left far behind. Joe, the wooer of Fran, painted FRAN DOES IT on the garage. Hardly Cyrano de Bergerac, but it pleased Fran enormously. She held Joe's hand and smiled. I was ready to go home but felt I had to press on with my mission.

At the next house, Jitters went into the garage and got out some gasoline and poured it on the lawn. Frightened, I hissed, "What the heck do you think you're doing?" He said he was going to burn a cross in the lawn. I said, "The Ku Klux Klan does that. We are *the opposite* of that!"

"Oh, is that right?" Jitters said. He smiled a chilling smile and then said to the others in a tone of mock seriousness, "This bitch says the Ku Klux Klan does that," and they all killed themselves laughing. And then he lit the grass where he'd poured the gasoline. Fortunately, it was a damp night and the flame didn't spread.

When Jitters began to pour gasoline in the bushes as well, I said, "Get out of here right now! You have no idea what we're trying to do here."

He yelled at Joe, "Get her out of here before I throw her in the bushes and bang her like a screen door in a hurricane."

I was scared and humiliated. I began packing everything up to go home. Fran now saw that Jitters was one brick short of a load. She whispered to me, "Sorry, Jitters was a mistake."

I knew I had to abort the rest of the operation. I gathered my paint in the wagon and said to Fran, "If you know what's good for you, you will come with me now. I swear I will never speak to you again if you don't." No one moved. I continued, "This is serious stuff. It's not funny." My voice was shaking.

Fran refused to come home. Joe had one thick arm around her and was smoking. Fran said that she and Joe could get Jitters to behave.

I pulled that wagon at record speed all the way back to Fran's. Then I sneaked into the house and collapsed into the armchair in her room. I was sweating from running and my lungs burned.

Fran didn't come back that night. Finally, at seven-thirty the next morning, she appeared. All she said was, "Wow, it was cold out there."

I knew then that I had come to the end of the line with Fran. We could never be friends again. I didn't say anything. I just packed my bag and walked to an IHOP, where I planned to call my mother and ask her to join me for a Belgian waffle. As I walked along in the cold morning, I thought of how much I would miss the fun I'd had with Fran.

—⁓—

Two days later I staggered into the bathroom to take out my rollers and tease my hair for school and found on the closed toilet lid two cut-out newspaper articles from the local papers. They said that vandalism had cut a swath across Amherst and gave the locations involved. The damage was reported to be in the thousands of dollars. My heart began to pound when I read about the money, and I had to sit to read the rest. There was an interview with the bewildered man who had a cross burned into his lawn. The part that really scared me was in the last paragraph, where it said that they had called in downtown detectives because what looked like random destruction might be linked. The occupants of the targeted homes had received anonymous letters stating that they were under surveillance because of their lawn ornaments. I couldn't believe that the paper never mentioned that the ornaments were offensive black jockey statues! One article claimed that the detectives were looking for a French connection to the defacement. How had this gone wrong? French plot? How stupid were the police? I guess they were focusing on Joe's line, FRAN DOES IT. Maybe they thought Fran was short for France? The sad part of this whole episode was that I could go to jail for this and they didn't even get that it was a civil rights issue. What a mess.

Anyway, my mother probably figured it was me, because she'd cut out this article. And I knew her. She wouldn't get involved with this — nor would she cover for me if the chips were down. She would say, "You cooked your own goose" or something to that effect. My father would simply think I was insane and be appalled if he found out that my mother had been in on the letters. Best not to incriminate her any further.

That morning, when I left, I simply yelled "Bye" over my shoulder. Mother lay on the couch, reading the way Madame Defarge kept knitting.

---

A few days after that, when my mother and I pulled into the driveway, I noticed a police car parked at the curb. It followed us into the driveway and parked behind us. Two policemen flashed their badges as I got out of the car.

I said, "We get it. We saw the car." Then I realized I'd better change my tune. What if I was sent to Industry? Was there one for girls? Maybe it was called Homemakers or Industryette. It was probably on the same site and the girls had to make supper for the boys in Industry and then send it in tunnels in Tupperware containers.

"Won't you come in?" my mother said, smiling at the policemen.

It was four o'clock. Mercifully, my father wasn't home yet. I had one hour to get these cops out. For a brief second, I contemplated coming clean. I actually wanted to just tell them what I had hoped to accomplish, and explain how it had all gone wrong. But I didn't have the money to pay the damages. Surely the jockey owners' insurance would cover it. My father was acting strange about money lately — in fact, strange altogether — so I decided I had to remain silent.

My mother came back into the living room in an apron. God, that must have been a wedding present. Where did she dig that up? What a great touch. Maybe she *was* on my side. She shook hands and offered everyone a Tab or a Coke. I took one, as did the heavier of the two cops.

They asked me if I knew anything about recent vandalism in Amherst. The total in damages, they said, was in the "five digits." My heart was going like a jackhammer.

"Jeepers," I said. "This was some angry man."

"Man?" one of them asked.

"That was my assumption," I said.

"You're probably right. No one else could have carried some of those statues and thrown them in the swimming pools."

Thank goodness I wasn't there for that.

"Do you help your dad a lot?" the other cop asked.

"I've worked for him since I was four."

"The reason I'm asking is a pale blonde teenage girl bought some white paint from Hector's Hardware last weekend. The boy who worked there said it was you. He remembered you from track and field."

Holy moly. What now? He could identify me.

"Yes, I did buy paint. I was going to paint our doghouse. The paint is in the garage. Would you like to see it?"

"We'll check on our way out. Ever heard of Tom Drescher? Nickname Jitters?"

"No."

"He's our culprit, and we just wondered who was with him. He's been placed in a foster home in the downtown area. He was just out of Industry a month ago. Nasty piece of work. I can see you're not his type." Then he looked at my mom. "It's a good thing too." (Later, in the 1980s, Jitters was convicted and received life imprisonment for being a hit man for the leaders of the Hare Krishnas. The whole episode was described in a book called *Monkey on a Stick*.)

As they stood to leave, my heart was pounding so hard my ladybug pin was actually fluttering. I tried to make eye contact with my mother, but she just looked straight ahead with a Betty Crocker smile on her face.

I opened the front door for the officers and kept talking, hoping they would not go back to the garage to see the paint (or lack of it). Thankfully, they never mentioned it, and just waved and drove away.

I went back into the house and straight to my room, where I stayed until it was time to go out for dinner. My father pulled in and beeped, and Mom and I popped out to the car to go the Four Seasons Restaurant, just as we did most nights. Neither of us mentioned any police visit.

One thing I did notice was that the jockeys we painted were retired and that even the ones we never got to slowly disappeared.

CHAPTER 6

# fried

Nineteen sixty-three was shaping up to be the most boring year

God ever created. I was fifteen years old, and grade ten was beyond

deadening. You had to sit at a desk in an overheated classroom

that smelled of disinfectant and floor polish while some teacher

droned for an hour. Then the bell rang and we somnambulated

like the living dead to the next overheated room. It was worse than prison, because at least there you could read what you wanted.

I continued to do no homework. I copied my French every day from Leora and wound up at mid-terms with a D. *Quel dommage.* No one said anything about my abysmal report cards. I told my mother that I had no desire to learn a dreary little language that only worked in their tiny country. In the films we saw in French class, they were always emerging from bat-infested winery caves with glasses of Bordeaux, saying, "*Magnifique.*" Then the dutiful children of the drunken sods who went from winery to winery to "discover different regions" would have a sip of wine and say, "*Oui, maman.*" I used to regale my mother with descriptions of the French film clips we were supposed to memorize for *La dictée.*

When you don't do any school work and want nothing to do with boys, you have a lot of time on your hands. Restless, I decided to become an entrepreneur. I was a natural at the cosmetics trade, since we had supplied most of Niagara Falls and its tourists with makeup at the drugstore, so I returned to it that year as an Avon representative. One thing I had learned in our drugstore was that no one liked makeup as much as teenage girls. So I never entered my homeroom without saying "Avon calling." I had a captive market. I seemed to have been born to work, for soon I was toiling until the wee hours and ranking as a top saleswoman, before moving on to the big time — Mary Kay cosmetics. I would have been awarded a Mary Kay pink Cadillac to drive if I'd been old enough. At Mary Kay's pink school I learned a great slogan: *Fake it till you make it.* I have used that concept ever since in most of my endeavours. It eases the learning curve and lowers anxiety.

My father's restlessness paralleled mine. He worked like a fiend on his lawn, which was the size of a postage stamp. He made what little there was of it look like a putting green. He bought an enormous number of lawn power tools, the kind you would use if you were the head gardener at Buckingham Palace. He had a machine that plowed snow and another that had a bucket that carried firewood, even though we had no fireplace. He spent a lot of time in his huge garage, sitting in a lawn chair, labelling garden tools with a machine he'd bought called a Dymo, a plastic gun that cranked out small red plastic labels. He labelled every tool and machine he owned, and delineated parking spots with red plastic lines. The label on the screwdriver said, SCREWDRIVER OWNED BY JAMES MCCLURE.

Occasionally he made a brief foray outside the garage to cut the grass with his riding mower. The lawn was so small he had trouble even turning the mower around without hitting concrete, but he persisted with this, as well as with his massive electric edger, which he used while wearing safety glasses. This deafening machine dug little gullies like a mad gopher along the driveway and up the walk. When I saw him edging his way up and down the street, I suggested that the neighbours might not be as wild about edging as he was. To this he replied, "Good edges make good neighbours." When I told him it was Robert Frost who said, "Good fences make good neighbours," he said it was Jim McClure who added the "edging component." My mother hoped no one wearing high heels would stumble into those gullies and sprain an ankle.

One day, after hitting concrete too many times, my father sent us into the bowels of the city to get a new blade for what he referred to as his "self-propelled." After travelling through a labyrinth underneath the elevated thruway system, we finally got to the parts store and requested the gigantic blade. The salesman asked us if we'd come in from a farm. He said he'd have to go through the warehouse and it would take a half-hour.

My mother and I decided to have dinner while we waited. We were in the Puerto Rican part of the city and there were mostly warehouses and rundown bars. Finally we came upon a doughnut shop. We figured if we got something more expensive out of the cooler under the cash register instead of a doughnut, it would be enough for dinner. I dined on a chocolate éclair with a cinnamon bun as a second course and washed it down with a Tab.

There were no tables, only a U-shaped counter with stools around it. We could see through a window from the shop into an attached doughnut factory. It was interesting watching how all the doughnuts were made in huge vats and fryers. The cream- and jelly-injecting machine looked like a turkey baster for *Tyrannosaurus rex*.

A small, swarthy man who looked like he might be the owner, since he wasn't wearing a uniform, entered from the factory. As he got closer, I could see he had parted his hair almost at his ear in a lounge-lizard attempt to cover his bald spot. He focused on three nervous-looking girls who were sitting at the counter. He eyed them as though he were Chief Justice Earl Warren of the Supreme Court making a momentous decision. Finally he said to them, "You the girls applying for the waitress job?"

They nodded.

My mother and I watched in fascination as the interview pro- ceeded. All three sat with their elbows on the counter, dragging on cigarettes. My mother whispered to me, "Never smoke at a job interview."

The owner said, "Okay, dame-sels" — a cross between dames and damsels — "I have a little test for you."

The girls looked around, then realized they were the dame-sels.

The owner was carrying a timer. "The first one to figure out how to work the coffee machine — that is, grind the coffee and make a full pot — is hired. Who's going first?" he asked.

One eager beaver said, "I will."

I piped up, "I'd go last so you can learn from the mistakes of the other two."

The prospective waitress said, "Hey, why didn't you say that before I said I'd go first?"

"You should send the others out of the room to make it fair," I suggested to the owner.

He shot me a look that said I should shut up. But he did send two of the girls into the factory while the other took his test. The first one couldn't work the machine at all and after two minutes he said, "Time is up and so long, Cisco."

I had grown up in diners. I had no idea how to boil an egg, but I had seen hundreds of pots of coffee being made before most kids had given up their bottles. I stood up, leapt behind the counter and did it in record time, with a second pot ready to go and a third on top set to boil for tea.

The owner lifted an eyebrow. My mother clapped, and the one toothless skinny man who was drinking coffee with a shaky hand, said, "She's your girl, Mr. B."

The other two applicants took well over two minutes each. One even ran the pot with no grounds. "Mr. B." then had them wait in the factory, and asked me what I'd do if there were no customers. I said I'd refill the napkin holders, the sugar containers, the salt and pepper, run the dishwasher, clean the counter and fill up the doughnut trays. I'd seen waitresses do this for years while they "chewed the fat" with Roy. When the other applicants came back, one said she'd make sure everything was running smoothly and see if any customers wanted seconds. I guess she forgot that in his hypothetical example there were no customers in the store.

"You eighteen?" he asked.

"Nope, but I'm over sixteen." It was not quite true, but fifteen was close enough.

I heard my mother gulping her coffee.

"Start this Saturday at 4:30 a.m. Same on Sunday. Friday start at 3 p.m. It's your problem how you get out of school."

"Salary?" I asked.

"Minimum wage."

"Which is?"

"$1.15 an hour."

"What?" I asked, disgruntled.

"You're a doughnut waitress — not a rocket scientist," he said over his shoulder as he headed back into the factory.

"What if I do the work of two waitresses and you don't have to hire a second?"

"If that happens, you should open your own place." Then he closed the door.

Thus began my career at The Dunk.

When we pulled into the driveway, my father's car was already there. I guessed he had missed dinner. My mother wondered how we were going to tell him that I had a job in the Puerto Rican part of Buffalo, starting tomorrow at four-thirty in the morning at the illegal age of fifteen. We both knew better than to include the part about my early school departure. That had been a hard sell even to my mother. I'd finally convinced her that nothing important happened at school on Friday afternoon. The only thing I would miss was study hall and French. All I did in study hall was sell cosmetics. Actually, that was all I did in French as well. My mother suggested that someday I might want to speak French more than having had the experience of being an underage doughnut waitress, but in the end she did agree to write a note to the school saying that I had a standing appointment every Friday. When she worried about lying, I told her that it *was* an appointment and I would, after all, be standing.

I was happy to be able to get back in the saddle. I had worked full-time for most of my life, and staying at home seemed slack to me. I had lots of energy and generally hated sitting around. Sitting for seven hours a day with teachers blathering at me about what to do and what to think was like wearing a hair shirt in the heat.

I could sit for long periods if I was reading. That was different. I needed to read because it did for my mind what physical labour did for my body. If I didn't read at least two books a week, I would feel restless or like I'd had too much coffee. My mind would be going too fast to listen to others. Reading stretched it and made me feel good, or at least normal. When I read, I did more than imagine the country or era I was reading about. I'd be there and enter the character's bodies, just as the Holy Ghost or my guardian angel entered mine. I was ready to relax after I'd finished a novel like *A Tale of Two Cities*. I'd been to France and England, fought in a war and stood on a guillotine (whew). I would often see people on the street that I imagined to be the characters in those books.

My mother was equally happy to get me back to work. The trouble I was getting into now at school was the same sort of trouble I got into when I was a preschooler. When I was three, I climbed trees and the fire department had to come and get me down, and at four I did imitations of Ed Sullivan and bacon frying for money at the dry goods store. Now, as a teenager, I had gone over the top in some of my "broadcasts." And I had ignored rules. The ski lodge had called to say I was skiing "dangerously" and not staying on the trails.

All of this behaviour was due, my mother said, to "overexuberance." She said I was really the same girl at fifteen that I had been at four. When we lived in Lewiston, people used to say, "Who lit a fire under her?" Mr. Wallens, who owned the clothing store at the corner near my father's pharmacy, said I had *shpilkes*. For many years I thought *shpilkes* was a condition, like diabetes. Only later did I find out that it was Yiddish for nervous energy or "being on pins and needles." My mother pointed out to my father that work was important glue for me, and it used up my excess energy. Though my father didn't even know about the lawn jockey escapade, he finally agreed to the job.

When I thought about my behaviour as a small child and my work history, I realized that my mother was, as usual, right. When I worked I got into far less trouble.

——

When you work at four-thirty in the morning in a Puerto Rican neighbourhood in an all-night doughnut shop, you see four kinds of men — truck drivers, policemen, men who are lonely and men who have no real home — and one kind of woman: the kind that's hit hard times. The factory wasn't so much a hole in the wall as a hole in the ground. The Dunk was a perfect name, for it was located far below the skyway, between two steel girders. It was surrounded by elevated forks holding up the New York State Thruway, the Niagara Expressway and the exits for the route to Canada. All the highways surrounding the shop formed an inter-woven cup, and The Dunk lay like a soggy doughnut at the bottom under all the intertwined concrete. If you'd landed at The Dunk from Mars, you would have had no idea that nature existed. Coffee cups vibrated when a big transport truck rumbled over-head. When there were trucks on all the exits, the cups rang like a wind chime. The upside was that when it rained, the parking lot never got wet, and when it snowed you never had to plow.

All the employees had lockers. I was given a salmon-coloured uniform and within the first week it had *Cathy* embroidered on it in maroon cursive writing with a little curlicue at the end of the *y*. It was starched to the point of giving me a burn on my neck, and I threw it in the laundry bin marked SOILED after each shift. We all wore white aprons, and you had your choice of either a black hairnet, which made me look as though Spider-Man had caught my blonde hair in his web, or a weird little white peaked frill cap that was starched to attention.

When I saw my embroidered name, I said to Mr. B. (which stood for Bertinelli), "Now you'll have to hire another girl named Cathy if I ever leave, but I hope I'm irreplaceable!"

Mr. B. yelled, and I mean *yelled,* "You just take care of the cus-tomers and remember you're on trial here. Don't go gettin' above yourself. Go on — git!" He pointed to "the front," as the restaurant was called. I was offended that he would speak so rudely. Plus, it was ten minutes before I was even supposed to start working. I was having my first taste of what people had to put up with when they were hourly wage employees with nowhere else to go. Maybe I had become too used to being the boss's daughter.

I was working with Puerto Rican males, most of whom didn't speak much English. Only the head cook, José, spoke English well. There were only two people there besides me who weren't Puerto Rican. One was a man named Wendy who had a tattoo on his arm of cherries on a stem. I guess you have the right to be weird if you're a man named Wendy. He described himself as "just your basic goddamned American" when I asked him where he was from. The other non–Puerto Rican was a waitress named Mary Ellen Edgar who had worked there for years on weekends, starting at 10 a.m. to catch the after-church crowd. Mary Ellen was big and lumbering, with sallow skin, dyed orange hair with dark roots and frizzy ends fried by a home permanent. She looked like she was made of cartilage and had no bone structure at all. She spoke only in monosyllables and never made eye contact. She was the first person I'd ever met who turned her whole body away when she talked to you. When I asked if she lived near the shop, she said, "What's it to ya? Why don't you go back to your fancy suburb and stop slummin'."

The first thing Mr. B. told me was that all policemen get everything for free — no matter what they order. Mr. B.'s car had a bumper covered with POLICE PAL stickers. Naturally, the place was a police hangout.

Another regular was a man who talked to anyone who would listen, and if no one would listen he talked to himself. He spoke in a strange singsong cadence, almost as though he were an original rap singer or Billy Graham delivering the gospel. He wore a baseball hat with a multitude of oversized pins with sayings on them. The button in front read, SOMETIMES PARANOIA IS JUST HAVING ALL THE FACTS.

The first time I met him, he said his name was Pontius Pilate because he had washed his hands of the world. Then he dipped his fingers, with his long, curled, dirty nails, into a glass of water. He often quoted from the Bible and from literature and clearly had been an intelligent, interesting man before he was debilitated by mental illness. The Pilate, or Pilate, as he was called, lived nearby in an empty warehouse under the highway.

The Pilate referred to Dayanara, a local prostitute, as Dulcinea. He said she was a saint who gave the undeserving a piece of herself under the Peace Bridge. When she felt down, usually after a few drinks and a fight with a new boyfriend who usually turned out to be a pimp, the Pilate would say to her: "'A knight errant without love entanglements would be like a tree without leaves or fruit, or a body without a soul.'" Years later at college, I would realize that Pilate had been quoting the classics.

Truck drivers came in, and they liked to talk to me. I was curious by nature, so I often asked them about their routes and life in different places. These guys were from all over the United States, and I learned about travelling through the Louisiana Bayou and how to carry explosive gas through the mountains. As my father used to say, you can learn from everyone if you ask the right questions. I also laughed a lot and tried to have a good time. I mean, why not? I was there anyway. I may not have been Groucho Marx, but it didn't take a lot to be slightly more engaging than Mary Ellen, whose hobby was biting her lower lip until it bled. I was a fast worker and plied people with fresh warm doughnuts even when they didn't ask for more. No one ever complained about the cost. I also knew how to drum up sales at the takeout counter, saying to mothers who came in after church with swarms of kids hanging off their full, colourful skirts, "You don't want to have them fighting over that last peanut twister on the Lord's day. You better take two dozen."

One day, as I was carefully counting change, one of the policemen, Kevin Donovan, said, "Ask one of the spics in the back when the plain twisters are going to be ready."

I informed him that "spic" was a racist slur and I had no intention of responding to a racist's requests. I also suggested that policemen were supposed to uphold the laws, not break them.

"Suppose I just tell your boss you think you don't have to do anything you don't want to do?"

"My boss is Jesus Christ and you'd be wise to remember that," I said. Suddenly I was speaking in tongues — the tongue of my grade-school teacher Mother Agnese. It is amazing what comes out of your mouth in anger. Anyway, it buttoned up Kevin Donovan in his bulletproof vest mighty quickly.

I later saw Kevin out the window in the parking lot talking to Mr. B., who was loading trays into the truck. Mr. B. came in and slammed the door behind him, giving me a dirty look.

After my shift he told me that if I ever insulted a cop again I would be out on my keister. He also said I had to apologize. I promised to talk to Kevin Donovan when he was in next.

—

We would relax as soon as we saw Mr. B. drive away in his truck with the motto AT THE DUNK WE WATCH THE DOUGH-NUT NOT THE HOLE painted on the side in pink letters, with doughnuts for all the Os. José would say, "It's time to watch the hole," and then we would all lay off. Mr. B. never gave anyone a break. Even if you weren't busy and had cleaned everything, you still couldn't sit down. A lunch hour was unheard of.

I thought of how differently my father's store had been run. Whether or not he was there, everyone did their job in exactly the same way. We all took a break at ten-thirty or when we needed to. No one ever minded putting in extra time at Christmas and Easter or when there was a flu epidemic. When I told my father how everyone slacked off at The Dunk when Mr. B. left the premises, he said that if you tyrannize people you have only their labour — you never have their loyalty.

Whenever Tito Puente came on the radio and Mr. B. wasn't around, José and the other Puerto Ricans would scream, "El Rey del Timbal!" Immediately everyone would roll the cooling trays into the corners, clear a space and "set up" as they called it. The maracas would come out — large bottles of nutmegs for shaking — the conga drum would be an old industrial-sized shortening container turned over, and the bongos would be flour containers of different sizes — one full and one empty, for different sounds. José would beat out a rhythm with claves; with two huge wooden spoons, he would make all kinds of amazing sounds. In the summer, we would open the back doors, which faced east. At sunrise the view no longer looked like a series of intersecting highways. Instead, it resembled a pink desert with orange mirages. We watched the dawn cast neon pink and orange shadows on the thruway. The sun reflected off the skyway girders like a spinning nightclub light. The beams danced off the steel and bounced through the door. The street cleaners would have just finished washing the streets and all the filth from the night would have swirled down the drain. It was time for a cigarette and *la bomba*, the traditional music of Puerto Rico.

After watching the Puerto Ricans for a month or two, I caught on to the beat and started joining in. I stamped and dragged my feet, and the rock sugar we sprinkled on the floor would crinkle with a marvellous sound under my shoes.

When I told my mother about our dawn dances, she said it was good to know all those years of tap dancing weren't for naught.

Although The Dunk had its drawbacks in terms of a mean boss who exploited everyone, I learned there how hauntingly beautiful the dawn could be. Forever after, I would be an early riser. I also found that, with the dawn, there are no distractions. You can do a whole day's thinking between the hours of 4 and 7 a.m.

—

I was at work one dreary Friday a few weeks before Thanksgiving: Buffalo at its worst. Everything was raw, newly dead, waiting for a decent burial with the first snowfall.

I was making coffee and Dulcinae was telling me that I shouldn't go for the first guy I laid my eyes on. Kevin was chatting with a Texan trucker and showing him all the pockets he had in his new vest.

I said, "I guess since you get all your coffee free, you don't need a pocket for your wallet in that bulletproof vest."

The paying Texan at the counter snickered.

"I need a bulletproof vest to deal with *you*," Kevin said, lifting his complimentary coffee.

The Pilate came in saying the chill had gone right through him and he couldn't get the warehouse heated up no matter what he burned.

I remember that moment, and everything that followed that day, and can replay it in my mind in slow motion. The memory is so vivid that the smell of reused peanut oil fills my nostrils.

José rushed out from the back, howling, "President Kennedy was shot. He's been shot in the head in a motorcade in Dallas. He's dead. It was an assassin."

We all stopped moving. I felt my vision narrow. I couldn't even ask José any questions. I just looked down at the connecting rubber mats on the floor, which were sprinkled with sugar and had become dirty with footprints. No one said a word for a full minute. I thought of how sad my mother would be.

Dulcinae laid down her spoon and said, "Why, when something good happens, does someone have to kill it? I liked that thing he said about our country not doing for us — you know that thing he said."

"'Ask not what your country can do for you; ask what you can do for your country,'" Kevin reminded her. He added, "Jack Kennedy was the first Irishman, first Catholic in the White House, for Christ's sake."

He and I exchanged same-clan glances. I had never felt anything but American before, but suddenly at that moment, with Kevin, I felt Irish Catholic.

Kevin had no Kleenex in any of the innumerable pockets of his bulletproof vest, so I slipped him a napkin as he fiercely blinked tears away.

After a long silence, the Pilate began slowly spinning on his stool. He said, "This is the beginning of the end, ya know."

No one answered.

I knew that the Pilate was crazy, but he was on to something.

I felt it too — we all did. I could not have articulated it at that moment, but I sensed the stillness in the air, the grumble under the earth as my innocence was pulled out from under my feet.

Later that day, José got the TV out of Mr. B.'s office and brought it out front — something we'd never done before. We justified this office invasion by saying that the police and the other customers wanted to see it. Passing trucks pulled in from all over the country to catch the live coverage. It was the first time I saw a TV turn a place into a town hall. I later read that 93 percent of Americans watched the coverage. Kennedy was the first president we knew well — or thought we did — because we'd seen him in our living rooms.

"Who's going to be president now?" Dulcinae asked.

"Bobby Kennedy, I hope. He was tough on Cuba. He can do it. It should be Jack's brother," Kevin said.

Apparently Irish cops thought they could call the dead president Jack.

"I think it will be the vice-president. I mean, that's the line of succession," I said.

"That guy from Minnesota?" Dulcinae asked.

"Is it Humphrey?" someone asked.

The trucker from Texas spoke for the first time. "Lyndon Johnson, a big cracker from the Lone Star state."

We all exchanged glances. Him?

The front was soon packed, and we began running low on everything. José had to come and work the counter and wait on the lines of disbelieving people who'd pulled off the highway. They were willing to stand along the windows to see the TV. I didn't charge most of them, and when José looked at me questioningly, I said, "Hey, we're all Americans."

———

Two days later, when I was filling the dishwasher, José ran to the front and started yelling in Spanish, causing Dulcinae to throw up her arms and scream in Spanish.

Kevin snapped, "What the hell — shut up, José, or speak English."

José flipped on the TV just in time for us to see a replay of someone shooting Lee Harvey Oswald on the television screen.

The Pilate screamed, "How in tarnation did that guy get into police headquarters?" As he kept watching, he added, "Who walks into police headquarters and kills a heavily guarded assassin in front of a police force?" The Pilate got up on his feet and told the shop that this was a set-up. His eyes were bulging and he was agitated as he said, "Some group promised to get rid of Oswald before he talked. Oswald botched the crime and now they sent someone in to shoot him before he talked."

I asked the Pilate who "they" were.

Kevin and the other policemen who had just come in from their squad cars got angry at the Pilate. "Shut up, Pilate. You're nuts and this is a time of national emergency. Nobody wants to hear your paranoid ravings. History is unfolding, so shut the frick up."

"History is unfolding. I like that," Dulcinae said.

"Actually, we are getting dribbles of information from NBC, who got their information from the FBI and CIA," Pilate said.

One of the policemen said, "Don't make me come over there, Pilate, or I will."

Dulcinae said, "You've had too much coffee, Pilate. You know how you get."

As the days rolled by, we all watched, over and over, as Jackie got off the plane in her Oleg Cassini outfit. We saw the rider-less horse whinny down Pennsylvania Avenue, and we all felt for three-year-old John-John as he gamely saluted his dead father in the horse-drawn casket draped with the American flag.

At the time of the assassination, my mother barely mentioned it, and she left the room during any of the TV coverage, which went on for months. No matter how many times people called her to be involved in politics again, she politely declined. In fact, she had very little to do with *anyone* after that. The outfits purchased for her political activity were placed in dress bags, and every year the mothballs were replaced. A decade later, she put Dymo labels on the permanently zippered plastic bags that said, GOODWILL — SIZE EIGHT.

I felt her wound over Kennedy's assassination and watched it spread into a general listlessness. She stopped buying clothes in the way she used to and rarely got her hair done any more. When I asked her why she no longer went to her weekly salon appoint-ments, she said, "Surely it will not mar the aesthetic of the Four Seasons Restaurant." *Why bother?* became her refrain.

—

Buffalo is not called the snow capital of America for nothing. One winter morning in 1964, everything was blanketed in almost three feet of snow. I was fairly immune to the weather because I'd spent my childhood working outside the drugstore at six in the morn-ing, selling newspapers. Also, I knew how to dig myself out of any snow that God put in my path. When I worked with Roy, we liked a snowstorm — considered it a challenge. Interesting things happened in snowstorms because nature pried you out of your everyday routine.

It never occurred to me not go to work at The Dunk. Mom drove the long way, knowing that it would be better than the skyway, which would have more ice, wind and whiteouts. As my mother and I inched along, she said everyone made too much of a fuss about snow. She said she'd ridden in rumble seats all the way to New York City when she was a teenager on worse days than this one.

When I got to The Dunk, I was surprised that I was the only employee to have made it in. When I'd worked at the drugstore, not making it in hadn't been an option. The Pilate was the only customer, and he was wearing old hip boots the firemen down the road had given him. It was strange to see the empty factory. Mr. B. called to say that the snow was so bad where he lived in East Aurora that the roads were closed. He was trapped in his new, palatial home. Ah, at last, relaxation at The Dunk. The Pilate and I sat down and had a coffee together.

When the phone rang, I thought it might be Mr. B. again, so I turned down the radio, which was playing "He's So Fine" at top decibel. It was José, in a flap. When he was riled up, his English went to pieces. I finally understood that his car wouldn't start and he couldn't pick up Jésus and Luis and the others — and the buses weren't running. I told him not to sweat it because nobody was in. He insisted the doughnuts had to get made. It was Sunday and the Jehovah's Witnesses and the Catholics would be in later when the roads were cleared. The dough was prepared and ready and all I had to do was turn the Beetle on high (the black iron fryer was called the Beetle because it was the size of a Volkswagen Beetle). Then I was to drop the dough in the fryer in small circles, making twelve rows of twelve, and frost them with the Hershey's Chocolate Spread.

After I hung up, I heated the fryer until the oil started to bubble. I put the circles of batter in and they quickly started to sizzle. The next step was the tricky part. It was hard putting the chocolate frosting on the doughnuts while the dough was still wet and the doughnuts were wobbling and bobbling in a rough sea of boiling oil. When I reached the middle rows, my arm was getting splattered with hot oil, so I had to turn down the fryer until I got them all frosted. When I finished spreading chocolate on the 144th doughnut, I reset the timer and the oil began to simmer again.

I went to the ladies room and washed my hands. It took a long time to get the hardened chocolate off my arms and out from under my nails. When I looked in the mirror, I noticed my uniform was splattered with chocolate and dough, so I changed all my clothes, got a new uniform and redid my hair.

By the time I opened the lavatory door, the smell of burning chocolate was overwhelming.

The lavatory was the last room at the end of hallway from the factory. Our lockers lined the hallway and Mr. B.'s office was on one side and the storerooms and janitor's closet were on the other. A closed door separated this hallway from the factory. As I walked down the hall, I felt a wall of heat, and when I opened the factory door, flames shot out like a devil's tongue. I jumped back before they got me. Smoke billowed and began to fill the narrow hallway. I panicked, realizing that I had no way to get out of the hallway and into the front restaurant except through the factory. I remembered there was an emergency exit in the factory, but it was on the far side of the building. I didn't know how to get there through the smoke. Now the flames were shooting out of the fryer and hitting the roof, travelling like orange trapeze artists up the wires to the ceiling and along the wires hooked to the exhaust system. I wanted to turn on the fan, but I knew that air feeds a fire.

Then I figured, the hell with putting out the fire. How was I going to get out alive? I went back into the bathroom, climbed up on the sink and opened the small window near the ceiling. I wondered if I could slip through it. But I saw bars on the outside.

I began to smell smoke in the lavatory and my eyes were watering. I took off my apron, soaked it in the sink and put it back on. The smoke was coming in under the doorway. I got my soiled uniform from the bin and shoved it in the crack between the floor and the door. As I paced, it hit me that I was trapped. I was going to be fried and become the 145th doughnut. Everything Mother Agnese ever said about me was true. I would burn in hell, and this was it. I was so bad that hell couldn't wait. I thought of all those film strips we used to see in Catholic school, like the one where the boy went fishing instead of going to Mass and then in the next frame he was burning in the fires of hell, saying how a moment's, a day's or even a lifetime's earthly pleasure wasn't worth an eternity in hell.

Then I heard my name. The door burst open. It was a fireman in a gas mask. There was another fireman behind him with a hose spraying water at the fire. Kevin Donovan came barrelling down the hall, past the mops and pails. A fireman yelled, "I've got her. Good work, Kevin." They got the flames out in minutes, but the black smoke was thick and continued billowing and it was hard to catch my breath.

When I emerged into the factory, a dozen firemen were staring at me. They wrapped me in a large thermal blanket and took me outside. A few of them were Dunk regulars and said things like, "Hey, Cath, glad you're okay."

One fireman said, "Kevin called us from the phone on the thru-way as soon as he smelled the smoke." Fortunately, the station was only two blocks away. As he began folding up the hoses, he added, "A good thing it's a single building or it would have caught on like kindling."

About an hour later, as they were packing up all of their equipment, I went back in and took a look around. The walls were black on the fryer side of the factory. Water dripped from the ceiling. The trays of finished doughnuts floated in waterlogged trays. Some were actually stuck on the wall where the hoses had blown them.

The Pilate popped his head back into the factory and screeched, "We have all been anointed by tongues of fire!"

"Pilate, we have no time for your bullshit. This is serious. Cathy is about to get fired," Kevin said.

Fired?

"Her pale fire she snatches from the sun."

"One more word and I drive you to the bin and you can blather on in a padded cell about fire there. Pull yourself together and try and help Cathy."

The door closed and the Pilate was gone. A fireman appeared holding a clipboard. I knew him from the counter.

José, who had just arrived, the fire chief, Kevin and I all surrounded the ruined fryer. We stood around it like cowboys around the campfire. I was clearly on my last stampede.

José took the scoop and pulled out charred chocolate flakes. "Oh no," he said, and then he went on in Spanish. (He sounded like Ricky yelling at Lucy on *I Love Lucy*.)

Kevin said, "This is America, son, speak English."

"I was late for work. I called and told Cathy to fry the dough-nuts and to frost them with chocolate. She must have put the frosting on *before* they went in the fryer."

"No, I put it on *while* they were in the fryer," I said.

"What the hell do you think *frost* means?" the fireman asked me.

"Frost? I mean, I've had frosting on cakes." I hesitated, unsure what he was asking.

"Didn't you ever see your mother frost a cake?"

"No."

"Mr. B., he will go loco and have her head," José said, and the others nodded.

"Well, what's the worst he can do?" I paused and added lamely, "I mean, the fire is out."

We all looked around at the thousands of dollars' worth of fire and water damage.

Kevin pulled up his holster and adjusted his pants — the type of thing a certain kind of man does before he takes action. The snowplows had been out and the traffic was starting to move. Mr. B. had been called and the firemen were rerouting disappointed doughnut shoppers out of the parking lot.

Kevin said, "We have twenty minutes, tops, until the owner is here." He turned to the fire chief. "Could you wait out front and have a free breakfast and then come on in and file your report?"

When the chief left, Kevin turned to me and announced in an abrupt, official tone. "This was caused by a faulty wire in the fryer. Cathy, clean that chocolate charcoal gunk out of the fryer, bag it and dump it in the trunk of José's car. José, get a knife and splice those wires and then hold a match to the end. Cathy, scrape all that burned chocolate off the ceiling."

The fire chief was invited in after we'd organized and cleaned up the mess, and he looked around and wrote things on his clipboard.

Then Mr. B. stormed in, screaming in Italian, "*Ma cosa fate, cretini!*" while simultaneously hitting himself on the side of the head.

"We are trying to deal with faulty wiring here. When was the last time you had your fire extinguishers checked?" the fire chief asked, holding up an orange tag that hung off the extinguisher and indicated when it was last examined.

Before he could answer, the chief added, "And there was no fire extinguisher in the utility hallway."

Mr. B. said, "Why is the fryer destroyed?"

"You tell me. These frayed wires finally broke and were sparked by the fryer oil," the chief said, holding the burned wires.

Mr. B. touched the wires, which were still hot.

The chief said, "You don't ever wrap wires around an exhaust system."

"That was . . . temporary," Mr. B. said.

"So is fire," said the chief. Then he held up his clipboard and said as he wrote, as though he were the perfect bureaucrat, "Cause of fire — *dash* — faulty wiring in the fryer. You're lucky that it's product-related." He said the insurance company would go after the fryer people and probably split the cost. An insurance adjuster and the county fire inspector would come by in a few days.

Kevin said, "Your boy here," pointing to José, "did some good work, as did the waitress," nodding my way. "You could be looking at a pile of ashes."

Mr. B. said, "Please, everyone, have a doughnut — not the little ones. Cathy, get the big ones that are in the circulating refrigerator."

Big whoop.

Kevin, José and the fireman all refused chocolate éclairs. My comrades sat lined up, looking exhausted and covered in ashes, eating their Tutti Frutti doughnuts and Dutch apple fritters with whipped cream. As I poured the coffee, I knew I had to say something.

"So, if you guys ever want me to make a birthday cake, give me a call."

José, always the gentleman, said, "It was partly my fault. I should never have asked her to make the doughnuts."

The fire chief said something I'll never forget. "She is a real smart-ass — but really she's only a kid."

They all nodded.

To this day I wish that at this point I had thanked everyone. But I didn't.

Kevin stood up, adjusted his vest, checked his pockets for a toothpick and, by the time everyone was putting on their coats, said, "Let's just call it community relations at work."

I heard the traffic overhead and realized that the whiteouts were over and the highway was open. The sun was shining brilliantly on the snow outside; a thick layer of ice had formed over it, sealing in its purity. The ice on the girders of the thruway made them all look as though they were silver maypoles spinning with diamond streamers. With the red caution lights reflecting off the ice, the whole basket weave of exits and girders looked like a giant antique ruby ring. The Dunk was buried at the bottom of all of these jewels, and for as far as the eye could see, the world shimmered.

CHAPTER 7

# scars

Everyone knows that the social hierarchy in school is as rigid as that in the military. Staying on top of the heap in senior high school took aggression, cunning, humour and an ability to read what people wanted. I'd quickly made my way up the pecking order in junior high. By the time I arrived in senior high school at fifteen in 1963, I had established my place at the summit. I would not say I was popular, but I was a natural leader. In order to withstand the winds of change, I had to dig in my talons and frighten off all those who challenged me. Fortunately, I'd learned long ago how to plump my feathers. Females had a much harder job staying on top of the chain of command than males. Boys simply fought it out in the playground. Girls didn't use physical means to establish their position, so it was a new challenge every day.

One of the prerequisites to social acceptance in high school was to be in a sorority, which involved pledging, submitting yourself to a higher authority that you never could please. This was remarkably like Catholic school, so I'd had years of practice. During the pledgeship of six months, you had to wear a large green dog bone around your neck, to be reminded that you were no more than a canine walking upright until you became a full-fledged "sister."

I had to choose a sorority, which really meant I was choosing between the good girls from the advanced class who were on student council and the wilder girls who, although popular, made it clear that school was only a boring job. The wild girls lived for what they called "laughs." Theirs was definitely my style; the major drawback was that the wild girls had an enduring interest in "make-out parties," which necessitated fraternizing with the opposite sex. The goody-two-shoes girls were not overtly interested in the opposite sex. They were into academic success, school spirit and sports. I was interested in the latter two. I was a high jumper and broad jumper and did a routine on the pommel horse. I also planned assemblies with "the girls of solid virtue," worked on the poetry magazine and contributed to the yearbook, into which I inserted lots of pictures of myself. In the end, I chose the good girls' sorority and immediately buttoned down my collar and only wore the most collegiate of attire. I had no trouble fitting in, because I had learned how to *fake it till you make it* from my Mary Kay courses.

Boys remained incredibly tiresome to me. They were a lethal combination: anxiety-provoking when you were preparing to be with them and boring when you were with them. On the rare occasion that a male showed particular interest in me, I was able to ward him off by simply refusing to acknowledge his attentions. If any idiot persisted, I was forced into a full frontal attack so he would run in another direction. I refused to even kiss anyone goodnight, so I have no idea why boys continued to invite me anywhere. I had already seen boys' stunts and their fraternity meetings. I never, as my mother suggested, looked upon their attentions as a compliment. I'd witnessed Veronica Nebozenko, with her undefended heart, make that mistake. Whenever we had to pray for lost souls in religious instruction class, I always prayed for her.

Now that I was in senior high, with only a few years left until college, I had to put myself on the fast track to success. If I couldn't get there on my own, I would join a group that I hoped would stampede me along. I also hoped that, since they seemed so well adjusted, my strangeness could be camouflaged by their neon normalness.

Our sorority was called Theta, and its theme song was "It's Theta That Makes the World Go 'Round." I remember on one unseasonably warm September day, as we were clapping and singing the song, a girl who was tall, olive-skinned and willowy, with an Audrey Hepburn pixie haircut, looked over at me and whispered,

"Did you ever think that maybe Theta *doesn't* make the world go 'round? I'm buying in, but I think I'll hedge my bets." Her name was Leora Sterne. I had an instantaneous feeling that we had been identical twins, raised apart and finally meeting. I was bonded to her with an attachment that I knew would last.

Leora's parents were, as my father said, "some kind of liberals." Her father owned a photography, advertising and movie studio, and he flew often to New York, where he owned another movie studio. They had a stunning home, full of antiques they'd bought in Europe and a magnificent grand piano, and there was a greenhouse attached to their living room. Although I knew a lot of wealthy kids with luxurious homes, Leora's was the first I'd seen that had original art objects and paintings.

I fit right into their family because Mrs. Sterne loved to cook and I loved to eat. Coming from a family that *never* cooked, I ate copious quantities of anything that was offered. Leora's mother had a brimming refrigerator and food was a big deal in their home. Ironically, Leora didn't like to eat much. I probably ate at their home about twice a week for the rest of my teenage years. Her mother acted as though food were a virtue and those who ate a lot were virtuous. She would marvel, as though I had just saved someone from going over Niagara Falls, "Leora, look at all that Cathy is eating. Why don't you eat?" Leora once said she didn't like food that was chunky, and her mother put it in a blender for her. I was surprised by this focus on food and the notion that if you didn't eat your dinner, you might not wake up in the morning. My mother didn't care at all if I ate. If I said I wasn't going with my parents to a restaurant for dinner, she just said, "Okay, have fun."

There was also a big fuss made about Leora's homework and projects that were due. It was as though the homework had been assigned to the whole family. Academic success was the focus of their home. Leora was a perfect student and, as far as I could see, a perfect daughter. Whatever demands her parents made, she met them immediately, and she seemed really worried about disappointing them in any way. I had no idea why pleasing them was so important to her.

I would tell my mother, who was inevitably lying on the couch when I got home, about all that went on in the Sterne household and she would say, "Who cares what she eats or how much? How many people starve in Amherst, New York?" My mother's take on the school-work issue was, "Why are they concerned with Leora's school work? It's her life."

The Beatles were going to be on *The Ed Sullivan Show* for the first time on a Sunday night in February 1964. I planned on watching it at Leora's because, not only was she my best friend, but also she had a great RCA New Vista colour television. It had the biggest screen I'd ever seen. It had to be twenty-one inches. On the day of the performance, Leora started quacking that it was a school night and she had a history test in the morning and maybe she should study and miss the show. I told her that the Beatles coming to America was history in the making. Even Walter Cronkite had said that. I informed her that Walter Cronkite knew a bit more about history than her teacher Mr. Reed, even if he did teach the advanced program.

That night we locked ourselves in her parents' room and watched the Beatles singing "She Loves You." They had long hair that they kept shaking like bull terriers. Every time they shook their heads, Leora and I squealed hysterically and held on to one another as we jumped up and down on her parents' bed. Leora captured the glory of the Beatles in their collarless suits, peg-leg pants and weird and wonderful Liverpudlian accents when she jumped from the bed to the floor at the foot of the TV and shrieked, "They are so *not* Amherst High!" This came as a huge relief to both of us. She adored Paul and I took John and we were set — a double date.

After the show, we ate an entire package of Sara Lee brownies to celebrate. Why was that a great moment? I have no idea. Maybe we could let loose pent-up feelings of desire for these strange creatures from England while in the pressure cooker of puberty; it was acceptable and safe because we never in our entire lives had to set eyes on a real Beatle.

—

I studied the Sterne home as though I were Margaret Mead examining some strange island people. My mother was interested in Margaret Mead's books. She'd just finished *Coming of Age in Samoa*. She left it on the coffee table, so I read it as well and was fascinated for two reasons. First, the idea of being an anthropologist captivated me. I began looking at families as small tribes and studying the customs of everyone I visited. Why was one house so different from another? I also began to see that my parents were not at all like the Sternes. They rarely worried about what I was doing, or if they did, they never openly fretted about it. In turn, if I disagreed with my parents, I didn't worry about upsetting them. We were separate people in our house, while in hers they seemed to be concerned about one another all the time. I realized that I had no idea what a family was supposed to be.

The second thing about Margaret Mead's book that was mesmerizing was the content. She actually said that teenage girls in Samoa had sex before they married! It was no big deal at all there. Samoan girls thought the teenage years were a breeze. They eventually went on to marry, have children and be good mothers. There was no wrong side of the tracks for the rest of their lives. I told my mother that all the rules of North American civilized society made a teenager's life hell. She said Margaret Mead's theories were "a pile of hooey," and that Mead just wanted to be shocking and sell books. But Leora agreed with me. After I finished reading the good parts of *Coming of Age in Samoa* aloud to her, she said, "When do we start packing?"

The words of Marie, the prostitute in Lewiston that Roy and I delivered medication to, came back to me: "As long as the church runs this town, I'll have plenty of work. People will drag themselves in here because they are locked into human misery. Sure, the powers that be can make people into what they aren't, but it takes its toll. I can tell you that." I was beginning to see that both Marie and Margaret Mead were anthropologists of sorts. It was dawning on me that society was built of bricks that could be placed in any configuration. Leora and I used to stay up late and talk about whether there was an innate good and bad or whether we were just following someone's rules.

—

The day of our "Theta flying-up ceremony" was one of those freezing, overcast February Buffalo days when winter had lost its lustre and was now a chore. Leora and I were to become Theta sisters forever and be part of what made the world go 'round.

The small group of lowly pledges had to kneel, blindfolded, on the cold tile floor of a sister's knotty pine basement in front of the bar — at the communion rail of acceptance — and drink horrible concoctions called Theta Rickeys. Then we had to eat cows' eyeballs that were saved especially for us by Sue Werinsky, whose father was a butcher. The salty eyes were soft, with membranes on the outside and something crunchy in the middle. Sharon, the sergeant-at-arms, ran the show. She cracked the whip when one of us didn't relish the crusty vascular inner core of the eyeballs. It was amazing what cruelty could come out of teenage girls when the thin veneer of civilization was lifted. They took the rules seriously, and if you violated them, they could justify the most inhumane of punishments.

Next, something that smelled like raw meat was held under our noses. We were told it was meat with maggots. The first girl in line must have managed to down it, for they moved on to Leora, who was next to me.

She whispered, "I'm going to be sick."

I said, "It will be over in a half-hour." This was a prompting tool I'd already used many times in my life.

The third girl, named Heidi, threw hers up, and the sergeant-at-arms screamed, "Eat it or you will fail the initiation." Heidi, crying by now, tried again, but this time she aspirated because she was also crying, and the food went into her lungs; she began gasping and choking. We started to take off our blindfolds, but the sergeant-at-arms yelled, "Keep on your blindfolds, lowly pledges!" By this time, Heidi was making strange, unearthly rasping noises like a saw on metal. Then we heard her hit the floor and all was silent.

Leora and I took off our blindfolds and there on the floor was Heidi Sampler, turning blue. The sergeant-at-arms yelled, "One blackball for defying an officer."

Was she nuts?

We tried hitting Heidi on the back, but now she didn't make any sounds. Leora ran to the phone to call an ambulance. The sergeant-at-arms followed her and tried to press down the disconnect button on the Princess phone, saying she didn't want to get into trouble. I shoved her away as hard as I could and she hit the wall with a thud. The other girls all stood around in horror. Leora, following the instructions of the attendant on the phone, said to hit her hard between the shoulder blades. Someone did it, but it didn't work. By this time, Heidi had turned a sort of whale-skin grey. Finally, when a really tall, muscular girl lifted and squeezed her, Heidi started coughing and a large piece of raw beef flew out of her mouth.

She slowly regained her colour. As she did, I looked down at the cows' eyes: they were cocktail onions in Jell-O. The maggots were pieces of raw beef rolled in rice that was turning brown on the edges.

Leora looked at me and said, "Is it really worth dying to be in Theta? We could find another way to make the world go 'round. I mean, Copernicus managed to find one."

I said, "This is it. Pledging is over. We fly up now. I am not putting this blindfold back on."

We found it remarkable that no one thanked us for helping save Heidi's life. I don't think even Heidi ever mentioned it.

After that night Leora and I were slightly different people.

—

Becoming a cheerleader was one of the most important roles for a teenage girl in the 1950s and 1960s. It was, in fact, the only one that gave you any visibility. There were no girls sports teams that mattered. Since this sliver of power was all that was allowed a girl, a spot on the cheerleading team was highly coveted. It was one of the cornerstones of popularity. Dating was another. Since I didn't date, I really needed to be a cheerleader to maintain my popularity.

The previous year I'd made junior varsity cheerleading and was by far the best on the team because I could jump high and do the splits and backflips. I'd been doing this for years in gym. I had lots of spirit, smiled and was dramatic. I was tall, blonde and thin, which were not necessarily prerequisites, but they helped. There were twelve junior varsity cheerleaders and only three would be picked to move up to varsity to replace graduating seniors. I was confident that I would make varsity because I was team captain and even the varsity cheerleaders came to me so I could advise them on new moves. I practised day and night in the garage, which was the only place big enough for a running broad jump and flip.

The day of the cheerleading tryout, where they picked the squad for the following year, came in early March and the senior girls all wished me good luck, telling me it was in the bag. I had to do a backflip and land without a mat, which would really hurt if I came down on my back on the gym floor. The tryout went tickety-boo. The results were to be posted on the wall outside the guidance office the following morning.

The time came and all the junior girls crowded around the list; they told me to take it down and read it aloud. Some of the boys from the football team were hanging around to see who they'd be lifting into the air and putting on their shoulders for the next three years at pep rallies. Then a large crowd began to gather. The seniors seemed to be interested. Even the gym teachers were there.

I read off the names of the girls who'd made it to varsity and, as I got to the end, realized I wasn't on the list. My voice caught and I prayed for the first time in a long time. *Please, God, don't let me cry.* Then I read off the names of the girls who were to remain on junior varsity. I wasn't on that list either. I was being cut from *junior* varsity? I was sure it was a mistake. Finally, I read off the names of the four girls being cut from the junior squad.

People moaned when they heard my name. Then everyone went over and congratulated the girls who had made it. Sally Wren was crying she was so happy. She could barely jump or kick and she had the spirit of a sloth. But she was very pretty and had waist-length blonde hair and perfect skin, and I'd taught her all she knew.

I forced one saddle-shoed foot in front of the other and walked forward to congratulate the winners.

Sally said, "Oh, Cathy, you should have made it. You're so much better than me."

Feeling the tears well, I looked at my watch as though I were late and said I had to run. I hurried to the lavatory, stood on a toilet so no one would see my feet, and sobbed. While I was there, two senior varsity cheerleaders came in to comb their hair.

"God, I felt sorry for Cathy McClure."

"She took it well."

"She was by far the best."

"I know, but we had to listen to Mr. Herstammer. He *is* the head of athletics and varsity faculty adviser. Besides, he was dead-on when he said, 'No one looks at how high you jump. Cheerleaders have to be pretty — the prettiest girls.' Cathy's face is full of acne."

I waited for the other girl to disagree or tell her friend that she was exaggerating.

Instead she said, "Her face looks like a piece of pizza. It's embarrassing. She can't represent the school looking like that."

I held my breath until they left.

—

I never told my mother or father what happened. I just said I hadn't made the team. When my father asked, I snapped that I didn't want to talk about it. I knew that my mother would suffer more than me from the acne comments, and I didn't want her to feel sad. I never had anything more to do with the athletic department. I buried my acne-scarred head in the sand. I had been deluded enough to believe that cheerleading was about athletic talent.

I had known my face had broken out and looked bad. But my mother had always told me that when I put on pancake makeup you could hardly see it, and I'd believed her. After the cheerleading episode, I stopped going to the general practitioner who had suggested one derma scrub after another. I realized I needed the best dermatologist in town. The doctor I went to prescribed tetracycline, an antibiotic that I took for some time, but to no avail. I was told I couldn't have any chocolate or shellfish. That made no difference. My face was deep purple, with huge cysts that lasted for months and then disappeared as mysteriously as they had arrived, leaving crater scarring on my face, and then the process started all over again.

A few hopeless months after the cheerleading calamity, a

dermatologist who taught at the University of Buffalo and who was on Mom's master's bridge team referred us to the world's authority on acne, at Johns Hopkins Hospital in Baltimore. While my mother sat in the chair opposite the examining table, the doctor looked at the giant red and purple boils on my face from every angle under a light. He said the type of acne I had was usually hereditary. My mother replied that neither she nor my father had ever had a blemish, nor had anyone in the extended family. He asked if I was adopted, and my mother said no. (Did he think if they were going to adopt a kid they would have chosen me?) I guess this stigma was wrought upon me by means other than genes. Then he asked if it was on any other part of my body and I told him it wasn't. He nodded thoughtfully.

I figured in order to feel better, since I liked to bludgeon people with optimism, I would ask the following question, "Have you ever seen a worse case?" He was the world's authority on acne. Surely someone in New Jersey had to have had a worse case than mine. I figured he'd say, *Oh, of course, this is just teenage stuff.* That way, my mother would feel better.

He thought for a painfully long time and then said, "Once, in Pittsburgh, when I was a resident."

I can still see the table I was sitting on and smell the heat from the light he used to examine my inflamed face. I can see my mother in the green leather chair and hear the crinkle of my paper gown. As the seconds ticked by, I began to realize how bad this acne was. It was as though I'd been engraved with one of those pens used in art class to burn designs into wood. Having had a loving family had allowed me to feel that what I saw in the mirror wasn't really there. When I had complained about the acne, my father had said, "You just see it as terrible. Girls your age always do. Girls used to come in the store with prescriptions for acne medication and I couldn't even see any blemishes. No one else notices it. You're seeing every blemish through a microscope. It's called social insecurity."

I'd believed him. In reality, I had raging acne, the kind that stumped a world authority.

The Baltimore dermatologist recommended radiation. My mother was wise enough to ask if there were any side effects, to which he replied, "None that we know of. It seems perfectly safe; however, it is a new procedure." He referred me to a cancer hospital in Buffalo, where I went every week for the rest of high school for a blast of radiation to my face and neck.

Later, when I was about twenty-five, I received a letter from that hospital saying that I was at risk for thyroid cancer because I had had so much radiation. They were no longer using that form of therapy for acne because it had proved to be unsafe. They suggested that I get tested immediately and then every six months thereafter.

—

The only fight I ever had with my mother followed that Johns Hopkins appointment. I was unusually quiet in the car on the way home.

My mother asked, "Cat got your tongue?" and I let her have it.

"You should have told me how disgusting this acne was instead of letting me think it wasn't bad," I shouted.

"What good would it have done?"

"I wouldn't have tried to be cheerleading captain and would have saved myself embarrassment. In the future, don't tell me what I see in the mirror is not true when it *is* true. That's how they make crazy people. Next time, just be honest."

"Well, how did you like the honesty of the Johns Hopkins doctor? Feel better?" she said as she tightened her hands on the wheel.

After thirty desultory miles on the New York State Thruway and watching tiny tears roll down her face, I finally managed to mutter, "Sorry for yelling."

———

When we got home from Baltimore, my mother went to bed with a headache. It was only mid-afternoon then, and later, when she didn't get up for dinner, my father and I went out to Your Host together.

One of the things I hated about restaurants in Buffalo was that you never saw the same people twice. In Lewiston, when we went out, it was like walking into the large kitchen of an extended family, especially on Friday for the Catholic fish-fry. Eating at Your Host meant dining with travelling salesmen on really minuscule expense accounts who ate the blue-plate special alone, with their papers propped up on the napkin holder. Who had dinner alone with their father in a greasy spoon? No one, that's who. I prayed no one I knew would come in. Teenage girls went to greasy spoons to smoke and meet boys, not to have the daily special with their dad.

The waitress ambled over wearing a tan uniform with dark brown trim, and the insignia across her chest read, RELAX! WE'RE YOUR HOST THIS EVENING. She stood leaning on one hip, holding her order pad, with one lifted eyebrow.

My father beamed a tobacco-stained smile and asked, "Well, angel, where do you hail from?"

I longed to drop through a trap door and fall into the pit where all teenagers go whose parents give the word *humiliation* a new meaning. Dad still thought he was the big cheese in the small town of Lewiston. He really didn't get that now he was a tiny cog in a huge drug conglomerate in the boring city of Buffalo. We were not in a family restaurant with home cooking; we were in a greasy food chain in a suburban strip plaza along the constantly whining thruway. He didn't seem to be remotely aware that no one knew him or wanted to know him — let alone give him their family tree.

After we ordered, I prayed he'd be silent and read the paper, but he had to start with the small talk, and I mean small.

"So, how was Baltimore, peaches?"

"Fine."

"Okay, you don't want to converse. Is there a law against my speaking and you listening?"

"There is no law against you speaking, but there is a law against my having to listen. At least, *my* calendar doesn't say 1984."

"I stand corrected. I will talk and you may or may not listen."

He didn't say any more after my subtle hint until our food arrived. Then he tried again. "Everything happens for a reason, you know?"

I jabbed my fork into my french fries with a great deal of force. I wanted him to realize that if he was going to start on "God's grand plan that we may not understand now but it will become apparent in the afterlife," I was going to use my fork for more than a french fry. He knew that I didn't mind scenes and I'd caused many in my lifetime. I also knew neither did he. (It was my mother who would do anything to avoid one.)

"You know something — I'm glad you have acne. It's a blessing."

I continued to study the paper placemat assiduously. It was a map of all the Your Host restaurants in Buffalo, marked with pictures of a man's head wearing a large white chef's hat.

"You've had it pretty easy. Boss's daughter at work. Everyone loved you. You're blessed with smarts and humour and are as pretty as a picture."

Who was he talking about?

"Everyone likes a pretty, happy girl. You could have gone through life like this without ever having had anything happen to you. Pain does two things. Suddenly you realize that everything you are is not enough. You have to grow. Second, it makes you empathize."

What the hell was *empathize*? Typical of him to use a word like that.

"It's easy to care for people far away who are poor or discriminated against. Now, when people suffer from something like shyness, or they're not so smart, or socially awkward, you might reach out to them, knowing what it is to be excluded."

"Unfairly," I muttered.

"Everyone who's excluded feels it's unfair."

"Well, if you think pain is such a growth experience, how come you lied and told me my terrible acne was all in my head?" My voice was involuntarily rising. "I believed you, you know."

We continued eating and I stopped reading the placemat. That was as much as I was willing to do to admit I'd heard him.

"You now have the opportunity to see something that is invaluable. You will learn who your true friends are: the girls and boys who like you for you, the ones who don't want a perfect friend to make them feel prettier or more popular, but the people who really value your great qualities, which, by the way, haven't changed. Looks are transitory anyway. As a case in point, I was once prom king myself."

"Where was that . . . Braille High?"

"If you count on your looks to get you by, they'll eventually let you down. Ask Marilyn Monroe. She's still beautiful and warm in her grave."

As he signalled for the cheque, he said, "Now you've had a growth experience."

"Please. I experience things all the time. It's called living."

"Real experience is what you get when you don't get what you want."

My father stood up and grabbed the cheque to pay while I finished my coffee. "I'm not going to say there are people worse off than you; you already know that." His face suddenly lost its good nature and he added, "I will say something that you had better hear: if you ever make your mother cry and have to go to bed like that again, you'll have more scars to worry about than acne."

My father so rarely reprimanded me, and I so rarely hurt my mother's feelings, that I had to fight back tears. Looking back, I realize that the most important thing to my father and to me was to protect my mother. Saying or doing anything to hurt her was a taboo in our family and always had been.

When we got into the car, I took off my new and slightly pinching Bass Weejun loafers, which I'd bought in Baltimore and hadn't broken in yet. I threw them on the seat next to me and stretched my legs out, my feet on the dashboard. My father lit a cigarette and then took some change out of his pocket and slid a dime into each slit in the shoes where the penny belonged.

He said, "It isn't easy to be young. It's hard to learn the ropes. Sometimes teenagers do stupid things and get into tight spots. I know I did. I am putting two dimes in these loafers — the price of two phone calls. If you ever get in over your head, call me. I will come and get you — no questions asked, ever."

As we pulled into the driveway, he said, "Now that the Liston fight is over, Cassius Clay has changed his name to, get this, Muhammad Ali."

"So?"

"Little strange, don't you think?" he asked.

"No." It had happened months ago.

"Well then, I think I'll change mine to Pope Pius the Tenth."

"Better than Jim McClure."

I knew what he was doing. The only thing we had enjoyed together in the last year was Howard Cosell's interviews with Cassius Clay. We laughed when Cassius threatened to knock off Howard's toupée. My father was searching for something to say that would bring back the mood we'd shared when we worked together side by side. He didn't get how totally gone those years were.

CHAPTER 8

# short order

Spring finally arrived, or was at least tentatively gathering some steam. The tiny crocuses were poking their heads above ground with some trepidation because, even though it was April, it wasn't April in Paris, but in Buffalo. Even April could betray you in this town. Still, I was relieved to have the car windows open. A sure sign of spring was when Ted's hot dog stand opened for the season. Ted's was more reliable than a groundhog.

My father and I were dining alone because my mother had another headache. As we drove by Kip's house, we saw him in the driveway Simonizing their old Ford Fairlane. My father yelled out that we were going to Ted's if he wanted to come along. My father knew I wouldn't talk to him at dinner; besides, he liked Kip. While we scarfed down our foot-longs and curly fries in the parking lot, Kip regaled my father with details about the souped-up cars that surrounded us.

On our way home, he asked my father if he wanted to see an amazing new car, one that would make it into the Automotive Hall of Fame. We pulled into Stephens's car dealership and looked at a new robin's egg blue Impala 409 convertible with four on the floor. It had a stereo with huge back speakers for when the top was down. Mr. Stephens, whom I hadn't seen in years, since I stopped hanging around with Fran, came forward and greeted me as an old friend. (No one wanted to mention her underage marriage to Joe, the guy who was with us the night of the lawn jockey escapade. She ran away and married at fifteen, and she wasn't even pregnant.)

Kip asked to see under the hood, and he and Mr. Stephens started talking about single four-barrel cast-iron intake mounting, a Rochester four-barrel 4GC carburetor and a hydraulic-lifter camshaft. They were getting more excited by the second. We took the car out for a spin and headed back to Ted's for ice cream. A number of teenage boys surrounded us, looking at the car and touching it like it was a flying saucer that had just landed. Kip and my dad jumped out and gladly lifted the hood. Kip was the guy who knew and cared about car motors. My father had never been interested, but clearly he loved being top dog at Ted's hot dog stand.

When we sped back into the dealership parking lot with the radio blaring, Mr. Stephens came outside, leaned on the driver door, patted the car and said, "Did you ever feel pickup like that?"

My father was wearing his red plaid hat, the kind that buttons down in the front and has a little belt in the back. He adjusted it on his head, smiled at Mr. Stephens and said, "Wrap it up."

Kip was jumping up and down in the front seat, yelling, "Jesus, Mary and Joseph!" I was pleased too, although I had a slight feeling of trepidation. Hadn't we just bought a Lark? Now we had two beige Larks, neither of which even had a radio, *and* a 409. I quickly filed away any anxiety, assuming he knew what he was doing.

Kip and I blared the radio, which played "I'm Henry the Eighth, I Am," and screamed all the way home with the top down; my father seemed equally pleased. He tore off from a signal light, leaving everyone in our dust.

When we got home, my mother seemed more quizzical than excited and asked how much it was.

My father said, "Well, it wasn't cheap, that's for sure," and started laughing. "Cathy is only a teenager once and I thought since she got her licence it was time for some fun around here."

"What did you do with the car we just bought?"

"I'll trade it in tomorrow. Janet, you don't seem happy," he said, sounding hurt. "The car is for the girls in the family. I'll drive the Lark."

"I am happy," she said. "It's just that I thought you went out for a hot dog."

My father figured if I wasn't going to do my homework, there was no point in my sitting home stewing about acne that showed no signs of abating. He said it was best to stay busy, for the saying "idle hands are the devil's workshop" was written in my honour. I had walked out on The Dunk a few months earlier, after a fight with Mr. B. over tips, so I was presently unemployed. Within a week of the cheerleading ordeal, my father saw a HELP WANTED sign at Howard Johnson and encouraged me to apply.

I piled on my Acnomel pancake as thick as Zsa Zsa Gabor's and easily got the job at Howard Johnson as a short-order cook. After all, I'd had previous experience at The Dunk. I didn't bother mentioning that it was as an arsonist. When the manager asked if I could short-order cook, I said, "In short order."

The manager was a twerpy Cornell graduate in hotel management who wrote on his name tag *Mr. Sloan Swath-Roan.* No one called himself or herself Mr. or Mrs. on their name tag and the only people who had hyphenated names in those days were in P.G. Wodehouse books.

Ours was the busiest Howard Johnson in New York State. HoJo's, as it was called, was perfectly located where several thru-ways intersected. No matter how bad the food was, the place was always packed with snaking lineups — to say nothing of the locals who ate there. After all, what was the competition . . . Your Host?

As I was leaving for my first day of work, my mother looked up from *The Source,* her latest Michener novel, waved jauntily and said, "Good luck. Don't frost the clams before deep-frying them."

My father said I looked like a rare albino parrot in my green outfit with the orange frilly hairband on top of my blonde head. Then he added, "Pardon my ignorance, but why are you a short-order cook instead of a waitress?"

I explained that it all had to do with tips. I'd heard that there was a three-year waiting list to become a waitress. The most valuable job there was that of hostess, the one who seated the throngs. She dressed up in a snazzy outfit and got a cut of each tip. Every hostess there was a member of the same family: mother, sister or aunt. It hadn't gone out of the family since this particular Howard Johnson opened eighteen years earlier. One was a teacher who had quit teaching because she made more money as a hostess.

—

Within fifteen minutes of starting the job, I realized the cooks were low on the totem pole. They got no tips and had to work non-stop in a small, boiling-hot kitchen. The waitresses were all white and the guys in the kitchen were all black.

Everyone in the kitchen wore white pants and long jackets like straitjackets and large white paper hats that would become so wet by the end of the evening that they were mush and had to be thrown out. There were nine guys in a space as narrow as an apartment corridor and about fifteen feet long. To my amazement, they never ran into one another. One guy yelled out the orders, and it was a mystery to me how anyone knew who was making what dish. There appeared to be no system. It seemed total chaos. Yet no order was ever duplicated or missed. There were eight deep-fryers going at once, loaded with clams or french fries. Every few seconds someone would yell, "Got it." The dialect was so thick I had only a vague idea what any of the cooks were saying.

The head of short orders was a man named Grover. He was huge and had hands like paws. He wore a black stocking cap on his head under his white chef's hat and never took it off. Soon after I started, I heard him say, "Maongrilllch — may'atfellow white-nowyahear," which I found out later meant, "Make one grilled cheese, lightly toasted."

I think I could have eventually caught on to the dialect, but it really didn't make any difference what I understood, because I had no idea how to make a grilled cheese sandwich. Grover pointed me to cheese and tapped a huge vat of butter, and then turned to fill the next order. The bread I figured out myself. I put the butter on the inside and tried to grill it. While that was burning, some-one yelled, "Western." Grover nodded my way. What the hell was a Western? I'd eaten them many times — but what were the ingre-dients? I knew they were yellow and flat, but what made them that way? To top this confusion, I found out that while I was making one thing, I was supposed to start on another. Now they wanted a club sandwich! How was I supposed to know that a club sand-wich had bacon and chicken in it? I had never taken one apart and examined it under a microscope.

I knew I had to ask the whirling Grover for help, so I tried to find an opportunity. Grover was always doing four things at once — he didn't even use an oven mitt for the cast-iron fry pan. He just grabbed it and never so much as winced. He could break an egg with one hand and place it on the grill sunny side up while he popped the fryer with the other hand. I gently tapped him on his wide back.

He wheeled around. "Don't be touchin' me."

"Excuse me, Grover. Could you possibly advise me on the ingredients of a Western? I used to work at the downtown Dunk, but for some reason I forgot how to make one."

The head of short orders looked at the mess I'd created, yelled, "Out the way!" and grabbed the fry pan, shaking it until the sandwich I'd concocted flipped into the garbage. "Who hired Goldilocks?"

Someone yelled back, "Sloan."

Grover said, "What I ever do to that man to deserve this chil' here on my detail? Honey, I don't know what you made down The Dunk way, but you ain't never seen no Western. Now don't you go botherin' me again."

Another cook said, "You say you been one short-order cook? Them must have been some short orders."

Soon the complaints started coming in the long, narrow short-order window.

"Where's that club?" one waitress asked.

"This grilled cheese is a disgrace," said another waitress, slamming the plate on the shelf in front of the short-order window and ringing the bell loudly.

Another angry face popped into the window and yelled, "There's a whole family gummin' up the works out here. They're on dessert and their son doesn't have his Western. What are you boys doing back there?"

A few minutes later Sloan hissed in the window, "What is the problem in short orders?" No one said anything. "Grover, I'm asking you something."

Grover just shook his head, looked at the ceiling and shook his head again.

Finally I owned up. "I guess I made different orders where I used to work," I said sheepishly.

"Grover, can this be remedied?" Sloan asked, pointing to me.

"Not in no short order." Everyone was laughing as they twirled like tops.

Sloan said, "Grover, cover for her." Then he looked at me and said, "You're fired. Put your uniform in the bin." And his face disappeared from the window.

No one looked at me.

I said, "Well, I guess he'll have to hire two men to replace me." Everyone broke up.

Even I had to admit it was sort of funny. There was no way I could have done that job. I could do several things at one time, but one of them would never be cooking. Because my mother had never cooked, I hadn't even seen most ingredients. Kitchens looked to me like the lab of *The Sorcerer's Apprentice*.

I went back to the girls change room and got on my street clothes. I donned my baby blue Villager shirtwaist and my blue Pappagallo shoes, tied my blue ribbon around my ponytail and walked through the kitchen toward the employee exit.

Grover yelled out, "Now, you take care."

Right then Sloan ran into the kitchen. I heard him say that the hostess had fallen over the cocktail trolley and hurt her ankle. It was swollen up and she had to go home. Now there was no hostess and the lineup had turned vicious — customers fighting over who was next. "The lineup is so long it's into the parking lot. I need a dang hostess."

I popped my head through the short-order window. "I can do it. I can tell people what to do, I just can't cook."

He really had no choice.

So I set to work. I had the lineup organized lickety-split. A man, a New Yorker, began yelling and saying his family of four had been waiting longer than some couples. I told him there were more tables for two. He asked in a loud voice why we couldn't put two tables together. I said if he didn't like it he could catch his own clams.

This was the job for me. For some unknown reason, I'd always loved arguing.

The first thing I noticed was that the bullies blew in from the east — New Yorkers often cut in line or said they were there first. But I had a list and I *knew* who was first. I'd say, "You want to bully someone? Go to Brooklyn." And I'd go back to work.

My father laughed that night when I told him I'd been fired and then promoted to the highest-paying job in the place. As he said, "When you get fired, the most important thing to do is leave slowly, since you have no idea what opportunities might arise."

Suddenly I was making a lot of money. I was really friendly to the nice people and I always asked customers where they were from and created a folksy atmosphere. But if customers got out of line or complained, I either threw them out or gave them short shrift so that things could run smoothly. I was in charge of the suggestion box at night, and I always tore up the bad things people said about me and left only the good notes. Needless to say, the manager revered me in no time. My only concern was that I would have to leave after the other hostess's ankle healed.

Three or four weeks later, a man came in and said he would like a seat for one. I said, why not sit at the counter, and he said he preferred a table. Fine. When I seated him and gave him his menu, he asked what was good. I said, well, we were famous for fried clams. He said he was allergic to shellfish, so I said, "Got me, then. I always have the clams."

"How about the Salisbury steak?" he asked.

"I never tried it. I'd rather have a shoe with salt than Salisbury steak. However, I have to say people buy it all the time — so don't listen to me. Usually older people buy it, but, hey, you're not so young."

I suggested he get the sirloin steak. "It's a little more expensive, but you've probably been travelling all day on that boring thruway. Just relax and enjoy it. I mean, you deserve a break. Besides, you only live once." I was simply parroting the words of my mother as she looked at the menu every night at a restaurant.

When he had finished his HoJo Cola (Howard Johnson fought the Pepsi and Coca-Cola cartel and won) and I was pouring him a coffee, he said, "Boy oh boy, are you guys ever busy!"

I said, "Believe it or not, it's slow now."

He said, "Do you guys ever run out of food?"

"No, never. It arrives frozen and we have a walk-in freezer the size of a house in Beverly Hills."

"Is it always good?"

"It is always the same, and that's what people care about. Plus, those guys in the kitchen can make sawdust taste good. They are amazing and fast. They should be working at the Waldorf."

He then asked, "How is the manager?"

"Penny-pinching and humourless, but he's fair and knows how to get the best from people, because I'll tell you, moss doesn't grow under anyone's feet in this place. Plus, he is always the last to leave — and in a business that's a good thing. No one stays in business if you leave before the employees." That was a line I'd heard from my father when I worked in the drugstore.

The next day I found out that this customer was Howard

Johnson himself. I thought of all the times I'd heard the parable about the Good Samaritan — be kind to the traveller by the side of the road, for he may turn out to be Christ.

Howard Johnson was a nice guy, and the best part was he really liked me. He thought it was great how I had talked him into a more expensive meal. He even approved of me sending the overflow to the next Howard Johnson down the pike. He had watched me during the rush, handing out menus to the long lineup in the parking lot. First, it gave them something to do so the wait would seem shorter, and second, they could order right away when they sat down. It sped things up. The name of the game for Howard Johnson and for waitresses who wanted good tips by the end of the night could be expressed in one word: *turnover*.

To my astonishment, Howard Johnson told Sloan I'd said good things about him, and that I was to have a job there for as long as I wanted one. He also told Sloan that if and when I went away for college, I could always have part-time hours. Plus, right then I got the three-year wage increase, even though I'd only been there a month.

Our tips improved significantly after I revamped things. If big families came in for dinner, I would say that the wait looked pretty long. If they really needed a booster seat or high chair, I'd tell them it was best to go down the road to the next Howard Johnson, where there'd be no lineup. Big families with children were poor tippers and a lot of work. You wanted single males on expense accounts. They were the big tippers. The way to get them was to pull the tables apart and have only one or two for big families. The kitchen liked me because I'd tell people who were being seated half an hour before closing that we were closed but that if they wanted a short order we would try to accommodate them. I did this only on the sly, so Sloan never heard me. The result was that we all got out nearly an hour earlier.

While Sloan got paid a salary, we got paid by the hour and only until midnight. After that, "the boys," as the cooks were called, still had to clean the fryers and the whole kitchen.

When everything was done on hot nights, we would all sit out in the parking lot at 2 a.m. and watch Booker and Grover play soccer with the iceberg lettuces. The next day they'd peel off the outer layers and use the lettuce for salad. If I had ever thought for even one second that restaurants wash the lettuce, especially when it's busy, I now knew better. Garnishes were moved from one plate to another when cooks were in a hurry. When chefs were hungry, since they never got a dinner hour during the rush, they just grazed from the plates that were set up under the hot lights, referred to by the health department as "Salmonella city."

I learned a lot from that job at Howard Johnson. And I didn't know it at the time, but the substantial money I earned there was not going to be just pocket money. It would eventually enable me to go to college.

CHAPTER 9

# the loafers

With less than a month left in my junior year, the petty pace of June 1965 was killing me. The only highlight remaining was the class skit to kick off the United Way campaign. I was writing the skit with Kip, and it was a takeoff on Batman. Kip was Batman and I was the Riddler, and we had a lot of laughs while writing it.

I had to have a business meeting with Rhonda Levitt, the class treasurer to find out how much class money I could spend on set design. Rhonda was a math whiz and was in all advanced classes. She had a notebook labelled for each class and she underlined possible test items in coloured pencil. I barely knew her, other than that she was in my geometry class. I actually liked geometry and found the axioms and theorems comforting. I liked that for every statement there had to be a reason and you could ultimately prove something. You could see it in black and white and there was no faith involved. It was the opposite of life at Catholic school.

When I arrived back at school after dinner with all of my stage design and storyboards, she said she couldn't start the meeting until she'd solved some proof we'd been given for homework. She seemed riled up and asked me if I'd solved it. I told her I never took the geometry book home — it was far too heavy. I had the feeling I was not reassuring her as she wound her thick, black curly hair around her green pencil.

She looked genuinely worried and said, "I worked on it for three hours last night until my father finally had to call Mr. Eagleson at home. He told my dad not to worry about it. He said we would go over the solution in class on Monday."

"Your father called Mr. Eagleson over a geometry problem?" My father would no more call the teacher at home over a math problem than he would call President Johnson over a pothole.

"My father goes over my homework every night and corrects it."

After working on the class ledgers for hours on a Friday night, and working and reworking my scenery and costume budget, I offered to drive her home, because it was dark. As we walked through the parking lot on that muggy June evening, I decided I'd stop off at Brunner's, the neighbourhood bar where every-one-who-was-anyone in the wild group congregated. (Although I had identified with a conservative group, I had still kept one foot in the wild group.) I thought it only polite to ask Rhonda if she wanted to come with me. After all, Buffalo was a bar town. Most kids had a neighbourhood bar where they hung out. If you were underage, you had fake ID in the form of a sheriff card. Everyone bought their fake IDs from Bobby Holmes, the best artist in our school. His brother took the pictures and did the laminating. This counterfeit business paid for them both to later go to design school.

Rhonda looked appalled. She said she didn't drink alcohol except at Passover. I said I didn't even drink it then. I would just have a Tab — but I liked seeing everyone, chatting for a while and then heading home. At twelve I'd made a personal vow to never drink alcohol. Kissing a priest's neck and almost falling over Niagara Falls after a few cocktails had been enough for me. I wanted all of my defences intact.

She said, "No, thanks, I have a test to study for — just drop me off."

School work on a Friday night?

"Wow, is this your car?" she asked as she placed her small hand on my blue convertible.

I jumped in without opening the door — one of the only bene-fits of being a washed-up high jumper. After she got in the tedious way, by opening the door, I pushed in the lighter, blared the radio and peeled out of the school parking lot on two wheels like I did every day.

As we approached the signal at the corner, I saw Kip Rogers hitchhiking. "Stop! In the Name of Love" blasted over the radio. Kip had a great voice and sang at the high school dances. At the light, I slammed on the brakes and shoved the car into park. I stood up at the wheel and held up my hand to mimic Diana Ross, and he and I sang along. The timing was perfect. He jumped in the back seat and announced that he was going to Brunner's.

"Me too. I'm just dropping Rhonda off."

We continued singing as loudly as we could and holding up our hands at all the stop signs. Rhonda seemed overwhelmed, but she was laughing too.

A few minutes later I pulled into the driveway of her family's mock Tudor home, with its small panes of wavy leaded glass in diamond grids.

"Have fun at Brunner's," she said, getting out of the car. Hugging her advanced class books close to her chest, she stared up at the heavy barred dormers. "I've heard about Brunner's, but I wouldn't know anyone there."

Kip said, "You'll know Cathy and me." She still looked hesitant, so he continued, "Rhonda, you are still going to get into Wellesley even if you take Friday night off."

She continued up the walk and onto her front stoop, then turned and called out to us, "Would you mind if I came for an hour or two? I already told my parents I'd be really late studying with Barb Gold from the advanced program. Her older brother said he'd drop me off at home — no matter the time. I'll call Barb from Brunner's and tell her I'm not coming."

— —

Danny Wright was the first person we saw at the entrance to

Brunner's. He was perched on a bar stool by the door, casually checking sheriff cards for proof of age. In exchange for this, Doc, the bartender, gave him free drinks. He never really checked the proof, but only held it in his hand and greeted everyone as though he were host of the Inaugural Ball and their sheriff card was an engraved invitation.

Danny was the best-looking boy in the school. He always had extra money and drove a British-racing-green Triumph TR3. Although he denied responsibility, it was rumoured that he had gotten Arlene Nickeerbaum into trouble. She'd left school and gone to a home for unwed mothers in Batavia, and no one had ever seen her again.

Danny was accompanied, as always, by Frank Metz, whom everyone called Shaky because he was born with a bit of palsy. One side of his body was slightly weaker than the other and one arm shook involuntarily. His mind was also palsied in a way that no one could ever really put a finger on. People just said he was "not right in the head." His look was one of constant derision. His unpredictable rage focused on the very few who were weaker than he was. No one could predict what would set him off, but when he was on a cruel streak, his mind was as bent and shaken as his arm. I never understood why Danny and Shaky were inseparable. All I could figure was that Shaky basked in the glory of the friendship and Danny didn't mind a jester in his court.

Inside the bar it was hot, humid, smoky and crowded. All the doors and windows were flung open, and those lined up outside had their friends hand them beer through the casement windows. Some girls sat perched up on the beer fridge, letting their legs hang over the glass doors. Doc, the bartender, parted their dangling calves to get to the fridge, muttering, "Ladies, you are not making my job any easier."

I had spent many a happy hour in Brunner's. It was great to have a place to go where I knew everyone. It wasn't anyone's home, so there were no parents or family to deal with. It was neutral turf.

I went to the bar with Kip to get a Tab. We watched from afar as Danny leaned against the wall, chatting with Rhonda. Shaky stood there pretending to be part of the conversation. Danny laughed easily and touched Rhonda's arm, gently reeling her in.

Kip looked at me, shook his head and said, "Poor old Rhonda has no idea what hit her."

Rhonda was rather plain, but she had a head of long, beautiful curly hair. She was petite and had a large bust. It never ceased to amaze me how important breast size was to boys.

By the time I got back with my drink, Danny and Shaky were all excited about going to the Idle Hour, a roadside tavern out in the middle of nowhere. It was an hour away and you had to take a series of winding roads before ending up on some rocks by Lake Erie. The Idle Hour was a cavelike place that smelled stale no matter how long the windows were open. It was furnished in old picnic tables that were carved up with defunct declarations of love. In the summer, it was cooled by the lake breeze and it had a huge patio for dancing that was decorated with faded paper lanterns ripped by the wind. At the height of cottage season, the tavern occasionally enticed big entertainment acts.

"Guess what? I talked to Rick James in the parking lot and he booked Chuck Berry into the Idle Hour next week. We ought to go out there now and check it out with your friend Rhonda," Danny said.

"If we went now, we'd be a little early for Chuck Berry," I said.

"Come on. It's hot in the city."

"No, Danny. I have to get Rhonda home."

Rhonda was sipping a Singapore Sling through a straw and gazing up at Danny.

"It's going to be ten degrees cooler out there. Lake hasn't warmed up yet. Come on," he wheedled.

"That place is a dump and when no one is performing there it's depressing and full of drunks — not the interesting kind of drunks, the boring lifers. Besides, it's an hour's drive and it's already late."

Shaky said, "You never want to do anything. We gotta case the place for Chuck."

Rhonda agreed with Shaky on this one, saying she would love to check it out.

While having another drink, Rhonda, Shaky and Danny really got onto this Idle Hour rant. Finally I agreed, just to shut them up. Besides, I didn't know if Rhonda would ever get out of her house again. I tried to get Kip to go with us, but he admitted to having designs on a girl from Sacred Heart Academy who was sitting at the bar, and in whom he'd already invested two gin and tonics.

——

The four of us headed out onto the thruway in Danny's two-seater Triumph with the top down, with Danny at the wheel, Shaky in the passenger seat and Rhonda and me perched up on the boot. We had a harrowing ride out there because Danny had already been drinking and Shaky always encouraged any wild behaviour that he didn't have to take the rap for. We came upon the exit suddenly, so Danny crossed three lanes to make it off in time and

Rhonda and I almost flew out the side. We thought this was as thrilling as an amusement park ride. We screamed when Danny made the car jerk to the beat of "Help Me Rhonda" on the radio.

We walked into the Idle Hour and I saw regular townie drunks slumped over the bar. Rhonda, never having been in a bar before, thought the whole scene was fascinating, but I had been around bars long enough to know full-blown losers when I saw them, so I went out to the patio by myself to get away from the stale beer smell. For a while I hung out at an old cigarette-burned picnic table, listening to the waves hit the rocks and watching the coloured lanterns strung up around the periphery pick up the moonlight off the waves. Amazingly, nature could dress up even the Idle Hour.

By the time I went back inside, Danny and Shaky were drunk. They had been drinking shooters with union men from Bethlehem Steel. They had ordered french fries that they hadn't even eaten. I told Danny I had to get home.

Danny told me to "cool my jets" as he pulled Rhonda onto the empty dance floor. "You've Lost That Lovin' Feelin'" by the Righteous Brothers was playing as they began weaving around, staggering and laughing. Rhonda was tipsy but didn't seem nearly as drunk as the boys.

I tapped Danny on the shoulder as he danced and said, "Guys, we have to get going. It's late, and we have a forty-five minute drive ahead. Danny, I'm driving your car and you're sitting up on the boot."

"No way, you can't drive stick shift. Don't worry — my car knows the way home."

I knew we were in trouble.

I went to the ladies room, which was labelled Mermaids, and looked in a grimy full-length mirror. There I was, with my blonde hair pulled back in a long ponytail with a dusty rose grosgrain ribbon. I had on my John Meyer of Norwich sleeveless pink flowered shift with pleats down the front and my Bass Weejun loafers. I stared down at the dimes shining in my shoes. I had driven home with many a drunken driver, but never one who couldn't even walk. Danny could probably get home, but it wasn't worth the risk. I took a dime out of my shoe and marched down the hall; the stink of Pine Sol failed to camouflage twenty years of old beer, urine and regret. I made the call.

"Hi, Dad."

"Mmm." He'd been asleep.

"Remember, ages ago, when you gave me those dimes for phone calls and put them in my loafers."

"Yup."

"I'm calling in the right foot tonight."

"Everything okay?"

"Yeah. I don't want to go home with dead-drunk drivers. Would you pick me up? And then I have to get the 409 at Brunner's."

"Where are you?"

"The Idle Hour, about an hour out of town in Lakeview."

"I'm on my way."

"Don't come in. I'd die of humiliation. I'll wait on the outskirts of the parking lot."

"I'm leaving now."

I went back out to get Rhonda, who was leaning on the bar, giggling. I pried her away from Danny and led her to the Mermaids room. I told her we couldn't go home with those drunks. I said I'd called my father and he was on his way. She looked stricken. I had never seen the colour drain from someone's face like that.

"You can't be serious." She covered her face and leaned over the sink as though she was going to be sick. "I can't believe this is happening to me." She straightened and grabbed my shoulders and shook me, saying, "Did you tell your parents I was here?"

"No." What was her problem? "I know it's embarrassing, but there is no way around it. We are in the middle of nowhere."

She let out a sigh of relief. "Thank God you didn't tell him I was here. I can't go home with your father. He would tell my father where we've been. It petrifies me to even think what he would do if he ever knew I was in this tavern."

"My father won't tell him. He'll just drop you off and watch to make sure you get in safely."

She looked terrified. "I can't take that risk. My father *cannot* know I was here."

"Some guys got drunk. You called for a ride. Worse things have happened."

"You're sure you never mentioned my name?"

"Positive."

She was quiet for a few moments. "No. I have to go home with Danny and Shaky."

"They are really drunk. Listen to me. They've downed a dozen shooters since we got here. They don't care what happens to them or anyone else."

"I don't care. They'll sober up when they get out in the air."

Her father scared her so much that she just couldn't hear what I was saying. I tried several other routes into her mind but finally had to give up. Her brain was frozen with fear and I was on the outside without an ice pick. She walked out of the Mermaids room and returned to the bar.

Alone, I headed out to the parking lot and waited on the edge of the woods. A raccoon sat on some rocks and looked at me. We exchanged glances. *Yes, I really am this stupid teenager waiting for my father to pick me up.*

Almost an hour later I saw the headlights of my father's beige Lark, which might have been the least cool car in the world. I guessed I shouldn't complain, since I got the Impala. He pulled up and I got in the car and slammed the door, not saying a word. We drove along the back roads, making hairpin turns along the jagged shores of Lake Erie. We heard the constant lap of the waves, providing a heartbeat for the forest. I turned on the radio. Danny Neaverth, the deejay of WKBW, announced it was the hottest day in June in New York State since 1936. He said people do strange things in the heat. I thought my father might say something at that point, but he didn't.

I was worried about Rhonda but told myself that odds were everything would work out for the best. Danny and Shaky got drunk all the time and they had never had an accident. Besides, I had promised I wouldn't say anything.

As we hit the thruway, "Stand by Me" came on. My father sang along as he smoked his cigarette. No one I knew had a father that sang along with popular music. How embarrassing was that? I looked at him like he was a mental case. "I've Got You, Babe" by Sonny and Cher came on the radio when we were a few blocks from Brunner's. Dad started singing, but I ignored him completely, looking out the passenger window and clinging to the armrest. As we made the turn into St. Benedict's Church parking lot, across from Brunner's, at three-thirty in the morning, the last stanza was blasting, and I heard him pause after he sang Sonny's part, waiting for me to sing Cher's. I looked at him and could feel how much he wanted me to sing the duet, but I remained silent.

He belted out the last line alone: *"I've got you, babe."*

—

I never had to use the other dime. One was enough.

And Rhonda made it back that night without her father finding out where she'd been. He assumed she had been working on a school project all night at a friend's house.

Three weeks later, when she made the same trip, she wasn't as lucky. The car flew off the road on a thruway exit and hit an embankment. Rhonda was left a paraplegic.

## CHAPTER 10

# a vial in the sunshine

Somewhere in my teen years I woke up one day and looked at my

parents, especially my father, and realized I'd rather have been a

survivor in a plane crash in the middle of the forest, reared by a

wolf. At least a wolf would have remained in the forest and not

committed atrociously embarrassing parental acts in public.

When my father had been at the drugstore, he was mostly locked away behind the Plexiglas shield of the prescription counter fourteen hours a day. However, once he had a nine-to-five job at the drug company in Buffalo, he had time on his hands. I wasn't sure if the extra time was the problem. To be honest, I had no idea what was causing the dramatic change. All I know is that when I was a child he was normal and by the time I was a teenager he was the village idiot. It was like someone from the Twilight Zone had implanted a moron rhizome in his brain and it had formed a tenacious system of roots.

My mother assured me that all teenagers found their parents annoying. She said it was normal. She left articles on my bed about primitive tribes in which teenage sons had to move to a special boys' house when they hit puberty because two men of reproductive age could not live in the same hut.

She really didn't get that my father was not just annoying — everything he did sent me into orbit. She said I should calm down and eventually I would be like Mark Twain, who famously said that as a boy of fourteen he found his father so ignorant he could hardly stand to have the old man around. "But when I got to be twenty-one, I was astonished how much he'd learned in seven years."

I used to love to spend time with my father, and I had logged many childhood hours with him. My mother said he was having a hard time understanding why I was perpetually angry and no longer wanted to be with him. The donnybrook over Donny was years ago now. She added, "Remember when Dr. Small said that all that time spent with your dad and not with other little girls would come home to roost when you were a teenager?" She paused. "Well, welcome to the chicken coop."

My mother said Dad needed more to keep him busy. He was used to working over sixty hours and now with a normal workweek he was at loose ends. He had no friends in Buffalo or hobbies other than lawn care, and my mother was certainly not up to providing any. Thank God she suggested he work at a drugstore on the weekends and fill in for vacationing pharmacists in the summer.

—

One day I had to use my father's car while the 409 was having the brakes relined. (I hadn't cottoned on to the idea of slowing as I approached a light. Instead, I would slam on the brakes if it turned red. I'd done this through four brake linings.) When I opened the glove compartment to check for loose change, I found a pile of unpaid traffic tickets. I thought this was strange, because although he was a fast driver, Dad was also a careful one. I'd never known him to get a ticket.

When I got home, I unrolled eleven bright yellow tickets and asked him what was with the Road Runner routine. With that many tickets, I told him, he could lose his licence. He said he didn't know how he'd received so many and laughed it off. My mother looked concerned as she silently made out cheques for each violation.

About a week later he pulled into the driveway, as he did every night at exactly 5:18, and beeped the horn, signalling that we were to join him to eat at the Four Seasons Restaurant. On this particular evening he'd added a new twist. Instead of the regular horn, we heard the ear-piercing harshness of *a-oo-ga, a-oo-ga*. I nearly jumped out of my skin. He blasted it again. Neighbours came out onto their front stoops. I looked at my mother and flapped my hands at my sides, indicating that this was exhibit A in the case I'd been mounting about his ridiculous behaviour.

All my mother said was "Yikes."

Later, she said that because he had lost status in his community, he was trying to bring attention to himself. She said, "You know, like you."

"I am not a raving lunatic who humiliates his daughter with an *a-oo-ga* horn from the 1920s. What's next, a fox tail on the aerial? I mean, aren't *you* embarrassed?"

"No, I'm not. He was the most popular boy in our class at the University of Buffalo, and I guess he's returning to those glory days. He had more varsity letters than anyone else." She said it as though she were Sandra Dee talking about Bobby Darin.

"Well, I don't see you dressed as a flapper."

"I was never popular. I was studious and quiet."

What is the point of talking to someone who is stuck in the era of letter sweaters? He *a-oo-ga*'d again and we dashed out just to shut him up.

When we arrived at the restaurant, Dad chuckled and *a-oo-ga*'d several times in the parking lot. My mother laughed as well, although she sounded more nervous than truly amused. Diners in the restaurant gawked at us — my family of *a-oo-ga* idiots — through the window.

My father entered the lobby, still chuckling, and seemed unconcerned that no one else was amused. He acted like he was some college boy engaged in frat boy shenanigans. He seemed oblivious to the fact that he was a bald, overweight man in suspenders who had been making an ungodly racket in the parking lot of a chain restaurant.

When the hostess seated us away from the window, my father asked, "Don't you have anything better for the cat's meow?" She grinned and seated us by the window.

As I looked around to be sure no one I knew was there, I saw two guys from my school who were working as busboys. They stared at me with an expression that said, *Oh, we always thought you were an idiot, and now we see it's genetic.*

My mother said I was being too sensitive and that Dad was only having fun. "No one in our family is really that important. No one cares what we do. An *a-oo-ga* horn is just another sound in the cacophony of urban life."

One night in 1965, after working late at the Howard Johnson, I fell into bed thinking of all the homework I hadn't done and how I really had to get to school early to borrow Leora's chemistry notes and learn some formulas. It was bad enough that I didn't do my homework, but now I hadn't even left enough time to copy it. I was going to have to cut down on my hours at work for the last few weeks of school, buckle down and pull off some good grades. In my breaks at work, I'd studied for the New York State Regents Exams. Good marks on those exams could bury most of my daily academic sloth — at least, that was what I was banking on.

I couldn't believe that I'd have to start applying to colleges in the fall. It seemed like every day of high school had crawled by at a painstakingly slow pace, but now suddenly the curtain was drawing closed on high school. I had to start thinking of the next step in my life. How could the days have seemed to move at a snail's pace, yet high school be almost finished?

It was one-thirty in the morning when I finally had my hair

wound around my orange juice cans to straighten it and turned off the light.

A while later the light snapped on — not the night light but the overhead light, which was bright enough for a police interrogation. My father's head craned around the door.

"You awake?"

"It's almost two in the morning," I said, squinting at the clock radio.

"I didn't want to wake your mother."

"What do you want?"

He sat on the edge of the bed with a self-satisfied grin, apparently dying to tell me something.

"What?"

"Well, I have a great idea. I wanted to tell someone before I forget it."

If he thought I was going to ask what it was, he had another think coming.

Finally he divulged the big secret in a stage whisper: "Garbage potatoes."

"Garbage potatoes?"

"I knew that would take even you by storm. I've been reading about them. In other countries they have realized that there is no land left and potatoes grow perfectly in garbage. I am going to invest in growing potatoes in garbage dumps."

"No one wants to eat potatoes that are grown on cigarette butts and old paint cans. This plan rivals the time you invested in paper underpants when we were in Lewiston. Remember those? You made Mom and me wear them and tell everyone how great they were, while we got paper cuts every time we crossed our legs.

Then Mom's ripped in half when she genuflected in church. It's late and I'm tired . . ." He still looked excited, so I sat up, made eye contact and said, "Listen, it's a bad idea. Drop it."

"Well, you'll be sorry when we go to Kronbach's German Restaurant and order German garbage-potato salad."

As he stood up to leave, I felt a bit sorry for raining on his garbage parade, so I asked him what he thought of the shocking draft card burnings that had recently taken place at Berkeley. He shook his head at the disgrace and said it was proof positive that nuts travelled west and wound up in California.

I settled back into bed, thinking that garbage potatoes were weird, but that he'd gotten into far stranger things in the past, like playing music to wheat.

—

One summer Sunday my father filled a prescription at work and brought it home for the Redkins, our neighbours. When he sent me across the street to deliver it, I noticed that there were many colours and different-sized tablets in the tinted vial. I read the label, which said STREPTOMYCIN. Concerned, I returned home with the prescription and asked him about it.

He looked blankly at the pills.

"Are these all streptomycin?" I asked.

"What do you mean?"

"Are these all streptomycin?" I asked louder, shaking the vial.

His brow furrowed for a moment and then he said, "Yes. I think so."

Still worried, I went into what he called his den, which was really a corner of my parents' tiny bedroom, got *The Physicians' Desk Reference* and matched up the pictures with the tablets. They were not all streptomycin. Some of the tablets were not even antibiotics.

I hugged the big red book to my chest. What was happening to my father? Was he having a full-blown nervous breakdown? I thought that maybe, hopefully, someone else had filled the prescription and he had just signed off on it. Mistakes happen.

I returned to the living room holding on to the vial. I spoke in the first kind tone I'd used with him since we moved to Buffalo. "Dad, these pills are not all streptomycin."

He looked up from the *Buffalo Evening News*. He smiled — probably at my tone.

As soothingly as I could, I said, "Why are they all in the same vial?"

"Look, peaches," he said, taking them from me. "Hold them up to the sunlight and shake them. Aren't the colours festive? I just love all the different colours when the sunshine hits the vial."

At that moment things tipped over the edge for me. I can still see my mother lying on the couch, reading *Parade* magazine from the Sunday paper. Willie was perched on his needlepoint ottoman in the picture window. My father stood in his seersucker blue striped suit, shaking the pill vial and holding it up to the picture window. Everything slowed down. Even the dust particles that spun in the light from the window seemed suspended in the air.

My father had lost his mind.

In Lewiston my father had been the town's most solid citizen, and in our family he'd been the rock who held it together, despite my shenanigans and my mother's lethargy. He'd worked hard, had never been unhappy, had never said an unkind word or had an irrational moment. That man had disappeared. I had no idea what a toll the loss of home, status, job satisfaction and friendships had taken on him. I had been too wrapped up in myself. I was his only child and all I ever did was criticize him. My next thought was, what was I going to do? My mother was not going to be the rock. I knew that. It had to be me. Who else was there?

I tried to think what my father, if he were still my old father, would have done. I saw myself standing at the prescription counter of our drugstore, and I could feel his warmth, his comfort and his confidence in me.

A scene from Lewiston drifted into my mind. Mrs. Gray, a neighbour whose husband was president of the bank, went crazy. She thought that her hairbrush was poking holes in her head and that Harpo Marx was sending her "filthy" messages through his horn. Irene, the drugstore cosmetician, said Mrs. Gray was dangerous. My father disagreed. He said she had a disease of the mind and was no more dangerous than a diabetic, who had a different disease. He said, "Irene, it is hard enough to be mentally ill without us adding to the burden." I recall that comment because he rarely judged people, so when he corrected someone, they felt it. I remember Irene slinking away at Coke break.

I had been unspeakably mean to my father about his strange behaviour. I should have seen all those parking tickets and his driving like Mr. Magoo as a warning. I was like the daughter in *Imitation of Life,* who publicly denied that her socially unacceptable mother was, in fact, her mother.

Suddenly, a vial in the sunshine had booted me into adulthood. I was no longer the carefree teenager I'd been yesterday. It was a luxury I could no longer afford.

I went back to my father's den and sat for a long time hugging the drug compendium. I could hear the voice of my normal father in my head. He was saying, *Okay, so you were mean. Don't cry over spilt milk. Get on with it.*

The first thing my dad would have done was to address public safety. I would have to deal with his weekend job as a pharmacist. He couldn't fill prescriptions in this state. I didn't even know who owned the store where he worked. I had to get hold of a doctor. I thought of Dr. Zukas, for whom I babysat. He knew my dad because he called in prescriptions to him.

As I stood to leave the room, I had a fantasy that when I walked out of that den I'd see my normal father again, and my mother would say, *Don't worry about a thing. I'll handle this between making meals.* It was the first time in my life I ever wanted my mother to be anything other than the person she was. Immediately I felt overcome with guilt. After all, she had never wanted me to be someone else — someone who did well in school and never got in trouble, who was a cheerleader and who dated boys instead of being a crater pit of acne and abnormality. Through all my folly in Catholic school and high school, she had never acted as though I was not the kid she wanted. So if she needed someone to lean on now, she had it.

As I walked back to the living room, I knew I had to file away my fear. I had just turned seventeen. Some prairie women were married at that age. *Come on, Cathy, grow up.*

My father had gone outside to use his electric edger. My mother continued reading. I assumed she'd heard my father's speech on the kaleidoscopic beauty of the multicoloured pills. But a full minute passed and she didn't say anything. I told her my concerns and showed her the vial as corroborating evidence. She suggested

that maybe he ran out of one brand and used another. I told her
I'd checked and some of them weren't even antibiotics, but all she
did was shrug. I said that we had a serious situation on our hands.
She still looked blank.

Finally I said, "You were right there on the couch!" Then, showing as little alarm as I could manage, I said, "I guess you weren't
listening. When I confronted him, he said he liked the colours
when he shook the vial in the sunlight."

"Oh dear," she said.

"He can't fill prescriptions like this. Something is wrong with
him."

"Oh, Cathy, for heaven's sake, calm down."

"Mom," I said. "I have to stop yelling at him, and you have to
stop denying there is a problem. He could kill someone."

"Jeepers," she said.

—

Dr. Zukas was there within the hour. My mother and I went outside to greet him and my father turned off his electric edger.

The doctor used the excuse that he'd forgotten to pay me for
lifeguarding at his daughter's pool party and wanted to drop by
and give me a cheque. We invited him into the living room and
we all had lemonade. My father acted completely normal and
even cordial. He asked the doctor how his practice was and how
he liked the new hospital. Now I was feeling like an alarmist
nutcase.

When Dr. Zukas finally got up to leave, he told my father his
eye looked swollen and asked if he could have a look. He pulled
a pen out of his breast pocket and held it to Dad's left side. He
said, "Tell me when you see the pen," and slowly moved the pen

to the centre of my father's vision. Dad seemed to see it perfectly normally in his peripheral vision. Then the doctor did the same on the other side, and to our astonishment, this time my father couldn't see the pen in his peripheral vision. In fact, he couldn't see it until it was right in front of his eye.

"Hmm," Dr. Zukas said. Then he asked my father to touch his nose, and he couldn't find it.

Instead of being upset, Dad said, "I'm the boy who can't see his nose to spite his face," and started laughing.

"Jim, I'd like to see you in the hospital at seven-thirty tomorrow morning for tests."

"Sure thing," he said, as though he'd been invited for coffee.

Outside, as the doctor got into his car, he gave my hand a squeeze.

—

Dr. Zukas called me four days later. I answered the wall phone in the hall and stretched the long cord into the living room, where my mother lay on the couch. I sat opposite her in an easy chair to hear the news. He said he had purposely called when my father was at work because he thought we needed time to "compose ourselves" before he got home.

"Your father has a brain tumour."

"Does he know?" I asked.

"I told him and he took it well and said, 'You can't win them all,' but I think he has trouble absorbing and remembering things. While he still has a long-term memory, his short-term is greatly diminished. He will remember the past but forget what happened yesterday or even a minute ago."

"Can you operate?"

"No. We can give him radiation therapy, and that will shrink it, but he will never be the same."

I tried to keep my voice from shaking. "How long does he have?"

"Judging by the tissue changes, it's slow-growing. How long have you noticed marked personality changes?"

What was I going to say? Since the age of fourteen I had found him unbearable, but that had just been teenage stuff. However hard it was, I had to separate abnormal behaviour from teenage loathing.

I told the doctor about the tickets and how Dad's driving had deteriorated over the past year. Then I remembered how last year we had gone out for a hot dog and come home with the 409, so I told him about that impulse purchase too. I also mentioned the *a-oo-ga* horn and how he had acted like he was still in college.

Dr. Zukas told me to prepare for more personality changes, because my father had a tumour in his frontal lobe, which controls memory and behaviour.

He wondered if the drug company had noticed anything. I replied that they had never called me or my mother. Though, God knows what they might have said to him.

"I see," Dr. Zukas said.

"Should he still go to work?"

"At the drug company, yes. It's just research. But he can't work at the drugstore, filling prescriptions." He paused and took a breath. "There is an added complication. Clearly at one point your dad realized something was wrong with his thinking and his memory, so in order to sharpen himself up, he self-prescribed Dexedrine. I have warned him against that type of thing."

Now my father was a *drug addict* with a brain tumour.

"I'm sorry to saddle you with this, Cathy. Fortunately, you are a strong girl and can help your mother to get through it. I'm referring him to an oncologist, Dr. Kahn, at Roswell Park Cancer Institute. If you need my help, call me."

My mother lay on the couch with her *National Geographic.* She'd heard my end of the phone conversation, which included the words *brain tumour, operate* and *how long does he have?* Yet after I hung up, she didn't ask what the doctor had said. Instead, she held up a picture of a tribe in Burma called the Paduang. She said the women in this tribe wear rings around their necks from childhood. With each year of marriage, they add another ring. Eventually, they develop very long necks.

"Not your basic pearls," I said distractedly.

Minutes ticked by until finally she said, "I heard, so there is no reason to repeat it."

—

God knows what Dad did at the drug company or how he drove to work on the thruway, but I decided to tackle the drugstore first.

When I explained about the brain tumour, the manager was shocked. Once he thought about it, though, he recalled that they'd had a problem with a con man passing counterfeit money a few weeks back. The fake money had been pathetically obvious — almost like Monopoly money. Yet my dad hadn't picked up on it. When they found it in the till at the end of the night, all the employees laughed and my dad said it was a good thing he didn't work for the mint. In retrospect, the manager now realized this error was out of character for such a meticulous guy. He said my father had a way of laughing things off and making strange things funny, which was why no one had noticed. He said my father wasn't the type you would ever question; he was such a decent guy, so good with customers and an absolute font of knowledge about hand-made unguents and tinctures.

When I explained about the pill concoction in the neighbour's vial, however, the manager said he would have to let my father go. He assured me he would do it in a nice way.

When my dad came home from the store that Saturday, we asked him what was new, and he said nothing. He got up the next day and went in again as though nothing had happened. He had forgotten he had a brain tumour and he'd forgotten he was fired.

The next morning, when I got up for school, my father had already been up for hours in his suit and was doused with his Old Spice. I said, "Dad, you can't go to work."

"Why?"

"You have a brain tumour."

"A brain tumour?" He started laughing. "That's a good one."

"I'm serious. Do you remember going to Dr. Zukas's?"

"Sure."

I could tell he didn't remember it at all. I went into the bathroom to apply white lipstick, which I thought might toughen me up. When I came back out, as I passed the picture window, I saw his car whipping out of the driveway at a ridiculous speed.

I ran out into the backyard, where my mother was on a chaise longue, reading. "Why didn't you stop him?" I cried.

"He isn't going to listen to me."

"Do you have any suggestions about what we should do?" I asked, since she was clearly taking no responsibility and had gone back to reading the paper.

"I have no idea." She looked up from her paper and said, "Really, none."

The man she had loved for thirty-odd years had an inoperable brain tumour. Everyone knows what the word *inoperable* means, yet my mother honestly didn't look that upset about the whole thing.

"This is pretty bad news," I ventured.

"Well, no one gets out of this life alive." She slowly put down the paper. "Cathy, Jim has a brain tumour. I know that. I also know he doesn't have long. It could just be months. I am not going to take his last moments on this earth and grind him into it. He'll be part of it soon enough. However prosaic this may sound to you, I believe I will meet him again in heaven. We will only be temporarily parted. If you feel better trying to deal with all of this, then do it. I, however, am not asking you to."

"Mom, there are things that have to be done. He shouldn't drive a car. He has no peripheral vision on one side. And what is the state of your medical insurance? He could be in the hospital for months and it would cost thousands of dollars. What kind of pension does he have at the drug company? He has only been working there for four years."

"I can check those things out." She paused. "But in terms of trying to rein him in, I don't think he is going to have any part of it."

Once, in September during my final year of high school, we were driving to the Four Seasons Restaurant. My father was simply following the most direct route to his destination, paying little attention to the rules of the road. As soon as he saw the restaurant, he turned the car toward the parking lot, ignoring the median and oncoming traffic. In fact, he couldn't see it, because his tumour had the same effect as horse blinkers. I could tell by his driving that his field of vision had narrowed since his diagnosis. Two other cars slammed on their brakes and veered onto the median. Miraculously, no one was hurt. Then he turned into the parking lot of the glass-fronted restaurant and pulled right up over the cement barrier. We landed with a *thud* as the barrier scraped the muffler. The people eating inside looked terrified, as he'd come within inches of going right through the window. We were nose to nose with a table of six looking out at us in horror as they clung to their Hi-burgers.

Totally oblivious to the mayhem around him, he said, quite pleased with himself, "I told you if we came early we'd get a close parking spot." Then, as he jauntily walked toward the door, he asked my mother, "What day is this?"

"Thursday."

He smiled and said, "Great, chicken cordon bleu night!"

I wondered how he could remember it was cordon bleu night but forget he had a brain tumour.

When we got home that night, I took his keys. The next morning, when he asked me where they were, I told him he had a brain tumour and simply couldn't drive any more because he was a danger to himself, other drivers and my mother. I knew that mentioning my mother would give him pause.

He flopped down in a chair and said, "A brain tumour? Really?" He looked down at the fresh abrasion on his leg and said, "No wonder I fell off my bike." He'd ridden his bike over and into Convenient Food Mart. Much to the chagrin of the cashier, he'd forgotten to stop at the door, and then at the cash register, and had banged into the magazine stand.

I had become the ancient mariner of Amherst, issuing the constant reminder to my father of his upcoming demise. Each time I told him he had a brain tumour he would be shocked for a few seconds and then silent for about five minutes, and then he would forget about it. The same scenario would transpire the next day, and the next.

One morning when he couldn't find his keys to go to his non-existent job at the drugstore, I explained yet again that I had them and that he had a brain tumour and couldn't drive. He looked at me, fuming, the way any grown man who thought he was perfectly fine and was in a hurry to get to work would look if his bratty teenage daughter had confiscated his keys.

He said sarcastically, "Fine, I have a brain tumour. I'm running out of patience, Cathy. Give me the keys. This is getting ridiculous."

"You cannot drive." I was racking my brain for someone to call for help, but there was no one.

He began screaming that I had to give him the keys or I'd live to regret it. I had never heard him scream like this. This was the shriek of a caged animal who was going to make his leap at the circus trainer at any second. I refused to give him the keys. He shook his fist in the air and his face turned purple.

At that moment my mother came into the kitchen and, seemingly ignoring the scene erupting in front of her, said with mild annoyance, "That President Johnson is a real dickens. He said no Irish-Catholic males can drive their cars until the war in Vietnam is over. Doesn't that just beat the band? How are men supposed to get to work every day to keep the economy running? Anyway, Jim, I'll wait for you in the car since I have to drive you to work."

"What?" My father stopped in his tracks.

Keys in her hand, she added on her way out, "There are state troopers all over the thruway — at least, that's what Irv Weinstein just said on *Eyewitness News*."

My father didn't miss a beat, and said to me, "They should never have let that anti-Catholic Southerner crawl into the White House, pogeying behind Kennedy's hearse." He put on his Burberry, stuffed his hands into his pockets and walked out to the car, where my mother was already in the driver's seat with the motor running. He slid into the passenger seat and lit a cigarette, and off they sped.

My mother drove him to and from work at the drug company every day until he could no longer get out of bed. I never bothered calling his employer. As Dr. Zukas said, Dad just did research there. He worked on his own. I don't think anyone there had an idea that anything was wrong with him. As far as I could see, he never proved or disproved anything.

——

About three months after my father's diagnosis, Willie, who hated visitors almost as much as my mother did, heard a loud *bang* outside and immediately defecated on the carpet. And he began to repeat this disgusting behaviour whenever the doorbell rang. Anything that startled him, as our coarse neighbour who only wore undershirts said, "scared the crap out of him." He began to sob and shake if my mother was out of his sight for even a minute. She would have to hold him all the time and tell him that everything would be okay.

When she took him to the vet over what she called his "serial accidents," they found that he too had a frontal lobe brain tumour.

He was frightened and confused because he was losing his mind.

Strangely, while Willie was terrified about his condition, my father's disorientation didn't seem to bother him at all. In fact, he often found it amusing. Only humans have the strange symptom called la belle indifférence. Humans may exhibit an emotional detachment from or lack of interest in their physical symptoms or socially inappropriate behaviour. This clearly described my father's attitude.

We now lived in a home that had four units, two of whom had brain tumours. What was interesting was that Willie was suddenly afraid of my father. I think some part of him recognized that they were in the same sinking boat.

Only later, in 1978, did the study of Love Canal, a toxic dump situated in a neighbourhood of Niagara Falls near the drugstore and our home in Lewiston, reveal an increase in brain tumours, among other abnormalities, associated with those who lived on or near the dump site. President Jimmy Carter announced a federal health emergency. We were not on the site directly while I was growing up, but we shared the water and fumes. My mother played bridge with Mrs. Hooker of Hooker Chemical, the company responsible for dumping and burying hazardous waste where the homes of Love Canal would eventually be built.

Within a week of Willie's diagnosis, my mother said, "Willie is in horrible emotional and maybe physical pain."

"We have to put him out of his misery," I said.

The following week we gave him his favourite meal, which was bacon, eggs and a cinnamon bun from Your Host. (It was my father's favourite as well.) He started to wag his sorry little tail when he saw the takeout box. It was too much for my mother, so I didn't say anything to her.

I took Willie for a ride with the top down. He liked the air on his ears. This time, he didn't cry for my mother, and when I got to the vet he didn't growl in the parking lot and carry on as he always had in the past. He just came quietly into the vet's office and sat on my lap. When the vet saw him, he got out his huge mitts, which he usually needed because Willie, perpetually grouchy and anxious, often bit him. This time, Willie voluntarily jumped onto the stainless-steel table and just lay down. He shook slightly as he was put to sleep.

My mother had packed up all of his dog things, his favourite being Alexander Hamilton, the stuffed monkey he bit and shook every time the mailman came to the door, and put them in a box in the garage so my father wouldn't have any reminders of him.

My father never once asked about Willie or his whereabouts.

––

Around Thanksgiving that year, I was sitting at the dining room table, filling out my application for the University of Buffalo. When my mother arrived home from the bank, she placed her purse on the table and said she had a headache and needed to lie down. My father was his usual cheerful self and asked her if she'd like a Tab. She said that would be nice and then he forgot to get it.

My mother didn't emerge for the rest of the day. Later I went into her room and asked what was wrong. She explained that she had just found out that a few months before my dad's diagnosis, he'd withdrawn all of their meagre savings and cashed in their bonds. The bank records showed four withdrawals about a month apart.

"We'll have to find it," I said.

"It's gone. He bought some worthless stock in a business called

Rooting for the Environment. He invested everything in it. Now the company is bankrupt and the money is gone."

My mother was not old. She was only fifty-six. She needed what money they had left to pay medical bills, and to live on. I realized that somehow I had to have my father's bank privileges taken away. It would be a painful process. I would have to get all the required signatures to declare my father mentally incompetent, and then go to the bank and have them placed in his file.

I remembered that crazy conversation we'd had before school was out last June, when he woke me up in the middle of the night, rambling on about the future of garbage potatoes. If only I'd stopped him then.

—

One Saturday morning, when I was at work at Howard Johnson's, Sloan, my drip of a manager, asked to see me in his office. No one got called in there unless it was an emergency or you were being fired. As I walked through the kitchen, Grover hummed "The Death March," and when I shot him a look, he said, "I didn't say nothing," and all "the boys" laughed.

Sloan asked me to close the door behind me. He waited almost a minute before he spoke, and then told me the police had called and were at the bank waiting for me. He looked like he thought I was wanted for bank robbery.

I phoned my mother at home from Sloan's office. She told me that the police had called her at home and she'd told them I would handle it. She'd given them my number at work. She explained to me that my dad had gone to the bank to take out money and the teller wouldn't let him have it. The teller told my father that his daughter, Catherine, had had him declared incompetent, that he was now a ward of the state and had no signing authority. Dad refused to leave the bank and called the police.

I asked my mother to pick me up at work and drive me to the bank. I assured her she could stay in the car.

My mother said, "Cathy, I'm sorry that I've been so useless."

I looked up at Sloan, who was eyeing me suspiciously, said, "Forget it" and hung up.

—

When I got to the bank, people were milling around and my father was talking amiably to a couple of policemen. When he saw me, his eyes clouded and he asked where my mother was. I said he had to deal with me.

He explained to the police that I was an angry teenager who wanted to get back at him, that I had "my own personal vendetta." The papers had been forged by me, he said, so I could use the money. People in the bank lineup were watching the altercation, probably thinking the issue was forged cheques. I insisted we all go into a small office behind a closed door and discuss the problem. I told the officers that, although my father seemed fine now, he had a brain tumour and could not be responsible for his funds. My father calmly countered this, saying that I was lying and he was fully employed.

I told the police that they should look at the documentation and talk to those who had stamped it. I suggested they call Dr. Zukas and Dr. Kahn, the two doctors listed on the government form. It was not up to me to prove my father's mental incompetence — that had already been done by several experts. While sitting at the desk, I slipped a policeman a deposit slip on which I had written, *Ask him the date*. He waited about a minute and then casually asked my father that question.

My father confidently responded, "June sixth, 1944."

The policemen shot me an understanding glance for the first time.

I stood up to leave and my father ran at me. Being an old high hurdler, he leaped across the desk and jumped me. I was knocked to the floor. I had never seen my father raise a hand to anyone before, nor snarl the way he did then. The two police officers grabbed him and pinned him against the wall.

He looked at me with hatred and said, "Liar! Remember, what goes around comes around." He was breathing like a long-distance runner who didn't have enough energy to finish the race.

It was one of the worst moments in my life. I had humiliated my father and he had no idea why. I didn't blame him for being angry. He had no idea he had a brain tumour. Even if he were willing to accept that, he wanted his hard-earned savings.

He was beginning to panic, pinned to the wall like that. Since I was only upsetting him, I turned around and walked out of the small office. The police held him back as I left. I went up to the bank manager and told him to tell the police to keep my father for fifteen minutes and then to drive him home. I tried to write our address on a piece of paper, but my hand was shaking so much the writing looked like a spiderweb. The manager looked at my cursive mess and said not to worry, he had it on file.

Outside the bank, I got in the car and told my mother that the police had sorted things out and that they would drive my father home shortly, when he was feeling better.

The whole episode must have taken a lot out of him, because after they brought him home, he slept for more than a day.

—-

On Christmas Eve my mother and I were celebrating by sitting in the 409 with the heater on in the parking lot of Arby's, eating our lunch of roast beef sandwiches from waxed paper with red cowboys stamped on them.

She told me she felt bad that I had taken all the responsibility for controlling my father since his illness. It was time for her to step up to the plate. I was only a schoolgirl and I should never have had to deal with so much. She acknowledged that she could never have gone through this without me. She had no idea how I had made all of the decisions, read up on everything, dealt with the medical insurance and talked to the doctors. She knew the worst part was managing my father, who was obstreperous when he was confronted with what he saw as senseless limitations.

"I knew that reading up on aboriginal tribes in *National Geographic* wasn't helpful. It was simply all I could do."

My mother then surprised me by saying she had called the school's guidance department and found out that this year I had pulled myself up to the top third of the class. I was flabbergasted to hear this. I'd also done well on the SATs. She knew of the perfect school for me. Her friend and old college roommate's daughter was in a sorority at Ohio University and was enjoying it. It was in a college town with all kinds of school spirit and sports. She said it had everything I would enjoy.

Over Christmas vacation I'd taken as many hours as I could get at Howard Johnson's, working almost all double shifts. I would need it to pay the tuition in the fall. But as we sat there, Mom said she had known that my earnings were not going to be enough for room and board too, so she had sold her original prints of Niagara

Falls at auction last week. My heart sank. They were all she had from her pre–Tiny Town life. She cherished them and often asked me which one was my favourite. We both loved the one with the Indian in white feathers on a boat under the falls, calmly rowing a beautiful young maid, perhaps the maid of the mist.

I balked, saying that I thought I should stay home and go to the University of Buffalo, so I could take care of Dad, but she said he might not live much longer.

When I said I wouldn't go, my mother used an uncharacteristically firm tone of voice. "No! I want to know that I did something. You have been strong and now it is my turn — now that I have my bearings. Please go for me. Don't deprive me of this, Cathy. Jim will be in the hospital soon, and all I'll have to do is visit him every day. I mean it. I've ordered the applications. You have to apply before January first."

— —

My mother was being strong for me and I was trying to do the same for her. We both needed to do this. But I also needed someone to talk to, to hear my sadness. I had lots of friends, but I didn't want to cry on anyone's shoulder.

When we got back from Arby's, I put on my thick ski jacket and went out to the garage with my Lark cigarettes. I grabbed the huge blue tin cup that said BUTT OUT, which my father always left on his now dusty tool bench, and took it with me as I climbed the ladder to the garage attic. Icicles hung over the eavestrough, and as I looked out the tiny attic window, the sun shone through the ice so you could see their crystal formation and made strange rainbows on the attic floor. I sat on an old white wicker rocking chair that we'd used on our big Lewiston porch.

I blew smoke from my cigarette and watched the condensation from my breath in the chilled air, feeling like a dragon breathing fire. I sat alone, rocking and smoking but refusing to cry.

I found myself thinking of Roy. He and I had always had fun at the store Christmas party. We would be out late on Christmas Eve, delivering last-minute presents and medicine. Everywhere we stopped we used to go into people's homes and I would have a hot chocolate and he would have "a shot for the cold" and some fruitcake. I remember one Christmas Eve when we stopped at the apartment of Marie Sweeney, Lewiston's washed-up prostitute; she was all alone with no presents or a tree. Roy insisted on giving her a Santa Claus candle, and we sang "Silent Night" with her.

I looked through the smoke and saw Roy sitting in the other wicker chair on the far side of the room. The second I made eye contact with him, I began to cry. It wasn't *wailing* crying, just big, fat, rolling tears. I spoke in a whisper, knowing he'd hear.

*I've treated him like a leper since we moved here. I blamed him for everything.*

Roy just looked at me, and I heard myself saying things I had no idea I felt.

*He was ashamed of me that day at church years ago when I waited for Donny Burns. He acted like I was a bad girl who'd done bad things. I was furious at him for that. Until he got sick, I hadn't said one nice word to him since that day.*

Roy smiled. *It didn't have nothing to do with you or that young fella. He just didn't want to lose his little girl.*

Of course Roy was right. But I had been awful, had made my father's life hell, and now he was going to die and I could never make it right. I had yelled at him for being strange when, in fact, his odd behaviour was likely a symptom of his illness. I never once, not for one minute, gave him a break. Yet he never said I was hurting his feelings or making him feel as though he were a failure as a father.

*You can't put the Jack back in the box. Your father knows the score. He knows what teenagers get themselves up to. He was one once.*

*Roy, did you know my dad was also an only child and lost his dad when he was young?*

*He probably was thinkin' then what you thinkin' now.*

I couldn't see him as clearly now. *Roy,* I implored, looking across the room. I knew he was fading away for good. Once I left this attic and went away to college, he would be gone forever. I could feel it.

*You know, a relationship is a feeling. All the bad acts in the world won't destroy it. They might chip away at it, but it is pretty well buried in the soul, where no everyday sharp bits and pieces can get in and cut it out.*

I nodded, wanting to believe him.

*You got a lot ahead. You best be thinkin' about tomorrow, not yesterday.*

PART 2

# Eye to Buckeye

*And there came to him a sign of man's true home. Beyond the*
*ominous and cloud-engulfed horizon of the here and now, in the*
*green and hopeful and still-virgin meadows of the future.*

— Thomas Wolfe

CHAPTER 11

# leaving home

In the fall of 1966 my mother and I drove south for nine hours

before finally arriving in Athens, Ohio. There was something about

a small town crammed with students that appealed to me. The

sidewalks were so crowded with Ohio U. coeds that they spilled

over onto the streets and cars had to beep to get by.

The town itself was beautiful. My mother had smartly insisted that we make the long trip a day early and stay in a motel, so that we would have time to take a walk that evening. I marvelled at trees and plants I'd never seen before — there were several varieties of southern magnolias that would bloom in the springtime with huge white flowers like the kind Billy Holiday wore in her hair on her album covers. There were magnificent Georgian fraternity and sorority houses with white-pillared porches on huckleberry- and cherry-lined streets, and gigantic signs hanging on telephone lines everywhere that said, WELCOME, FROSH. All the stores sold football regalia, and even the bank had a sign that said, BOBCATS BANK HERE. (I didn't yet know who the Bobcats were, but they sounded sporty and exciting.) I was thrilled that there would be big football games and lots of school spirit.

Early the next day, my mother and I pulled up to a set of dorms that were mounted above ground with connecting bridges. Later I found out that this elaborate system was in place to protect the buildings from the yearly spring flooding of the Hocking River. There were hundreds of rooms in each complex, and male fraternity pledges were assigned to help freshman girls carry up their luggage.

Before leaving home I'd had all of my clothes dry cleaned and had hung them on an extendable clothes pole across the back seat of the car. I had brought an enormous number of outfits, mostly matching wool shorts and knee-sock sets and dozens of dresses. I had four London Fog trench coats, all in slightly different shades of khaki with my initials monogrammed on the collars, and boxes and boxes of matching Pappagallo shoes. I refused help from the fraternity pledges, figuring there really was "no free lunch," as Roy used to say, so I had to carry all of this up the stairs. I never wanted help, especially not from boys. When my mother and I grunted past a bewildered fraternity pledge as we carried a heavy trunk, he asked my mother, "Ma'am, why won't your daughter let us help her?"

"She's nuts" was all she said.

The rooms had cinder-block walls and triple bunks and three desks all smashed together. My mother told me to grab a bed and desk and the best closet, since it was first come, first served. There was not nearly enough room for the clothes in my closet and one set of drawers. I really needed a walk-in closet. I had no choice but to send half of my clothes home, which meant carting them back down to the car.

As we were making vain attempts to put everything away, a girl entered, carrying a battered suitcase. A woman, presumably her mother, followed, huffing and carrying a box that was wrapped in old newspaper and tied up with twine. EDWINA SMYTHE, RURAL ROUTE #3 was printed across the box in babyish letters.

"Howdee. Boy, I have one sore butt after climbing those stairs," the mother said while patting her ample behind. She looked at my mother and said, "Weenie and I didn't expect to see jigaboos here, did you?"

Jigaboos?

My mother looked puzzled. "I'm afraid you have the better of me."

"Jigaboos, spearchuckers . . . you know, darkies," she said as she threw the suitcase on my bed.

The daughter nodded in silent agreement. She had curly black hair and pointy-tipped glasses, and wore a white starched blouse and a straight black skirt that was the exact outfit worn by the women who worked at Fanny Farmer Candies stores. All she was missing was the hairnet. On her feet were white bobby socks and Hush Puppy shoes. She never said a word, nor did she look my way. She set a tiny beat-up portable record player on the bed I'd chosen and placed one red record on the top. The last time I'd seen a red record I was three. I glanced at the title: "I Ain't Nothin' but a Tom Cat's Kitten" by Wayne Raney. Who the hell was he?

"I believe that's my daughter's bed," my mother said, pointing to my pillow, and Lamby, my tattered stuffed lamb.

"Uh-oh, beaten by the North again." The woman looked over at her daughter and said, "They've taken Custer's last stand, Weenie." She didn't have a southern accent. She had a nasal quality that mimicked country comedienne Minnie Pearl, one I later came to recognize as an Appalachian twang.

My mother shot me a look that said, *Don't say anything, please.* "Well, Cathy, I think we should go out for lunch before it gets too busy in the restaurants."

It was only ten-thirty, but I knew my mother had to get out.

On the stairs, knowing I was about to sound off, she put her finger to her lips and whispered, "Sounds carry up stairwells."

When we were outside, I said, "Jigaboos? Did you *hear* that woman? Who says things like that?"

"Jeepers creepers," my mother said. Then, as an afterthought, she said, "Did she think Custer was in the Civil War?"

My mother started laughing and so did I.

—

We got out the map and looked at it while we ate lunch. On the way down we had followed the AAA TripTik, which showed only the road you were to take. We had not actually studied a map of Ohio, known as the Buckeye State, as it related to the rest of the states. It plunged below parts of West Virginia and bordered Kentucky, and took a major dip at the southeast corner. Athens was at the southern tip, far closer to Kentucky than Cleveland. My mother and I looked at each other in surprise. I was trapped in the Appalachian Mountains and surrounded by West Virginia coal mines.

Still studying the map, my mother said, "I hadn't realized how far south Ohio goes. Isn't it amazing that I know more about the geography of Africa than of the United States?"

The waitress, instead of saying *hello* or even *hi*, greeted us with "Haaaaa." Neither my mother nor I could understand what she said after that. She had the same accent as Edwina's mother.

We had barely finished our lunch when my mother announced that she had to get home. When we got to the car, she said, "Look, there are sixty thousand students here. Certainly not all of them or their mothers would refer to Negro students as jigaboos or we'd have heard the word."

"If all else fails," I said, "I can become a scout for Queen for a Day. I won't even have to travel."

"Good luck," she said, then got into the car with the top down. As she drove away in the now slightly rusty 409, she lifted her hand in a wave.

Neither of us bothered mentioning that she had to leave so quickly because she was paying a nurse to stay with my father. She was about to "shuffle off to Buffalo" to a man who thought he was going to sell garbage potatoes that had never been planted, a man who'd lost his mind, body and money.

Compared to that, dealing with Edwina and her mother was nothing.

But as my mother drove away, I realized that I was losing my best friend. I'd had no sisters or brothers, and she had functioned as both. We both had the Irish penchant for black humour and for teasing the one funny thread from a tangle of tragedy. Although my father's illness was catastrophic, we had found humour in certain situations — enough to keep us going. He'd forgotten words and now confabulated his own. He said "big skate" for car, "wheel bin" for garage, "Tontos" for Natives, "Rochesters" for black people, and he had hundreds more. My mother and I had adopted these word substitutions and begun our own idioglossia based on his linguistic lacunas. We would formulate sentences that only we understood; for example, I would say, "I got the big skate out of the wheel bin and drove down to hear music in the Rochester ghetto and sat with a few Tontos."

I hoped she would be able to handle being at home alone with my father and not miss me as much as I would miss her.

Well, I had what I wanted, I guess. I was out of the nest, fluttering, trying not to get coal dust on my wings.

—

On each desk in our dorm room there was a cut-out red construction-paper bear wearing a jaunty plaid vest, along with an instruction sheet. We were supposed to write our name on the collar of our bear. Each of the four floors in our dorm was represented by a different-coloured bear, and that first evening Edwina and I were to go to a dorm mixer with our bears pinned to our chests to meet the other Bears. Our third roommate never showed up. Her red bear remained on her desk, hibernating, until Thanksgiving, when his feet curled up.

Our resident assistant, or R.A., was a senior named Winnie. Now I had to deal with Winnie, as well as Weenie, which I soon realized was Edwina's nickname. When Winnie got us all together in the lounge that night, it was wall-to-wall Bears. She said she had never been as excited as when she got her job at the "Scott Quad Den." As I glanced at the sleuth of Bears around me, I saw a red one whose collar read, MARILYN FRICKIN' MONROE. I figured she might be worth talking to, so I parted my way through the ursine forest. She was beautiful in an exotic way, and clearly not local. She had waist-length jet black hair and large close-set eyes on a delicate face. She was wearing a white gauzy peasant blouse with puffy sleeves and red embroidery. It was the kind of shirt you might wear if you were a gypsy doing a dance with a tambourine in Romania, not standing in Scott Quad with a red bear pinned to your chest in southern Ohio.

"Do you prefer Marilyn or Marilyn Frickin'?" I asked.

Reading my red bear's collar, she said, "You look like a Cathy."

Somehow I felt that was intended as an insult.

Ignoring my question, she pointed to the bevy of Bears of various shades and said, "This must be what my father meant when he said, 'You'll pay in ways you cannot even imagine for not doing your homework.'" She walked over to an open window, away from the crowd, saying she couldn't face another plaid-vested bear. It was hotter than it had ever been in Buffalo in July, and it was September. "Jesus Christ, let's have a cigarette." She opened a Band-Aid can that held her cigarettes.

"Amazing case," I said, taking a Tareyton she offered.

"Well, I hate those soft packages that get all fucked up in my purse."

I had never heard anyone use the term *fucked up* in a simple declarative sentence. In fact, I had only heard the word *fuck* used once or twice ever, when some greaser from Industry was enraged. I was taken aback to hear it used in the context of a wrinkled cigarette package.

"Where are you from?" I asked.

"New York."

"Where in New York?" I asked.

"Manhattan. That's what New York *means*." She looked at me carefully and then asked, "Where are you from? I assume it's somewhere in New England. I can tell by your shoes it's somewhere east coast, but the pastels tell me it's not *too* east coast. No one east of Poughkeepsie would wear robin's egg blue."

"Buffalo."

"I rest my case." She took a drag from her cigarette. "I used to think Buffalo was the boonies, but boonies has taken on a new meaning since I met my roommate Larraine. Not to be confused with *Lo*-rraine." She gestured toward a plain girl wearing a starched and ironed white eyelet blouse that my grandmother might have worn to an ordination.

The R.A. stood up then, and Marilyn Frickin' said, "I believe we are about to hear Winnie whinny. Believe it or not she lives next door to me and, get this, 'hopes we'll be reeeeal close.'" She said this with a perfect Appalachian twang. "She listens to some *farcockteh* radio station that plays songs like 'Waiting in Your Welfare Line.'"

"Scary" was all I could say.

When Marilyn Frickin' stood up, I noticed she was wearing jeans that were tight at the top and wide at the bottom, like Popeye wore when he sang his spinach song. They seemed strange and quite unappealing to me, but I knew that if they'd come from New York, they were the latest and I'd better take notice.

Winnie twanged, "Okay, Red Bear Clan. I'd like my section of Red Bears to introduce themselves, give their major and tell us why they chose O.U."

Larraine said she chose speech therapy because her brother was a stutterer and she had always wanted to help him.

Edwina, a.k.a. Weenie, walked to the front of the room. She had a permanent taciturn expression and an unusual gait. She walked with her toes pointing out and she barely bent her knees. She said, "I'm going to be a nurse because it's steady work and I have a knack for sciences. I came to O.U. because it's close to home, where I have a fiancé." She spoke in a strange monotone with no modulation.

I indicated that she was my roommate and said, "I'll bet she has a knack for sciences . . . like making Frankenstein in the basement."

"Holy shit! That's your roommate? She must be engaged to Gomer Pyle," Marilyn Frickin' said.

Just then Winnie said, "Mary-Lynn, why don't you tell us a little about yourself?"

Marilyn Frickin' realized Winnie was referring to her and said, "I'm Sarah Roth. I'm majoring in art history because it's unsteady work. I came here because it's far away from home, and I got in."

"Thanks, Sarah. I can see you're going to keep me on my toes," Winnie laughed and motioned to me.

"My name is Cathy McClure," I said. "I'm majoring in English literature. I came here because I had a strange fantasy that I wanted to see Middle America."

I thought of Leora at the University of Chicago, and Kip, who was still in Buffalo, toiling away at his dad's bakery. He'd said he needed a year to decide what to do and to make some extra money. I was already missing them.

The following week Winnie sent out what she called a "growl." It arrived under each Bear's door in the form of a flyer. On it was a mimeographed purple bear wearing a large pointed party hat. On the hat was the message: *Mandatory meeting tonight: topic — rushing.*

Almost everyone was there that evening. Winnie explained that rushing was a six-week series of social gatherings sponsored by each sorority. It was their way of checking you out to see if they wanted to offer you a bid to join them. If they invited you, then you were a pledge. First, as a candidate, you would go to each of the twelve sorority houses for fifteen minutes. Then you were either cut or invited back for round two. This whittling went on for four cuts. In turn, you accepted or rejected bids. For each meeting you wore a different outfit: first a "school dress," then a suit and then a cocktail-length dress and, finally, to the last inter-rogation, you wore a formal gown.

I asked Winnie what criteria they used for selection. We had only been here a week and they didn't know us. I figured it was best to know what they were looking for. From what I'd seen so far of southern Ohio, it could have been anything.

Winnie said, "Oh, they have their ways."

It cost quite a bit of money to be in a sorority. After Winnie went over the finances, half the girls left. To the remaining half of us who were willing to fork over the bucks from our own savings or have our parents do it, she handed out the sorority information.

On the way back to our rooms, Sarah said, "It's all done on looks, obviously — a certain kind of Midwestern pie-maker plumpness. I wouldn't be caught dead in one of those sororities. Christ, they make Betty Crocker look wild." Looking at me, she asked, "Are you signing up for this cattle roundup?"

"You bet I am."

"I guess you're a 'when in Rome' kind of girl," Sarah said.

She had the same droll quality as my mother, but with her New York accent she sounded more acerbic.

Before arriving at college I had learned from my mother's old sorority sister, whose husband was on the engineering faculty here, that joining a sorority was crucial. The second we drove into town, I could see that all the girls who were dressed like me, and looked as I thought I looked, wore sorority pins, and all the handsome and athletic guys wore fraternity sweaters. At every turn, signs in restaurants read things like PHI DELTA FOOTBALL PLAYERS DRINK AT HALF PRICE. My initial impression led me to believe that, in terms of social hierarchy, you were either in a sorority or you were left on the hillbilly sidelines, rustlin' up vittles on the weekend.

I decided to put my time and energy that first semester into rushing. I would pay attention to my appearance every day over the six-week period; I would look perfect and be friendly and greet everyone. Sorority girls wore skirts and matching sweaters everywhere, so I did too. And they wore hairpieces everywhere, so

I emulated them; I bought a large braided hairpiece that I wore as a weird sort of bun. I thought I looked marvellously sophisticated, but really I looked like the Norwegian mother on the 1950s TV show *I Remember Mama*.

—

That semester I was assigned a biology lab partner named Patty, a sophomore who was already in the top sorority — which happened to be the only sorority I wanted to be in. She was very pretty and lively and laughed at everything. She was, however, terrible at dissecting the aorta of our piglet. When she was finished, it resembled steak tartar. I took over, but it was too late and we got a bad grade on our lab. After that, I was the queen of the scalpel and I never let her touch our specimen again. I could dissect everything perfectly, and she was along for a free ride down the inferior vena cava.

I asked her why the sororities had a formal evening where you had to wear an evening gown. She said you had to be able to handle anything that was thrown your way. As if walking around the four streets of Athens, Ohio, in a floor-length gown and high heels would be a real test of mettle, I thought.

I began accepting invitations only from Patty's sorority. It was the cream of the crop and it stamped out nearly all of the homecoming and fraternity queens. They had high grades, fantastic clothes and self-confidence. They were who I fantasized I was.

The night I entered their mansion on a hill in my formal gown, having made it through all but the last cut, they greeted me in long white gloves and later sang a sorority song while standing on the winding staircase. We were told that a member would sit down and talk to each of us for five minutes — I guess when they called it "rushing" they knew what they were talking about. When a tiny bell rang, the sorority member moved on to another rushee. We all wore name tags, so the sorority sisters acted like they knew us well. Many of the girls were nervous, but I could make conversation with a doorknob, so I wasn't thrown.

I sat down with a gorgeous smiling blonde sorority girl who told me in a southern drawl that she was from Montgomery, Alabama. I said, "Wow, the home of Rosa Parks." I figured knowing the history of her city had to be a good thing.

"Well, Cathy, I'm not sure if you're aware that Rosa was in fact a plant for the NAACP. She wasn't really a seamstress who was too tired to give up her seat on the bus."

"Well, couldn't you be representing the NAACP and also be a tired black seamstress? The two aren't mutually exclusive."

The bell rang and she moved on.

—

I found out, after having made it to this final stage, that I didn't get in. When I asked Patty why, she turned red.

"Cathy, people don't usually ask questions like that."

"So?"

"They just didn't think you were our type." You had to be, as she said, "all-round."

From that day I worked very hard. By mid-term I had all As. I found out, much to my amazement, that if you read and studied for exams you could do remarkably well.

In the second semester I tried rushing again, but was rejected early in the process. I told Patty that I wanted to know why I still hadn't gotten in, and if she wouldn't tell me the truth she could find another lab partner.

Finally she said, "Some of them think you wear too much makeup." She quickly added, "I told them that was because of your skin, but they wouldn't listen." Little did they know that my skin was peaches and cream compared to what it had been in high school. I would get rid of the acne for good during the next semester when I went to Florida, became badly sunburned and, looking like a blowfish, had to be hospitalized for second degree burns. When I left the hospital, my acne was gone and so were my freckles, and I'd left behind four layers of epidermis in Fort Lauderdale.

Pat still looked worried, so I asked if there was anything more to report. "Another part of the problem is you sometimes associate with the girls in your athletic group." I had joined the gymnastics club and had made the high-jumping team, where most of the girls were black. Patty hesitated. "And you read the Sunday papers in the lounge with the New York crowd — if you know what I mean. There is nothing wrong with those people, but they really aren't our type."

I looked at her blankly.

"Cathy, there is a Negro sorority and a Jewish one. They don't want us any more than we want them."

I just stared at her. I realized "New York crowd" must be a euphemism for "Jewish." I knew she was telling me the truth. I guessed you had to be perfect, and the acne was indeed an imperfection. I was used to having to deal with that. But I was speechless that they didn't want anyone in their sorority who associated with blacks or Jews. The blonde sorority girl who questioned the integrity of Rosa Parks should have been a tipoff. I had never in my life heard an anti-Semitic comment. I thought that was all part of the past. In my high school sorority, neither colour nor religion had been an issue. My idea of racists was uneducated outcasts who were threatened by, and terrified of, anyone they couldn't feel superior to, like the KKK, who wore white sheets and burned crosses on people's lawn. I was appalled that the girls in sororities who were at the top of the social heap were racists. In fact, the whole fraternity and sorority system was racist. Edwina's mother's comment about jigaboos had surprised me, but it was nothing compared to this institutionalized racism.

I thought of how disgusted my father would be by all of this if he were in his right mind. I was embarrassed that I'd traipsed around town in an evening gown, trying to please these people. I didn't want to be part of their club or even be friends with them.

——

I was failing to adapt in Ohio. I was out of step and now had no longing to be *in step* with those I had previously emulated. I had the right clothes and hair, but the "middle" had fallen out of my Middle America.

When I got letters from my high school friends who were away at college, they all sounded like they were having the time of their lives. I didn't admit to anyone that I was not having a good time.

To add to my feeling of isolation, it seemed no one I knew here had friends of the opposite sex. There was no one like Kip here that I could go out with for a casual drink. I had recently gotten a letter from him, saying he'd been drafted. When I talked to him on the phone before he shipped out, he said that at least when he returned he could use the G.I. Bill to pay for college. That certainly put all of my trivial sorority problems into perspective.

In an effort to get out, I went on the occasional disastrous date. There really wasn't much to do but go to sporting events or drink in bars, and neither appealed to me. Bars here weren't like they were in Buffalo, where people in the neighbourhood or from school went to talk. Here, you went to one only if you had a date. If you were alone, it was considered weird, eccentric or, worse, like you wanted to get picked up. No one went out alone on a Saturday night.

Once in a while I went to dinner with Sarah, but more often than not she was busy with a boyfriend of sorts. Plus, she was a self-proclaimed beatnik, as were her friends. I saw beatniks as having a negative attitude and I could never understand their passive feelings of cultural and emotional dissatisfaction. I saw them as poseurs, like the ones so well satirized by the goateed Maynard G. Krebs on *The Many Loves of Dobie Gillis*. Sarah listened to protest music by the likes of Joan Baez, Phil Ochs and Peter, Paul and Mary and went to beatnik guitar nights with other similarly grubbily dressed maladapted cohorts. There were rumours that they smoked drugs they'd purchased in New York when they were home on vacation.

I began to genuinely enjoy studying and blossomed in the sciences as well as the arts. I was taking an introductory course in sociology and I came across Durkheim's term *anomie*, which was defined as alienation and isolation caused by normlessness (a norm is an expectation of how someone will behave). That definition jumped out at me because I knew I was feeling it. I also figured that if some guy in France came up with a word for it, then I wasn't alone.

Late one night, when Sarah and I were having a cigarette together in our student lounge, I asked her what she did all weekend with her new boyfriend. I mean, what can you talk about all that time?

She said, "Who talks? We have sex."

"Sex? Are you kidding?"

"No. Haven't you seen these?" she said, pulling a little plastic circle from her terry cloth bathrobe pocket. It looked like a small blue clock, but it had yellow pills instead of numbers on it. "I got them in the East Village. They're for birth control." She spun them around and said, "This little wheel can spin a mighty good time."

I had no idea *where* you could have sex. Everything here was regulated. You had to be in by midnight on weekends and ten on weekdays. No males were ever allowed in the dorm. At 11:50 every Friday night, there was the wretched sight of couples kissing and petting in huddles near the door, as though they were cows in the rain. Eventually, the resident head would pop her head out the door and scream, "It's midnight!" and girls would peel themselves off the boys they were wound around. Then there would be a stampede of razor-burned faces pouring into the dorm stairwells.

Sarah said, "Oh, I'd never get involved with these little boys. At my high school in Manhattan I only slept with teachers, and I'm only doing that here as well. I go to their homes if they're single or their offices if they're married. I mean, these little towheads from the local farms have no idea how to make a woman happy."

Make a woman happy? "Is she supposed to be happy too?"

"See, you have no idea what's going on. Why are you involved with these eager beavers who are tripping all over themselves to have sex with you?"

What was she talking about? Were Sarah and I on the same planet? In the first semester I had briefly tried to fit in. When I'd made the occasional foray into the collegiate dating world, no one had even mentioned sex. A chaste kiss was all anyone expected and I had no desire to investigate further.

My future looked bleak. There was the route my first cousins took: two of them became nuns — which was one way of dealing with not fitting in. Another was being eccentric, but that simply made you an outcast. You were expected to get married between the ages of eighteen and twenty-four or you were destined to be a spinster like Balzac's Cousin Bette. You couldn't live alone. You couldn't earn as much money as a man, certainly not enough to buy your own home. All you could do was live with relatives or maybe rent an apartment. Then people felt sorry for you and invited you for Christmas as a charity case.

Eccentric people in New York, like Sarah, who lived on Park Avenue, could afford to be insouciant and even wild. Here, she could sleep with some boys from Cincinnati or some professors. No one back home would know. She could always return to New York, marry a surgeon and move to Westchester. Besides, if you lived in New York, you didn't have to worry about what the rest of America cared about. People who were unconventional moved to New York, for exactly that reason. But even in the movies and magazines, you never saw any pictures of old wild women who lived alone in New York.

People like Sarah and Joan Baez could be beatniks. They were beautiful, rich and exotic. The only lot available to me was life with someone who could cut the lawn and father children — neither of which I wanted.

My eccentricity had not seemed so obvious when I was at the top of the heap in high school. I never got the dating thing, but I could camouflage that with a general conviviality. I now knew

I was far stranger than Sarah had ever thought of being. My idea of a perfect evening was to read a book. And I enjoyed my labs, where I cut apart baby pigs and labelled their heart valves with small green flags. By contrast, Sarah was wild about men and sex of all sorts. She was as focused as the basic Buckeye coed; she just had different standards.

I wore perfect clothes and had perfect hair so as to camouflage my essential bizarreness, but I wasn't entirely successful. The sorority episode had brought that home for me. My mother was also strange, but not in the aggressive, bossy way that I was. Though we shared a sense of irony about convention, she had the brains to keep hers well hidden. After all, my mother had gotten into the sorority of her choice in college. She could have been a spy for any country or any planet. She was a perfect mimic. She married the man of her dreams, a pharmacist who helped her with her cover. She had one kid so as not to look totally peculiar. Otherwise, people would have said, *What does she do all day?*

She had to stay home so she wouldn't embarrass my dad by seeming like a "career woman." If married women worked, it was only because their husbands could not support the family. She would never have humiliated him by taking a job. He, in turn, left her alone to live the life of a closet oddball. My problem with duplicating this arrangement, I realized, was that I just couldn't stay in the oddball closet. The reason I was so upset was that I'd been outed for the phony I was. I had the right clothes, car and social manners, but I was not a member of the culture — I didn't share their values.

Once I more or less accepted that I was not an insider, it was easier to see what made people tick. I became "the smart girl" who studied a lot and watched collegiate life unfold. I no longer accepted horrible "fraternity mixer" dates and I didn't even make up excuses. I let myself off the hook by saying, "I don't know about you, but I don't have fun on those dates. I think you should ask out someone who is more your type."

There was a junior in our dorm named Candi, who signed her name with a heart over the i. She was pretty and was in the best sorority — the one I had wanted to join. She had never "made grades" and as a punishment was forbidden to live in her sorority house and forced to live in the dorm with us. One night Candi appeared at the door of the Red Bear study lounge, looking jubilant, and gushed to our study table that she was getting "lavaliered."

"What's that?" asked Thelma, a black student who studied the harp.

Candi flung open her jacket and on her ample chest was a small arrow pendant suspended on a chain. It had SIGMA CHI etched in tiny letters. "Bryce and his brothers will be here in a minute for the serenade."

We all rushed to the window, whipping orange juice cans out of our hair.

Bryce was a member of the rich-boy fraternity called Sigma Chi. They weren't into scholarship-type athletics, but played golf and tennis. They wore expensive clothes and had sport cars, bleached blond hair and trim, slight, Bobby Kennedy physiques. Most of them, as Candi said as a point of pride, "paid out-of-state fees."

About forty-five Sigma Chi men stood in a horseshoe formation three floors down, under Candi's window. Each guy held a candle. Bryce stood in the middle of the horseshoe, holding a huge candle, much like the one the priest held on Ash Wednesday when incense was thrown around. They sang a song about Helen of Troy. However, in place of "Helen" the name "Candi" was substituted, which made it a bit strained. The refrain was *"She is our Candi of Troy . . ."*

Afterwards, some of her friends came barrelling down the hall from other bear caves and started crying; one was sobbing and jumping up and down, squealing, "We saw from the window. It was so romantic. Oh my God, will you remember it forever?"

"I'll never forget it — that's for sure," Sarah said, then dragged on her cigarette.

"Are you engaged?" Thelma asked Candi, trying to place lavaliering on the hierarchy of marital commitment.

"No, not exactly." Candi explained that first you date, then you go steady, then you get lavaliered, then pinned, then engaged and then married.

Now everyone in the hallway was crowded into Candi's room. "When do you get to have sex?" Sarah asked in the tone of an anthropologist holding a clipboard.

"Not until our wedding night, Sarah. It's a long time to wait, but we agreed to give our virginity to each other as a wedding gift."

Thelma said, "Man, this is one complicated process."

Later in Sarah's room, I sank onto her bed in bewilderment and asked if she had ever seen anything more ridiculous. I wondered what would make a man drag dozens of men across campus at midnight to hold candles under a dorm window and sing *"Candi of Troy . . ."*

Not sharing my befuddlement, she said nonchalantly, "Oh, come on, Cathy. That whole exhibition was all about sex. Bryce wants her to put out — not the home run, but he wants to at least get to second base. She says hands off until you've made a commitment. The least pledge he could get away with was this lava-spearing thing. All the *boychiks* down there know what it means. She gets this ritual and he gets closer to getting laid."

I learned something that night. A man was willing to do a lot to, as Sarah termed it, "get laid."

A month or two after the lavaliering episode, I received a letter from Kip. It was a blue aerogram that arrived in a ragged state.

*Dear McClure,*

*I have no idea what the heck is up here. I wish I'd gone to college right out of high school like everyone else. What was I thinking? Somehow I feel I'll never get there now.*

*This place is hell. I have no idea who are the good guys and who are the bad guys. It feels like there are no good guys. I thought when I first got here the people would be happy to see us — like the farmers and those guys. No way! The only people who are happy to see us are the prostitutes and the merchants. I feel frozen out by everyone else. I got sent on a boat with a bunch of Diem's soldiers and we were shot at by the Cong on shore and those so-called soldiers ran below deck and laughed and refused to come out and fight. Who are these guys?*

*The Americans are trapped. Who is the enemy? Who are we supposed to shoot at? Anyway, everyone feels screwed up, so we smoke spliffs all day. They say it's to deal with the heat, bugs and humidity, but I think it helps to keep our heads*

*from swivelling. Shit, I'm out of room — should have written*
*smaller.*
    *Remember me and for Christ's sake write,*

*The Kipster*
*p.s. Wish I was buzzing to Brunner's with you for a brewsky in*
*the 409 right now.*

After I finished reading the letter, Sarah popped in, saying she
was going to a concert with her friend Betsy from Dayton. She said
a boy from Betsy's high school named Richie Furay was in town
and had given her free tickets. Betsy looked bizarre to me. She was
wearing beads and bell-bottom jeans (as I'd found out they were
called), fabric tied on her head like a sweatband, and an orange
tie-dyed T-shirt under a white buckskin vest. I thought she looked
like something out of *The Last of the Mohicans*. I had read about
"the hippie phenomenon," but I thought all hippies came from
New York City or San Francisco and were male. I had no idea they
could be female and emerge from Dayton.

    I had my doubts about the concert, but I had just finished
an exam. Plus, I'd received that troubling letter from Kip, so I
decided to just drag myself along.

    The band was playing on a Tuesday night in an old theatre that
held a few hundred people. I was surprised to see it almost full.
Betsy, Sarah and I went backstage to see Richie, and he hugged
Betsy and gave the three of us front-row seats. When we were
seated, Richie came on stage and introduced the group as Buffalo
Springfield. I'd never heard of them, but all the hippies in the
audience, who it turned out had travelled from all over to hear this

band, started screaming. He introduced his fellow band members, including Stephen Stills and Neil Young. He said they were making an album soon and he wanted to try out some songs on us.

Gradually I began to feel connected to those around me, and then I was on my feet, humming along and clapping and feeling a solidarity that I couldn't explain. It was as though these lyrics were perfectly describing the last six months of my life.

*There's something happening here*
*What it is ain't exactly clear*
*There's a man with a gun over there*
*Telling me I got to beware*
*I think it's time we stop, children, what's that sound*
*Everybody look what's going down*

The hippies around me no longer felt like strange friends of Sarah's. I realized at that moment that I no longer needed social camouflage. I might actually get away with being myself. Something had opened up, and I felt I shared more feelings with this group of "hippies" than with the mainstream collegiate set. Most of all, I felt relief.

Now Sarah and I were on our feet, stumbling with the new words, but trying to belt out *"There's something happening here!"*

*There's battle lines being drawn*
*Nobody's right if everybody's wrong*
*Young people speaking their minds*
*Getting so much resistance from behind*

*I think it's time we stop, hey, what's that sound*
*Everybody look what's going down . . .*

The verse that made me aware that others were feeling exactly like me was this one:

*Paranoia strikes deep*
*Into your life it will creep*
*It starts when you're always afraid*
*You step out of line, the man come and take you away.*

This band from Dayton was on to something, and it kick-started me. Inchoate thoughts began crystallizing. I wasn't alone; nor was Kip Rogers. Although, as the song said, it wasn't "exactly clear," I saw that there was more to the world than lavaliering.

CHAPTER 12

# the straw homburg

I was actually pleased to come home to Buffalo for the summer after my freshman year. When I say I was looking forward to returning to Buffalo, you have some idea how bad college was. Lots of my friends said how hard it was to return home to live with their parents again for the summer after all the freedom they'd had at college. I didn't feel that way. At school you had to eat within a certain hour. And you had to be in by midnight. If not, you were "campused," meaning you could not go out of your dorm for the weekend. I had more freedom at home, where I could eat when I wanted and stay out as late as I wanted. My parents didn't have many rules or punishments.

I was relieved by how little my father had deteriorated since I'd seen him at Christmas. My mother looked and acted as she always had. She was inscrutable, so you would never know if she was suffering. I had called every week while I was at school and Dad had always asked when I would be home. However, my mother told me that there were times when he would come into the kitchen in the morning, looking alarmed, and tell her that I wasn't in my bed. My mother would tell him I was away at college, and he would say with amazement, "Wow, she grew up fast!"

I was disappointed that my two best friends weren't going to be coming home for the summer. Leora was staying in Chicago to take a summer course called Human Speech Mechanisms. Her anatomy professor had singled her out to work in his lab, collecting data on stuttering rats. (How could you tell if a rat stuttered?) Leora had never been one to put herself forward or toot her own horn, so I was happy that her intellectual gifts were being recognized so early.

Kip was still in Vietnam. When I got home, the following letter was waiting for me:

*McClure,*

*I am writing you from a makeshift hospital. Before you flip out, let me tell you it is only for jungle rot on my feet. (The doctor, a*

card, said I would get the purple-foot-of-honour medal.) I had
been standing in water for too long and my boots were never
dry. My feet were four times their normal size and I couldn't
separate my toes. The fungus was so bad it ate part of the tent! I
was lucky I was medevaced here to dry out. Now I have a break
from the 120-degree jungle, rice paddies, snake-size leeches and
bugs that fall off the twenty-foot-high elephant grass. Every inch
of my skin was either bitten or sucked. I looked like a shrivelled
human pincushion with gigantic feet.

I had a bad one last week. My best buddy, Russ, hit a land
mine. No point in the choppers coming. We could only gather
up about twelve pounds of him. Cath — this place is hell. We
never see the "enemy" and I'm not quite sure who he is. He
shoots at us from trees, sets mines and booby traps, but he
never comes at us. It happens any second of the day and you
never know when. Instead of being more alert, we can't do it
any more and take whatever drug we can trade for American
cigarettes.

Sometimes we "take land" and then just leave it the next
day. I think this whole show is run by Elmer Fudd. Anyway,
enough . . . enough.

Best to your mom. My sister got into a dance troupe in
New York City called Twinkie Shark or something — never
heard of it — but everyone is thrilled, so I'm happy for her.
Hope first year of college was good. I couldn't tell from your
letters, but hey, I'm sure you made it happen. At night I lie
awake and think of the Buffalo snow and skiing. I can feel the
rhythm as we cut it close to the poles. I'm thinking of becoming a gym teacher. Those guys made a difference in my life.

*Amherst Tigers forever,*

*The Kipster*

*p.s. I almost forgot to tell you — to top off the leeches and bugs, Nancy Sinatra was here, singing "These Boots Are Made for Walking." I felt like giving her mine.*

I showed Kip's letter to my mother and we just exchanged glances and shook our heads. It was too sad to discuss.

—

I started my summer job with New York State Welfare as one of twenty interns in social work. My mother had a friend from college who'd pulled a few strings to get me the position, even though I had little interest in the field. The first day I walked into the high-rise welfare building, I saw that it was as big as a department store, except the elevator signs didn't say things like LADIES WEAR or FOUNDATIONS. All the welfare departments were in jargon and initialisms — like DSS (Department of Social Services), ADC (Aid to Dependent Children), FS (Food Stamps) or ILP (Independent Living Program). Instead of products, it had floors and floors of "services." I soon found out that everyone who was indoctrinated in the welfare office spoke using this social work speak. At first I had no idea what anyone was saying.

On the form that I had filled out in the training sessions, there was a space to list work preferences. I said anything that was downtown and didn't have to do with children. Nevertheless, I was assigned to ADC in DSS. In my office there were eight caseworkers. One was on long-term disability for "nerves" and another had been fired recently for "lolling over many a liquid lunch," or so said the caseworker, David, who sat next to me. That left six caseworkers and a manager. The manager's name was Mr. Shoomack.

On the day I arrived, Mr. Shoomack introduced me to the others as the summer intern and told David I needed a guided tour of the high-rises known as the Talbert Mall Housing Project, where I would be working as a welfare caseworker.

As in many North American cities, some urban planning board had had the idea that if you piled poor people with no life skills on top of one another, and then ripped down everything around them except other welfare high-rises, you could call it urban renewal. They figured that the people trapped inside would develop a work ethic, good schools and safe surroundings. It didn't exactly work out that way.

When I first entered the projects, I thought they resembled a movie set of London after the Blitz. The community was so poor and dangerous, the only businesses that could survive on the main street were liquor stores. Behind the facade of boarded-up storefronts there were open fields where high weeds grew and garbage had been thrown. The dozen or so apartment buildings rose like a mirage in a desert of litter and untended vegetation.

I walked through the empty fields of broken bottles and discarded hypodermics and the occasional burned mattress. Broken glass of different colours glittered in the sun. Wildflowers grew amid the tall grass, and I thought it looked beautiful in an urban trash kind of way.

David said it was always best to call the client ahead so she could get rid of the man who might be living there.

"Why is that important?" I asked.

"If she lives alone and has no way of taking care of the children, then she gets ADC. The more children she has, the larger
the income. Also, if she has a really big family, she can qualify for
a larger apartment."

"What if she works to supplement her income?"

"It's deducted from her ADC."

"What if she gets married?" I asked.

"Then she's cut off the welfare roll."

"So the system encourages you to not work, not marry and not
have a man around and to have lots of children?" I asked David.

"That is 90 percent of welfare and 98 percent of the projects."

The projects didn't look that different from other high-rise
buildings on the outside, but inside they were gutted and spray-
painted with graffiti. All the mailbox doors had been ripped off.
The elevator didn't work, other than as a spray-painted cubbyhole
or a urinal. In the stairwell that first day, I saw a black man out
cold.

It took me awhile to understand how the welfare system oper-
ated. It was clear when I worked a full eight hours that I was
upsetting not only my co-workers but also the clients. There was
a delicate symbiosis — two species of sloth covering for each
other. Mr. Shoomack looked the other way when everyone in the
office went home after lunch. In return, they covered for him by
never asking him questions or imposing on him in any way. Mr.
Shoomack didn't answer his phone. He had a pile of mystery novels on his desk, which he made no pretense of hiding, and he
spent the whole day reading. He was happy to stay in the office
and read until five because he had children at home and if he
went home he'd have to help. The clients never complained about

the social workers or about being neglected. In return, the social workers covered for them and never really made them look for a job or helped them tackle any work or life plans. No one complained, and no one, in all the time I was there, ever got off the welfare rolls.

The first few weeks I was on the job, I attempted to look busy, but it only seemed to annoy people, so finally I started going home shortly after noon like everyone else. During my second week of coming home early, my mother said, "This is a pattern."

She sat and listened as I told her what went on there.

She said, "I'm surprised." Then she got up and left the living room.

Was she surprised that the system was so corrupt, or was she surprised that I was so corruptible? I was sure it was the latter. I felt ashamed of my behaviour. Even Mr. Shoomack must have taken a few years to become jaded. David called it burnout. I guess they had all tried at some point and eventually given up on the clients and social change, but they hadn't given up the job, the salary or the pension.

I followed my mother into the backyard and told her that I was only there for a summer job. I had never wanted to be a social worker anyway. I had about as much empathy as a gnat.

She didn't say anything more. She didn't have to.

—

From then on, I decided, I would work a full eight hours every day and I would try to do the job well. I would look at the welfare office with new eyes and try to come up with some way I could be of use. I'd rather do hard work than feel like a lazy sellout.

Every week, social workers had a meet-and-greet luncheon for

the interns. It amazed me that this program was designed to interest college students in the field of social work. I guess you were
supposed to look around at the human wreckage in the welfare
department and say, *Wow, is this ever the field for me.* I said this by
way of introduction to the two summer interns next to me at an
early meet-and-greet, and they wholeheartedly agreed on the ludi-
crousness of the recruitment plan. Neither of them ever wanted to
be a social worker either.

One, a girl named Miriam from Amherst, was the daughter of
a judge and said she had gotten the job through *schlep.* I wondered why the daughter of a judge was wearing a homemade dress
thrown together from a Simplicity pattern. Annette, the girl on
the other side of me, was also from Amherst. I knew from her last
name that she was the daughter of a well-known mafioso I'd seen
on *Eyewitness News* walking out of court with a paper bag over his
head. She said she wanted to be in fashion design and had gotten this job through her father's *raccomandazione* (whatever that
meant — I was too afraid to ask). I told them that I got mine
through networking, a new term my mother had read aloud from
her *Reader's Digest* "It Pays to Increase Your Word Power."

Miriam suggested we form a carpool for getting to and from
work. Some days I could drive them in the 409 and other days
Annette could borrow her father's car (it was a black Cadillac
with bulletproof glass windows). But Miriam had a problem: her
father would not let her get a driver's licence until she was married. (When we heard this, Annette whispered to me, "I've heard
of getting married to get out of the house, but never so you could
drive.") So her father would drive us downtown every third day.
Miriam said she would rather not commute every day with her

father because it inconvenienced him and she felt his resentment. This seemed strange to me, because his court was only a block from the welfare office. What was there to resent? She was his daughter, after all.

I agreed to the three-way carpool because I felt sorry for Miriam. She seemed desperate to get away from her dad, and also this way my mother could use her car during the week. The three of us interns had little in common. Annette was at a junior college in Florida, and she seemed to spend the entire summer getting shoes dyed to be in lavish weddings on the weekends. Miriam had gone to my high school but was a year ahead of me, and was majoring in home economics at Cornell. She was quiet and perpetually anxious. Her family had a beautiful large white house — the type you would find in Nantucket if you were a chief whaler in the nineteenth century.

I wondered why she'd gone into home economics, when she had won a math award in high school. How hard could it be to measure sugar and flour? Annette pointed out that math would come in handy if you wanted to double a recipe. When I asked why she chose home economics, she said her father forced her to major in it because it was still state-supported at Cornell, and though he wanted her at a good school, he didn't want to pay very much for her tuition. I found this strange because her brother went to Harvard law school and had his own car, which he drove to his summer placement at city hall. Miriam could never go out to lunch with the rest of us. She said she couldn't afford to.

The Judge, as her father was called by everyone, drove us downtown in his black Lincoln Continental. He wore Brooks Brothers suits and a straw homburg-style hat with a black ribbon around it.

He didn't speak to us at all, and on the first day indicated with a gesture that we all had to sit in the back seat. I told him that I got carsick in the back. He didn't answer, so I slipped into the front.

A few days later at the office, Miriam said that she needed to talk to us. She had bitten her nails to the quick and looked ashen. She said, "This is really embarrassing, but my father doesn't like any talking in the car in the morning. He uses the time to think about his cases and the decisions he has to write. Also, he wants you to sit in the back seat, Cathy."

My father would never have done that. He would have been happy to talk to my co-workers, and even if he hadn't wanted to talk, he would not have imposed his will on others. This was utterly tyrannical. The job description of a father does not include subjugation.

"I'll deal with it," I said.

"Cathy, please! You have no idea what he's like. No one does. He's lethal."

*Lethal.* What a word to use for your father.

Furious, that late afternoon after work when the Judge came to get us, I got into the front seat. I told him I had no intention of being ill in the back seat and that this would be my last ride in his car. Annette and I could alternate driving and he could make his own arrangements for Miriam.

"Fine," he said.

I added, "In the future, if you have a problem with me or my views, please tell me. I'd be more than happy to accommodate you. I don't need your ride. It's your daughter who organized the car pool."

He glared at me. "How dare you speak to me like this. I am

your elder and a judge."

"We are talking about a driver's licence here. I have one as well. I'm not in your court. I'm in your car."

"Well, Rhonda Levitt's driver should have been in my court."

So that's what this was about. My name must have come up in synagogue. "Are you this indirect in your court? No wonder the system is so backed up."

"You led Rhonda Levitt astray and introduced her to undesirable youths. Then you abandoned her."

"Father, please stop," Miriam said.

"I begged her to come home with me," I said. "I also told her those guys were idiots. It's interesting that Rhonda had a father just like you. Did you guys go to the same parenting school?" I took a long breath. "And just as a point of clarification, I was not with her the night of the accident. It was weeks later."

His mouth was a thin straight line. He pulled off the road on the thruway — no one did that. He said, "Get out of my car." There was nothing for miles around but grassland. "Get out of my car," he repeated, this time louder. "I will not be spoken to in this way. Your parents are the ones who have never learned how to raise children or they wouldn't have such a rude child with no self-discipline."

Now I really shouted. "My parents had the good sense to tell me I could call them if I was in trouble — with no questions asked. I knew better than to drive with drunks. I'd been out in the world. You learn how to judge situations when you're not sheltered." There was silence. My voice returned to normal and I added, "You say one more word about my parents and you'll be sorry, Judge."

We sat there as the minutes ticked by. The car rocked every time a truck sped by. There was no way I was getting out of his car in high heels and struggling around thruway lanes.

I said, "I drove your daughter yesterday and you can drive me today. I will never accept a ride from you again."

"Me either," Annette squeaked from the back, as Miriam sobbed with her head in her hands.

"Are you getting out?" he asked, ignoring me and looking straight ahead.

"You want me out — throw me out." I knew he wouldn't tamper with the rakish angle of his homburg.

Finally, he turned on his signal and headed back onto the thruway. We drove home in silence.

As I got out of the car, I leaned into the back seat and said to Miriam, who still had tears streaming down her face, "My parents won't mind giving me the car every other day. I can pick you up at eight. Don't worry, I would never hold any of this against you, Miriam. That would be prejudice."

I slammed the door shut.

When I told the whole story at dinnertime, my mother said, "You had quite a dangerous day and it wasn't even in the projects."

—–—

Later that night I was reading the paper on the couch and I happened to notice that American Heritage Week (the week of the fourth of July) would be running an essay contest sponsored by the New York State "Boost Buffalo" committee. The deadline for submissions was June first. The winning essay would appear in the paper on the fourth of July and the winner would travel with the Boost Buffalo committee all around the state. One of the stops on the tour was New York City. You could pick one of five first lines and write a thousand words. Most of the suggested topics were about America's fight for freedom in various forms, such as, "We fought for liberty and we're still fighting." One line immediately caught my fancy: "Oppression wears many hats." I stood up, went down to the reek room and began writing. I wrote the title: "The Straw Homburg." I wrote about how your life could look normal. You could be a perfect student and a "good girl." Your parents could send you to college, not to a place you wanted to go or to major in what you wanted, but only so it looked good to their friends. I laid out the whole thing — the judge who made unfair judgments, the brother who got the car, the sister who had to sew her own clothes even though she lived in a palatial home. I included how she bit her nails until they bled when she had to ride with him, and how she had to ride in the back seat.

Under that straw homburg was a wealthy man who donated to causes and sat on committees and was written up in the paper for being "an active philanthropist." Under that straw homburg was a man of straw, one who oppressed his daughter so much that she was physically ill from her fear of being ten minutes late. Yet no one would call him an oppressor — he'd won philanthropy awards.

You could go to war and fight for the oppressed. You could make laws so blacks could vote. What about the "privileged" child who was tyrannized and oppressed in her own home? She was an appendage of the father who needed his family to be a reflection of his own imagined perfection.

I counted the words. It was five hundred too long. I wrote, *Cut out whatever 500 you don't like.* I put it in an envelope on the lined three-hole binder paper I wrote it on and mailed it.

Fury had jumped synapses and I'd come out with phrases I could never have written if I had done it in a measured way. Even the retelling of that story made my neck break out in red blotches. The judge had hit an exposed nerve when he mentioned Rhonda. Yes, I had suggested going to Brunner's. I did introduce to her to Danny and Shaky. Clearly, if she had never met me she would still be walking. There is no higher octane fuel than unconscious guilt layered with rage.

When I told my mother what I'd written, she said, "Well, 'Boost Buffalo' should love a story about an oppressive judge from Buffalo."

My father said he thought all of the buffalos had been wiped out. He also thought it was silly for buffalos to be judging a writing contest.

"Just buffaloing us," my mother agreed.

"Typical government boondoggle," I said.

My mother and I had long ago agreed that it was useless to correct my father. It was demeaning for him, and trying for us.

—

About two weeks later I was informed by a registered letter that I had won. This year had, for the first time, been a tie. They had chosen two winners who, strangely enough, had selected the same question and both used hats as symbols of oppression, yet expressed their ideas very differently. I ran into the living room to tell my parents.

My mother said, "Hats off to Cathy," from her place on the couch. She held up her Tab in a toast. "To a tie for oppression."

My father, still watching TV, said, "I wouldn't want that tie."

"No." She reached for his hand. "We'll get out your Fourth of July tie pretty soon."

"That's a swell tie — with Paul Revere riding on it," he said, brightening up. "Remember my St. Patrick's Day tie? The one with the tube that when you squeezed it the snakes of Ireland would come shooting out?"

"We had so much fun with that," said Mom.

"Maybe I'll wear it for the Fourth of July," he offered.

"What a wonderful idea. Everyone always loved it," she said.

I read part of the letter aloud:

> Catherine McClure and Laurie Coal will share the $1,000 prize and will each be funded to travel, all expenses paid, to tourist festivities in the following five New York cities: Buffalo, Rochester, Syracuse, Albany and two separate events and weekends in Manhattan and Brooklyn sponsored by the New York "Fun City" campaign, where they will read their essays on the different hats of oppression respectively titled "The Straw Homburg" and "Keep It Under Your Cap." The essays will then be published.

"Who is this goofy girl hogging my other five hundred dollars?" I said.

My mother and I laughed, and she said, "I knew you were going to say that. Now remember, you're doing a lot of travelling with her, so be nice."

"God, I hope I'm not sharing a hotel room with her," I said. "Laurie Coal? She sounds like some big calcified lump."

"Well, keep what you think under your cap. Whenever

something good happens to you, you start carrying on about something or someone," my mother said.

"I do? That's strange."

"Yes, it is," she said.

"You know I'm just kidding around, right?"

"I know, but I'm not sure everyone else does. I mean, she's not hogging your award. You're sharing it."

"A hog got your award?" my father asked.

"Yup."

"Well, I wouldn't want to hear his thank-you speech."

"Hers," I said.

I was, as my mother said, "carrying on," but I was also thrilled to have won the award. The Judge had behaved badly and hurt my feelings, and, what was far worse, he'd said derogatory things about my parents. Now he would be roasted in the paper, and *I* was turning the spit, which pleased me no end. Roy had been right when he said, *Don't cross Cathy and then meet her in a dark alley.* He would recite that rhyme "When she was good she was very, very good and when she was bad she was horrid" when I exacted revenge on customers who had crossed us in some way.

I was also happy for my mother, who was proud of me. She needed a lift. My father, who was perpetually convivial, seemed thrilled to see my mother happy. We had a delightful time that evening — feeling a joy that had been missing from our house for so long now.

—

About a week after winning the contest, I was cutting across the field to get to the projects when a very tall black teenager wearing large Coke-bottle glasses with white tape holding them together jumped out of the bushes and said, "I could attack you right now and no one would hear."

I looked around. It was true. Despite the population density of the projects, I was in an empty field in the butterscotch sunlight, with not a soul in sight.

"Heh, misses, I see your social work clipboard. You must be new. You coming 'round these parts, you better get a taxi voucher. Don't be walking 'round here without protection. I take you through the building today, but I ain't here all the time."

As we walked through the empty lot, I began, "My name is . . ." Then I hesitated. We had been told to introduce ourselves by our last name to ensure that a professional relationship was maintained, but he wasn't my client.

"I guess you done forgot your name. Since I remember mine, I'll go first. I'm Flaps."

"I'm Cathy McClure." I asked him how old he was and he said seventeen, though he looked younger.

"Is Flaps short for anything?"

"My lips be flappin' all the time. I like jawin' with people, ya know?"

"That could be my name as well. I also like flapping."

As we walked along, he said, "Where you from? The country?"

"No. The suburbs."

"Got any horses?"

"No."

"You got a horse on your shirt. That's why I stopped you. I thought you might be from the country."

I looked down at my shaded brown and white toile blouse with a scene depicting riders, horses and hounds on a hunt.

"I gots a thing for horses. Bad," he said.

"Ever read the Black Stallion series?"

"A book?"

"Yeah. About horses. They might be too young for you if you are seventeen. You can get them at the library. On second thought, if you're here tomorrow I'll bring them for you. They're just collecting dust on my shelves."

Flaps was there the next day too, and every day after that that I worked in the projects. He showed me the ropes. He told me to never get in an elevator if there aren't some old ladies or little kids in it. Never get on alone or with one man. Never get off at the fourteenth or seventeenth floors, as those are drug-guarded floors with Dobermans. He said, "They might do something to you if the door opens. I gots a brother workin' up there."

"Why are you in this field every day?"

"Got to get out the house. Can't get back in till later. My ma needs privacy."

I later found out from David that Flaps's mother was a prostitute named Tasty Foot. She had many children who were in and out of juvenile detention, and the daughters worked with her. The little ones stayed at their grandmother's down the hall. Flaps's grandmother was frightened of him because he was an epileptic, or "taken to fits," as Flaps described it, and she believed the devil was in him. He had mostly raised himself, spending time wandering the streets and sitting in the library or in theatre lobbies.

Back at the office I looked him up in Tasty's file: *Third son named Jameson Foot. Born 1951. Answers to Flaps. Father unknown. Not quite right. High fevers as a baby and from then on had seizures. No criminal record.*

Clearly, Flaps was an outsider. No one threatened him in any way because he had an older brother who was head of a gang, and another who ran a drug business.

When I took the Black Stallion books to Flaps, he lifted a mattress from the field and under it was a large piece of plywood. He jacked up the plywood and under that was a hole with a tent liner in it. In this dugout he had collected a number of pairs of sneakers and some rolled-up pictures of horses. He showed them to me. They were from advertisements for movies.

"I got all these movie posters from the man what runs Shea's Buffalo on Main Street. Whenever there was a horse movie, I went in every day and asked for the poster." He held up a crowbar and around it he had wrapped a poster. When he unrolled it, I could see it was for *True Grit* with John Wayne. He had Gary Cooper in the *Last Outlaw*, Gregory Peck in *The Big County*, Jimmy Stewart in *The Man Who Shot Liberty Valance*, Burt Lancaster in *The Rounders*, Roddy McDowall in *My Friend Flicka*. He had dozens more. "I gots more than this — but these are my prizes. Some is old, some new," he said as he carefully rolled them up again.

It was then that I conceived the idea. I realized that I couldn't reform the welfare system before I went back to school, but what I could do was disrupt its present stagnation. I would start an employment program for teenagers on my caseload.

I knew lots of people who owned businesses, and the journalist from the newspaper who wrote human interest stories now knew me because I'd won the essay contest. He could write an article on the project and mention every business that employed a teenager. The jobs would only be for two months, and the carrot for the employer was that I would spend a few hours per week orienting the student; since we were paid by the welfare office, it would be the equivalent of a week's free labour for the business.

I enlisted Annette and Miriam, but they thought the best approach was to find our most downtrodden and give them hope through a job. I said absolutely not. We needed to focus on the kids who were at the top of the heap — those who had made it in business, even if that business was drugs or extortion. They had business sense. And they had to have good attendance records at school. Annette and Miriam wanted to set up some point system of criteria. I nixed that as well. We knew nothing about these kids. We had no way to accurately assess their capabilities. All we could go on was past history of no criminal record. Flaps knew far better than we did who would, as he put it, "make it with the man."

I decided we should get the jobs first, and then, with Flaps's assistance, match the teenager to the position. Three things made me think that Flaps could manage this: the way he tried to create a little world of his own away from his dysfunctional family; his ability to get those posters and hang on to them; and the fact that he was never late to meet me.

I presented the plan to Shoomack. When I was in the middle of explaining, his eyes kept darting back to his mystery novel. Then he moved his hand in a circle, indicating he wanted me to wrap it up, and said, "Fine, fine," and went back to his book.

First I drove over to the Buffalo Riding Academy, the posh equestrian centre, and asked to see the manager. He was an old white man with a craggy face and navy blue jacket and tie. On his tie there were men jumping horses over hurdles. I explained that Flaps was black, disadvantaged and needed help — he loved horses and I would work with him for the first week for free.

The manager never even wavered. He said very politely, "That sounds like a good idea. Has he worked with horses before?"

I said he hadn't, but I explained about the posters and how much Flaps loved them.

He said, "That's a first step. Be here in the morning."

Out of the five places I went to that day, they all said they would take a summer intern. I was amazed. I think it was the timing that made them agree. The Civil Rights Act had been passed. No one in Buffalo had been hit yet with disadvantaged youth programs. People were still hopeful. Or perhaps they were simply kind and I hit the right ones. I leaned on three drugstores where my dad knew the pharmacists. Annette hit her relatives. She had all kinds of cousins in the grocery business and in waste management. They agreed. Miriam was surprised that most of her father's friends agreed. I said the secret was to approach small businesses or franchises where you could talk directly to the proprietor; no one could pass the buck and say, *Oh, I have to ask headquarters.*

I drove Miriam and Annette home from work that day with the top down, feeling proud of the Buffalo businessmen who were so overwhelmingly kind and had agreed to put their money on the line. As we pulled into the Sunoco gas station, I was banging out the beat of Aretha Franklin's "Respect" on the steering wheel, and Annette and Miriam were drumming on the dashboard. The gas jockey was at the blue and yellow pump, grooving to his own radio, which was on the same station, WKBW. It was a sunny summer day and we felt like the world around us was as hopeful as we were.

—

I went to pick up Flaps two hours early on the day of his interview.

I had bought him an alarm clock and shown him how to use it, and had listed it on my expense report. When I arrived, he was up, ready and wearing an ironed shirt patterned with horses and cowboys lassoing horses in a corral. He was also wearing one of those string ties with a horse clamp at the top, the kind Alan Ladd would have worn in *Shane* when he went out courting. Flaps had taken a black pen and darkened the tape on his glasses.

I asked him if he'd had breakfast and he said no. I asked him if he'd packed a lunch. No. Did he have money for lunch? No. At that point his mother yelled out from her bedroom, "Shut up."

I bought him breakfast at the downtown Howard Johnson. I told him that to work for eight hours he needed a hearty breakfast every day. I suggested bacon and eggs. He dutifully ordered them. The waitress asked him how he wanted them, and he said, "Just anywhere on my plate." I ordered a takeout sandwich for him for lunch.

After breakfast, I drove him to his interview at the Buffalo Riding Academy, which featured a ring in the middle where young girls wearing hard riding hats cantered in circles.

He was thrilled when he looked through the windows into the ring. "I never met anyone else in the world who liked horses."

"Isn't it great to realize you're not alone?" I was surprised how much I shared in his joy.

We waited in the lobby for Flaps to be called into his interview. The chairs were old saddles on stools and there were pictures of horses everywhere. The coat rack was stirrups on the wall. The attached restaurant was called The Tack Room. As Flaps said, "These people really like horsing around."

The craggy white-haired manager came out and shook hands formally and introduced himself to Flaps as Mr. Winters. Flaps said he was Mr. Flaps. "Well, Mr. Flaps, come in for a little chat."

I felt so nervous while he was in the office that I began pacing. It was all very new for him and I didn't want to have raised
his hopes for nothing. People had been such a disappointment to
Flaps, and he'd put all his faith in horses.

He was in the office for about thirty minutes, and when they
emerged, Mr. Winters smiled at me and shook hands with Flaps.

"Welcome aboard, Mr. Flaps. See you tomorrow at 8 a.m. You'll
find we all work at a canter here."

———

No one at the welfare office was happy or sad about the great
success of the candidates. Instead of being rocked to their very
core, the employees of the welfare department seemed relieved
that I no longer made any demands on them. When the program
was written up, I put the clipping, titled "Breaking the Cycle," on
Mr. Shoomack's desk, but all he said was, "Where is the rest of the
paper? I need the crossword."

———

A few years later, when I went back to the riding academy, I found
out that Flaps had worked at the club all through high school. Mr.
Winters, the manager of the club, told me that Flaps had "horse
sense." He would speak what sounded like nonsense to the manager, but the horses loved him. Although Mr. Flaps wanted to stay
at the Buffalo Riding Academy, Mr. Winters had some contacts at
Saratoga Race Track, and encouraged him to move up after high
school. Mr. Flaps started there as a groom and gradually climbed
the ladder. Mr. Winters said he wondered how he'd done up at
Saratoga.

Thirty years later I went to Saratoga Race Track in hopes of finding Flaps. The manager told me he'd died in the 1980s in a car accident. He never took medication for his epilepsy and denied to everyone that he had it. It was presumed that he'd had a seizure while driving.

Everyone there had heard of him. He'd managed an entire stable that was as long as a city block, the manager told me, and was a legend among the trainers and owners. There were still jockeys and managers who remembered him personally. The manager told me only Flaps knew if a horse was coming down with something, or was "bereft" (the word Flaps always used if a horse was not himself).

As I was leaving his office, the manager said, "You know, he was a man of particular habits. Sometime we'd have to move horses from track to track, so we would be on the road. He always stopped and had bacon and eggs for breakfast, no matter where we were or how rushed we were. Only that breakfast could get him to leave the horses alone." He thought for a moment. "You know, Mr. Flaps was a loner. Many a good groom and trainer were on the outside looking in to the human arena, but when they stepped into the horse arena, they were front and centre."

Tears came to my eyes as I stood at the door.

He continued, "You're the first person who ever came to see him. He wasn't a gambler, a drinker or a womanizer. I have no idea what he did with his income. One in a million has horse sense, and Flaps had it in spades."

I nodded in agreement.

"He believed the horse was his equal, and the horse did things for him not because he was the one in the bit, but because that trainer was his friend. And friendship is not something you can fake."

CHAPTER 13

# a fire in the cellar

When August rolled around, I presented Mr. Shoomack with my

bright green exit interview sheet. Sighing as though I had walked

into his personal study and interrupted him, he picked up a pen

and wrote on the full page provided for my assessment: *Began*

*teen placement program for ADC — result — successful.* He handed it back to me and then returned to reading his mystery, titled *The Lunatic in Charge*. He didn't ask why I was leaving early, nor did I offer an explanation.

When I got home, my mother and I looked over the itinerary for my reading tour. My mother was excited about this opportunity and had already read the schedule about fifty times — I felt bad that she had to stay home. I was at least familiar with the names, because we'd been to New York City together many times in the years since I'd learned to drive. Sometimes we'd make a last-minute decision to go to the city. We'd hop on the thruway at night, take turns driving and pull into Manhattan seven hours later with all the trucks that were delivering at dawn. I remember once, when we left at noon, we got there for opening night of *On a Clear Day You Can See Forever* just as the curtain was rising. My father usually took a pass on these jaunts, saying someone had "to hold the fort."

The first stop on the Boost Buffalo tour was New York City, for the Fun City Campaign. We would then wind around the state, returning to Buffalo for our final reading almost a month later.

We would spend eight days in New York City with five talks sprinkled through the week. I would be in a suite with Laurie Coal. Thank the Lord I had my own bedroom at least. My mother gave me a lecture on being gracious and offering to go to meals with her. She gave me her "be charitable, for God is watching you" spiel, saying maybe Laurie wasn't as outgoing as I was and might feel lost in a city the size of New York.

"If she's a jerk, I'm not taking her anywhere," I said.

My mother shook her head and flopped on the couch.

We would be staying at the New York Hilton on the Avenue of

the Americas. My mother said, "Those who know New York City at all call the Avenue of the Americas 'Sixth Avenue.'"

My parents drove me to the airport for my flight to New York; I was excited to be travelling alone as an adult. I had flown to New York alone in grade school for the state high jumping championships and had been billeted in Harlem. My mother prepared me for this adventure by sending me with a box of heart-shaped chocolates for the hostess.

My father was no longer venturing out very much, so this was a big deal. He'd become thin and bald from chemotherapy, and looked much older than his fifty-eight years. In fact, he bore an uncanny resemblance in gait and demeanour to Robert Duvall as Boo Radley in *To Kill a Mockingbird*.

As my parents walked me out to the tarmac, my father suddenly stopped and, holding on to a chain-link fence, started singing the Ethel Merman song "There's No Business Like Show Business." (My mother forever after referred to this as "The Airport Aria.") He must have remembered Gene Kelly's dance in *On the Town,* for then he pretended to hold down a sailor hat and began kicking back as though he were running, singing:

*New York, New York, it's a wonderful town,*
*The Bronx is up and the Battery's down.*
*The people ride in a hole in the ground.*
*New York, New York, it's a wonderful town.*

My mother and I looked at each other, mortified. Mercifully, they began loading the plane then, and I made sure I was one of the first to board, before he broke into another verse.

When I arrived at LaGuardia, a man was holding a sign that said CATHY MCCLURE. How did he know me? My first thought was that I'd finally been caught for painting the lawn jockeys. When I described my paranoia in a letter to my mother, she wrote back that she could imagine the headline: "Lawn Jockey Hunt Comes to End in Airport Chase." Well, not exactly a chase. Undercover cop dressed as a limo driver simply holds up sign with her name and she confesses, saying she "couldn't live through another day of the manhunt."

The driver had a white van that said FUN CITY on the side in big red bubble letters. He threw a FUN CITY T-shirt to me in the back seat and growled in a Brooklyn accent, "I been out here three times already today. Why the hell couldn't they have you all come in at the same time? No wonder the city is going bankrupt."

When I got to the Hilton, I checked in and immediately, without even unpacking, went out sightseeing and made sure to go to Saint Patrick's Cathedral to see if any Broadway stars were lined up for confession. I also read that Jackie Kennedy attended mass there now that she lived in New York. Exhausted when I got back to the hotel, I flopped into bed.

The following morning I wandered into the sitting area and looked around. The suite was spacious — as in bigger than my home — and luxurious; there was a black leather couch and a sleek black ebony desk. The carpet was white and when I walked my feet almost disappeared. The flocked wallpaper was grey and the pictures on the wall were all black-and-white photos of New York in the 1920s. I slid open the drapes and saw Midtown Manhattan in all its glory. The sun shot off the tall glass buildings at sharp angles. I was thrilled that we were right across the street from Rockefeller Center and Radio City Music Hall. I lit a cigarette and contemplated calling room service for some breakfast. I had always wanted room service, and my mother had underlined the sentence in the letter that read: "*All meals are included but receipts must be submitted.*"

I heard rustling in the other bedroom. Laurie must have arrived late last night. My mother's words came back to me, *She probably didn't want to share her prize with you any more than you wanted to share yours with her.* I tiptoed over to the door and put my ear to it. Nothing.

I said, "Laurie," then louder, "Laurie . . . can I come in?"

I heard a muffled sound that I assumed was yes. I opened the door and was taken aback to see an amazingly handsome black man sitting up in the king-size bed. He appeared to be naked except for the sheet that covered him from the waist down. He was leaning against the headboard, smoking a cigarette. He had a long, narrow face with taut café-au-lait skin stretched on high cheekbones. He was wiry and without excess, and looked like he could easily spring into action. He had intense hazel eyes. I had an odd feeling — one I found hard to define. It was sort of like I'd had too much coffee . . . but wanted another.

Laurie, wherever she was, must've spent the night with this guy. The only other girl (besides Veronica Nebozenko, who I tried to block from my mind) that I had ever met who slept with men before she was married was Sarah, and she was from New York as well. Evidently Laurie didn't need me to show her around the Big Apple. She'd already had a bite of the forbidden fruit. I don't know how long I stood there, but it felt ridiculously long.

Finally I said, "I guess Laurie is in the bathroom?"

"I'm Laurie — Lawrence Coal."

"You're not a girl," I said in my usual accusatory tone.

"Hope not, or I've been playing on the wrong team." He didn't say any more, just took a drag on his cigarette.

When I told him who I was, he nodded as though he'd figured that out. I didn't say anything else. I couldn't. I felt a bit weak and strange, and didn't know what had come over me. He continued to smoke and look straight ahead.

I said, "Just what is going on here?" I have no idea why I began to interrogate him, as though somehow he'd tricked me and not told me he was a man and he hadn't even bothered to tell me he'd arrived.

He looked at me and spoke calmly. "You're in my room. You tell me."

He had a point. I was the one who needed to offer some kind of explanation. I was in his room uninvited, accusing him of not being a girl.

I managed to stammer, "I think they thought you were a girl, so they put us together for the trip. I mean . . . we share the suite." He nodded. At this point I figured a joke was best. "I hope you didn't think I was a guy."

"Not until you came in," he said softly, smiling.

He was the most striking man I'd ever seen. Instead of simply leaving, which any sane woman would have done, I continued blathering. "Uh . . . I was going to order room service, so I thought you might want me to order for two. We could eat in the sitting area. I mean, we don't have to eat in here. I mean, in this bedroom." I was now begging myself to shut up.

"No, thanks."

"Oh . . . uh . . . okay." I stood there, offering myself up to the God of social pariahs. Time ticked away. I heard loud horns and sirens outside. I still didn't leave. After an interminable amount of time I said, "Going out?"

"Yeah. I like New York in the early morning, especially on a weekend."

He had a surprisingly gentle voice for such a large man. I had to strain to hear him. I wondered if he was going to invite me along.

But he didn't. He leaned over and put his cigarette out in his ashtray on the bedside table and said, "Well, I guess I'll get into the shower."

I still stood there rooted to the floor — nailed by social incompetence. A long time passed, and then he smiled. I said, "Oh sorry. I'll just go call room service."

He nodded, probably relieved I was leaving.

I went back to my room and paced. I waited for him to go out into the hall and then I followed. One would have thought that after my ridiculous display in his room, I'd avoid Laurie for the rest of the tour. It was like someone had hit me over the head with an idiot stick and sent me on my merry way in New York.

"Oh, hi!" I said, as though I'd last seen him in the Arctic and it was really strange to have run into him.

He walked to the elevator and pressed the button. "Having room service in the hall?" he asked casually.

"No. I decided you had a good idea — New York in the morning — get out — bagel — Central Park — that kind of thing." What was I saying?

We got on the elevator together. We took the long ride down in silence. We got off in the lobby and he turned toward the revolving door. Why didn't I say at that point, *Mind if I come along?* I mean, the worst he could have come back with was, *No,* or, *I'm meeting someone.* Instead, I acted almost psychotic. I wish someone had driven by from Bellevue just then, taken pity upon me, put me in a white muslin straitjacket, thrown me into the ambulance, tied me down, turned on the siren and sped me to a locked ward.

I didn't know the first thing about how to flirt or to be "available." It was rare that I'd ever wanted to do this. He was only the second man I'd ever found attractive.

I followed him to the revolving door and was so confused that I missed my exit opening and went around again.

Outside I said, "Where are you eating?"

"Carnegie Deli."

"You're kidding . . . me too!" I said, hitting my forehead. "I always eat there."

He didn't say one word. He just nodded. The way you do when lunatics bother you on the street and you hope they will move on to the person behind you.

With each step my embarrassment grew, until finally, after a block or two, humiliation had completely saturated my body and I couldn't take it any longer. I looked up at him and exclaimed, "Holy moly! I forgot to cancel my room service. Bye." And I turned tail and clomped back toward the hotel.

I hadn't waited to see his expression. Probably one of relief. Anyway, he must have kept walking.

When I got back to my hotel room, I threw myself on my bed and crawled under the covers in my clothes. Later, when I could think again, I tried to talk myself down by hearing my mother's soothing voice echo within me. She would have said, *It's no big deal. So you were confused. You acted a little flighty. It'll soon be forgotten. Just start out from now on a different footing. Be businesslike. If you never mention the incident, nor will he.*

That's right, move on. I got up, threw water on my face and then opened the package that the Fun City Tour had left for us. In it there were comp tickets to some plays and art events, and a booklet describing all the winners of the contest from the different areas of New York State. I looked up Laurie's biography:

*Laurie Coal divides her time among New York, Buffalo and Ohio. She has been honoured at many festivals. She still finds time to study economics in college. At the tender age of twenty she has published three volumes of poetry. One has already been translated into French.*

Mine said:

*Catherine McClure is a college student. We eagerly await her first publication.*

I dug through my stuff and looked again at his essay, which was really a sort of poem. It was pretty good. Then I reread mine. It was so stuck in suburbia, with the rich girl whose father wouldn't let her drive the family's luxury car; it seemed laughable, especially here in New York. Laurie's was about races not really seeing one another. He used the image of the Yankees baseball cap blocking the sun so you could only see your team but never the light.

After rifling through the bag, I found a ticket for a matinee of *Cabaret* on Broadway. I decided it was time to put the morning behind me.

——

I took my seat in the balcony in the dark because I was late and the house lights had already gone down. Joel Grey was in the middle of "Willkommen." When he sang in a thick German accent about the nightclub girls taking off their clothes, the audience laughed. All except the guy next to me. I looked over.

It was Laurie.

That's when I gave a sort of demented yelp. Within seconds a flashlight was on me and the white-gloved usher asked if everything was all right. At a total loss, I said, "A mouse ran over my foot." He just snapped off his flashlight and walked away.

The woman on the other side of me yelled, "A mouse!" People began to turn around and say, "Shhh."

Laurie and I had been given the same Fun City promotional entertainment package, with seats next to each other. Again I had that horrible feeling of internal quaking. I felt as though my body had released battery acid — enough that one organ could consume another.

For most of my life I had kept my emotions, particularly about males, under lock and key in a cobwebbed basement below a trap door where there was yet another locked cellar — like the Underground Railroad on the Niagara River in Lewiston, where there was a series of locked cellars as you descended to the gorge. I only kept one emotion accessible in my back pocket — anger — and pulled that out whenever any emotion was required. Meeting Laurie had caused a fire in the cellar, and all of the stored emotions were rising and coming out like smoke and escaping through cracks in the floor. Somehow I knew there was no way I could ever gather them back up and return them to the cellar.

To calm myself down at intermission, I called Leora long distance, collect, at the University of Chicago, and told her I'd made an idiot of myself in front of a gorgeous poet named Laurie who had a velvet voice. Before she could say anything, I went on about how I had to travel with him all around New York State. She encouraged me not to worry, saying that poets have their heads in the clouds anyway. The five-minute bell sounded and I had to scurry back to my seat.

During the next part of the performance, I used my prodigious energy to block any feelings for Laurie. When I put my mind to something, I'm usually fairly good at it. I kept saying to myself, *Laurie is just a guy I work with.*

At the second intermission I got a Coke and bought him one without asking. He took it and nodded thanks, and we went outside for a cigarette. I started talking about the play and he listened. I pretended he was Kip Rogers.

On our way back to the hotel, I said, "So what are you doing tonight?"

"Going to a friend's, really an acquaintance's, play."

"Your friend wrote it?"

He nodded. "Leroi Jones."

Laurie had a friend who had a play produced in New York?

"Got an extra ticket?"

He hesitated, then said, "Yes."

"Mind if I use it?"

"It's at the Black Arts Repertory Theatre in Harlem," he said. He looked less than thrilled.

"If you have plans for the ticket, I'll understand."

He looked regretful, as though he wished he'd never let the cat out of the bag about the two tickets. But he said, "Okay, you might as well have it."

"Great. I actually spent a week in Harlem, high jumping, around ten years ago." How could I keep saying such moronic things? I pressed on. "What's the name of the play?"

"*Dutchman.*"

"As in the cleanser?"

He nodded, and smiled ever so slightly.

"Want to eat on our way?"

"No thanks," he said.

The play was in what looked like an abandoned warehouse off a back alley. I didn't worry about safety because Laurie was well over six feet and I figured he could take on whatever he needed to. We entered up a cement staircase that was littered with old flyers. When we got to the top and opened the door, there was a lobby that held about five people. After going down a dark, musty hallway, we came upon a minuscule theatre that held twenty people tops.

I whispered, "I was beginning to wonder what we were getting into, weren't you?"

"No."

"Sorry, Mr. Off–Off Broadway," I said.

He smiled a beautiful smile, his teeth straight and white, his eyes crinkled at the corners. "I've been called a lot of things, but never Mr. Off–Off Broadway."

I had made no effort to ask what the play was about before-hand. In the program it said that it took place on a subway car with only two people, one black and one white.

Three-quarters of the audience was black; the rest were New York white intellectual types, except for one red-headed Midwestern man in a polyester suit in the back row who looked like he had read the wrong theatre brochure and was meant to be at *Oklahoma!*

There was no stage, and we sat so close to the actors we could feel their spit when they yelled. The white girl was a sluttish racist who had sex with black men and then fantasized that she understood blacks. The black man was a college student who saw himself as a Baudelairean figure and really didn't acknowl-edge that he was black. The white woman taunted the black man until he exploded, screaming racist taunts at her. She eventually killed him, and in the end you assumed she was moving on to her next victim.

Not exactly what I'd bargained for. However, it was totally believable and spot-on for that moment in history. James Meredith, the first black student at the University of Mississippi, had been shot earlier in the summer while on a peaceful freedom march. I had never before heard black anger. I had heard Martin Luther King say things like "I have a dream . . . ," but this was new.

You could feel the audience identifying with the black charac-ter's fury. The dialogue was so tight and the room so small that the characters' rage spilled off the stage and flowed to every square inch of that theatre. I felt people were looking at Laurie and me, thinking we were the lead characters come to see ourselves.

—

After the show I suggested walking back to the hotel, because the night was warm and beautiful. It was a very long walk, but we had all of New York before us as we ambled up Lenox Avenue and cut through Central Park. The lights from the bridges reflected spectacularly in the reservoir. In the distance, the city was blue and twinkling.

We talked about the play but didn't mention the racist content. Laurie told me that the man in the polyester suit was from the FBI. He said that every night one FBI agent attended the play. We laughed because the fellow had been so obvious, with his too-tight suit and red hair. Laurie said that Leroi Jones's phone was tapped and so was Martin Luther King's. The FBI, he told me, was infiltrating the civil rights movement.

I said I thought the words in the play were seditious, if *seditious* meant questioning the established order. If people want things to stay the same, then artists like Leroi Jones are a threat. As we walked home, we talked about the power of the words in the play. Laurie told me he was on a campaign to use a new word each day. He was trying to find a way to make a large vocabulary an integral part of his brain, and eventually second nature. He looked up a new word each morning and made himself use it as much as possible. "The whole thing is fairly contrived, but you can't sculpt a poem with a dull blade," he said.

I said it wasn't weird at all. My mother had been doing the "Word Power" section in *Reader's Digest* ever since I could remember. Whenever she read a new word, she used it at dinner and made my father and me guess what it meant. She would sometimes have to resort to examples, like, "I'm chagrined. This french fry is wizened."

Hours later, when we got back to the hotel, Laurie stopped in front of the revolving door of the lobby and said good night.

"Don't you live here too?" I asked.

"I'm meeting some friends."

"At 2:30 a.m.?" I said, before I could catch myself. Then, realizing I was not his mother, I said, "So long" and beat a hasty retreat.

—~—

The next morning I got up and decided to get out of the hotel and run around. My high jumping coach had called this running laps. I had a nerve-racking day ahead, going to different places to read my one pathetic essay aloud to audiences for the first time. I'd learned that when I was riled up I should do something physical.

I opened the door to the hall and found a note that said:

*Cathy,*

*Found a word — "ephemeral" — in a poem by John Donne. I like the sound. New York is full of ephemeral joys.*

*L.*

An hour later I was lounging in the sitting area of the suite, highlighting the Whitney and Guggenheim galleries on a map of Manhattan, when the white Princess phone rang on my desk, which was as big as a skating rink. A Wagnerian blast came from the other end and identified herself as Mrs. Rose, the volunteer in charge of showing us around and shepherding us to the various performance venues. She said she had decided to give us a day to settle in and get over jet lag. Jet lag from Buffalo?

She cheerfully inquired where we wanted to go today. When I hesitated, she suggested we start at the Statue of Liberty. "Have you met Laurie?" she asked.

"Actually, there was a mistake. Laurie is Lawrence."

"Oy vey. Tell me you're not sharing a room?"

"No, we have our own rooms in a suite connected by a sitting area."

"What is with those *meshuganas* in Albany? You give civil servants a job for life and they can't tell the boys from the girls." She exclaimed as though there had been an accident. "Oh no! I went out and bought lavender drawer freshener sachets for both of you as presenter's gifts."

"So — he'll smell better than most men."

"Exactly," she said. "He can give it to his mother. Who ever gives them anything? I know I have two sons, who are grown up, or so they say, and I'm still waiting for a gift." There was never a pause when talking to Mrs. Rose. "So bring a sweater. The Statue of Liberty is on the water. You don't want to get a chill."

"Um," I said, stalling. "Let me get Laurie."

I put down the phone and went over to knock on his door.

He mumbled, "Who is it?" He'd still been sleeping.

"Elizabeth Taylor." Who did he think?

There was no response.

"Mrs. Rose of the Fun City committee is on the phone, wanting to take us for a sightseeing tour — starting with the Statue of Liberty."

Silence.

"She wants to talk to you."

Nothing.

"She screams when she talks and she thought you were a girl and bought you a lavender sachet for your drawers." I figured he needed a full-blown picture.

He opened the door, wearing only cut-off blue jeans and no shirt. He looked much thinner in long pants and a shirt. I was amazed at how muscular he was. Every step he took defined a muscle group. I was so shocked by his sculpted body, I couldn't even speak, which for me indicated a shock that has gone into the most primitive part of my lizard brain. I pointed to the phone, made a face and pantomimed slitting my throat. He nodded in agreement. I grabbed a hotel notepad and wrote *No way*. I placed my map and brochures on the galleries in front of him. He nodded again and picked up the receiver.

"Hello, Mrs. Rose," he said. "No, I was reading in bed . . . Yes, we straightened out the Laurie/Lawrence thing . . . No, I suspected all along she was a female . . . I know how dangerous New York can be . . . Thanks, but I have research to do. We both have to go to the Berg Collection at the New York Public Library. I've called ahead and they've taken the manuscripts I want to see out of storage . . . I'm looking up an annotated edition of Poe . . . I'm sorry we can't. We have plans all week." He picked up the brochure. "We're going to the Whitney gallery today to see an exhibition called 'Single Men Room Reconstructions 1920–1965: An Installation' . . . The problem is that tomorrow I promised to take Cathy to . . ." He looked down at the page of my guidebook. " . . . the Guggenheim to see their surrealists." After a long pause, he continued. "No, no, that's fine. We don't feel abandoned . . . Never cut through the park at night . . . Not even a cab goes to Harlem . . . Got it . . . Just give them the wallet . . . Okay, great, six o'clock tonight . . . Green

Buick in the front . . . We will . . . You're right, the tow-away zone
is no joke . . . Thank you . . . Bye."

He placed the phone on the hook and let out a long sigh.

"That was close," I said.

"Really."

"Well, we'd better get going if we have all that to do this week,"
I said jokingly. It was seven in the morning.

"I'll have a quick shower and be ready in ten minutes," he said
without a shred of humour, and walked toward his room.

―

I'd been to New York many times, but it all looked different that
day. I felt like a New Yorker. I can still remember Central Park,
the way the trees blew in the wind, the timed chess matches, the
Lubavitcher baseball game, the kids learning to ride bikes with
their dads. I can still smell the pretzels cooking at outdoor stands,
hear boys drumming on metal garbage cans as they made their way
down the street. I can still feel the thrill of being in a Greenwich
Village coffee shop where "real writers" sat, writing sporadically in
notebooks with no lines.

In Lewiston, I had been labelled "too excited," "bossy," "keyed
up" and "a whirlwind." In Buffalo, they had just settled on "outra-
geous" (meant in a positive sense). The terms turned darker when
I went to Ohio: "argumentative" and "eccentric." I always felt I was
on the outside looking in at all the normal people. Those people
had looked to me like they were moving in slow motion, and I'm
sure I had looked hyper to them. The hard part was that they were
always in the majority. When I talked to Laurie about it, he said
it was alienating — a new word for me. Yet after all these years, I
felt normal here in New York. New York was an escape hatch for

everyone who was never going to be at the pinnacle of normalcy on the bell curve in their home town. You could look around and see others who'd made the pilgimage from all the Tiny Towns, U.S.A. to Grand Central. For the first time, I fit in.

Laurie had to make some phone calls, so while he was in one booth I went to an adjoining one and called my mother. She asked how "the Big Apple" was, indicating she didn't want to mention the name of the city for fear it might set off "our own local Gene Kelly"; she wasn't interested in a morning medley. She asked about Laurie, and I explained that, unbelievably, he had turned out to be male.

She said, "Well, doesn't that just beat the band."

She asked where Laurie was from, and I said, "How would I know?" When she asked where he went to college, I replied that I had no idea. Then the operator interrupted us to say that our time was up.

My mother's parting words were, "Well, he certainly sounds fascinating. Bye."

When we got to the New York Public Library, I was amazed by the size and beauty of the building, with its two lions perched on the steps, protecting the thousands of volumes. The place was packed with researchers and nearly every chair in the reading room — each with its own little light — was taken. I decided right then that I wanted to do some kind of research. I felt at home.

I thought of how much my mother would love this library. Her cataloguing of research information in my father's old pharmacy drawers, piled to the ceiling in the basement, had seemed strange in Lewiston. Where most people had nails sorted by size and shape, she had stored thousands of three-by-five file cards and labelled the drawers with titles such as "The Mau Mau Rebellion" or "Alchemy AD 35 to Present." She would have been considered totally normal if she'd lived in New York.

When Laurie asked to see the original Edgar Allan Poe papers, he found out that they were out — not out of the library, since no one could remove them, but out in the reading room.

I said, "Wow. Do you believe that someone else wanted to see the original annotated manuscript of Poe's most obscure poems at the exact moment you did?"

"That's New York," he said, as though he felt the same way that I did about it.

<hr>

At six o'clock we met in the sitting area of our suite, all showered and prepped for our readings. I was a bit nervous — not flipped out, but on edge. I wore a Ladybug flowered sleeveless pink blouse with pleats in the front and a rose-coloured hopsack A-line skirt with matching pink Pappagallo flats. I pulled my hair back and tied it with a dusty rose ribbon. Laurie appeared in chinos, a tucked-in blue oxford-cloth shirt and loafers with no socks.

He said nothing about my appearance, so I asked, "How do I look?"

"Pink" was all he said.

As soon as we got out to the carport in front of the hotel, there was a mad rush for cabs because the dinner-theatre crowd was all leaving at once. Valets were trying to flag down taxis for customers and people were arguing about who should get the next cab. You could hear a cacophony of horns and voices under the carport as cars and cabs and people jockeyed for space.

Then a voice blasted above all other sound, jarring everyone: "Cathy! Are you Cathy? Hurry up — I'm in a tow-away zone."

Laurie and I ran toward the voice and a nearby car, and he politely opened the front passenger door for me and waited until I scooted in.

Mrs. Rose, a large older woman in a leopard-pattern blouse, with dyed orange hair and large red-rimmed glasses, yelled to Laurie, "Thanks, hon," leaned over me and gave him some change.

He just stood there with his long, slender hand open, looking at the tip. Cars were beeping for Mrs. Rose to move, because she was holding up everyone behind her. I was appalled: she thought Laurie was a valet.

"Close the door, please," she said, turning to face the front and flipping the car into drive.

I thought for a moment that Laurie would close the door and walk away. Instead, he leaned down and spoke softly through her front window.

"Mrs. Rose, I understood we got paid by the New York Fun City committee at the *end* of the tour."

She whipped around, about to yell something else, and then saw her mistake. "Oy vey, what have I done? Laurie, first I thought you were a girl — and now this. I am so sorry. These idiots treat us volunteers like cattle, tell us nothing. They are such schleppers. Get in, please."

The captain of the valets, who wore a red coat while the underlings wore green, stormed up to her and snapped, "Listen, lady, what the hell are you waitin' for — Christmas? Git movin'."

She slammed her foot on the gas, the pedestrians walking by jumped back, and she headed out onto Sixth Avenue. "This is the reason I don't drive into the city any more. Now I'm totally *fermisht*. You take your life in your hands, and your pocketbook goes to traffic court."

Laurie was in the back seat and didn't make eye contact when I looked back at him.

Mrs. Rose went on without taking a breath. "Okay, okay — so, Laurie, where are you from?"

She ignored me and interrogated Laurie all the way to our venue. I think she was trying to make up for mistaking him for the valet. Her assumption seemed to be that if she talked long enough he would warm up and forget her faux pas. She was wrong.

After about half an hour, I noticed we'd passed the Sloan–Kettering Institute twice. That's when she admitted she was lost. Laurie had to direct her to the Triborough Bridge, and we arrived at the event in Far Rockaway just as we were being introduced and had to run up the aisle.

After the presentation, which went well, Mrs. Rose introduced Laurie to all the officials as "Laurie, the other girl from Buffalo," and then laughed hysterically when people looked at him blankly. She never bothered explaining that the gender mistake was a clerical error.

During our time in New York, we read in all five boroughs. My favourite reading was at Battery Park on Sunday afternoon. I wore a big straw hat so I wouldn't get dizzy in the sun. Hundreds of people were out for a stroll along the boardwalk, and the planning committee knew how to draw them in with food and music. They dropped Fun City helium balloons and blasted "New York, New York" out of loudspeakers, followed by "Summer in the City." They gave out free hot dogs and Tang. All ten of us from around the state read our essays and poems.

We were followed by a youth orchestra that played "Rhapsody in Blue" as the sun set over the Hudson. Hundreds of people filled the folding chairs set up by the Fun City committee, from kids to the elderly, and hundreds more sat on the grass. I stood by the water, held my hat in the wind and spun around in a circle with my arms outstretched from the sheer joy of being alive on a summer's day in New York.

I tried not to think about Laurie as a man; it just made me nervous. I fought to concentrate on the present. We weren't on a date or anything like it. We had been thrown together and both of us were making the best of it. Yet things did hover near the periphery of my subconscious that undermined my party line on Laurie as a "colleague only." He knew the city intimately and took me to avant garde art galleries in Soho and an intimate poetry reading in a factory loft. Everything I liked, he liked. And when I was with him, time flew.

I can still remember the smell of the subway, the graffiti on the walls of the linked cars that made them look like decorated circus wagons. The idea of New Yorkers not being friendly seemed ridiculous to me. Everyone was friendly and the shopkeepers we visited remembered us from one day to the next.

One night, after Mrs. Rose had brought us back from our Scarsdale reading, Laurie and I went to hear Lena Horne at Birdland Theater. Again we sat up close. When she sang "It's Almost Like Being in Love," I felt my face flush. My throat had red blotches that began to spread to my cheeks. I knew it was ridiculous, but I felt that Lena Horne knew how I felt about Laurie and was singing the song to him from me. I had tried to keep a lid on this thing, but it was leaking out of me, pore by pore, with every song I heard and every pair of lovers we saw in Central Park. Even my epidermis was betraying my feelings.

Suddenly I understood songs that spoke of love. I understood what it meant to long for someone to simply take your hand as you crossed the street. Laurie never did anything like that. Sometimes I would bump into him as we walked, get jostled by the crowd and fall against him, sort of rub against his arm. The more I tried not to do it, the more it happened.

The only time anyone referred to us as a "couple" was in a mom-and-pop deli. We were at the counter at noon in a lineup of people holding trays. The old man making the sandwiches asked if we were together.

Laurie and I froze.

His wife, who stood next to him, picked up on the tension and said, "Sol, mind your own business and take the order. There's a lineup! We're running a deli, not a dating service."

He shrugged dramatically and addressed the whole lineup. "What's the problem? I'm asking so I know if they want their hot pastramis delivered to the same table. That's such a crime?"

I finally said, "Yes, we are together."

"See, Sol? Now ya happy?" she said. We all laughed, and she yelled, "Next."

On our last night in New York City, at about two in the morning, we walked into Washington Square Park. It had rained and there was so much fog that when we sat on a bench we could barely make out the huge arch at the entrance. There was someone somewhere in the park singing "Somewhere Over the Rainbow" really loudly. There were skateboarders, something I'd never seen before, but even they had had to sit down because they could no longer see the sidewalk ahead of them. As the rain subsided and the fog lifted, the marvellous Flatiron Building came into focus. We could make out the singer, a Puerto Rican drag queen who looked and sounded just like Judy Garland.

I turned to Laurie and said, "I'm having the best time of my life so far — what about you?"

He leaned over and placed his elbows on his knees, looked straight ahead and said, "It doesn't get much better than this."

CHAPTER 14

# the mirror room

We travelled around the state, eventually winding up where we'd
started, in western New York. Our last talks were in Syracuse,
Rochester and, finally, home in Buffalo, "the Queen City." I was
looking forward to reading in Buffalo. It would be like playing
hockey on home ice. The audience would be large and friendly.

They would be proud of me as another Buffalonian, so I wouldn't have to do a hat trick to be loved. Unfortunately, I didn't have time to go home before the performance, because we went straight from Rochester to the venue.

We were going to read at the Albright–Knox Art Gallery. My mother, who had taken still life classes when she was younger and knew art history, had brought me there dozens of times. I was sorry that my mother couldn't come to see my reading. She couldn't leave my father alone, and he was "too much of a wild card" to take out in public, she told me over the phone. When I pointed out that she took him out all the time, she admitted that she didn't want to bring him because he got agitated around me and he might "act up." Although he forgot *why* he was angry at me, he remembered that he *was* angry. Somewhere, in some cell that had yet to be gobbled by cancer, he'd stored the knowledge that I had taken away his driver's licence and his money. When my mother had told him I was back in town, he said, "Lock the glove compartment."

As the curtain rose that night, I looked out at a legion of empty chairs; only nine people sat under the crepe banner that read BOOST BUFFALO, IT'S GOOD FOR YOU. Hadn't the committee advertised our reading anywhere? It was bad enough that my family wasn't here, but where were my friends? Hadn't they heard about this?

One of the few people watching was Miriam's mother, the wife of the judge in the straw homburg. She was on the Albright–Knox festival committee and must have had something to do with planning this non-event. My heart was pounding as I read, and I made sure not to glance her way. Laurie watched me from the sidelines with a quizzical expression, knowing I wasn't myself.

After the reading as I was moving away from the dais, I saw Miriam's mother coming toward me. God, now she was going to chew my head off. I guess not advertising the reading hadn't been enough revenge for her. She was delicate and wore a simple shirt-waist and a string of pearls. (The judge probably made her dive for them herself.) She never mentioned the essay, but for some reason she gave me a honey cake, saying that Miriam had told her how much I'd liked it when she'd packed one in her lunch. She asked me to share it with my family. When I thanked her, she said the cake was for all the extra driving I'd done earlier that summer.

When I'd read my essay all over New York State, we had usually had full houses; that's why it was so sad to have this disappointing turnout in my hometown. My essay had definitely resonated with people. Laurie said it always got the loudest applause, and often people in the audience, always women, asked for a copy. I had thought everyone would be repulsed by Miriam's father's behaviour. But by the time I'd given dozens of recitations and taken even more questions, I'd begun to understand that my father's egalitarian view was an anomaly.

Once, in Brooklyn, a woman came up to me after my talk and handed me a tattered paperback. She said, "What you are trying to describe doesn't have a name, but it is perfectly described in this book, written a few years ago. I think the ideas in it are catching on. I want you to have it, as long as you agree to share it with others." As I thanked her, I looked down at the title: *The Feminine Mystique,* by Betty Friedan.

There was a guy hanging around after many of the readings. I'd seen him at some Brooklyn galleries and again in western New

York. He was white, although he walked like a black man from Harlem, with a kind of bouncy hipster gait, and spoke in strange couplets with a ghetto twist. He had teeth that looked like harvest corn and he smoked homemade cigarettes that smelled skunky. He wore a dashiki, a bright-coloured African garment that I hadn't seen outside of the pages of *National Geographic*. I'd forgotten his name, but I remembered he'd said he was "a dude from New York City who had gotten down with a heavy installation."

I thought most of those installation guys were major bullshit artists. They hadn't bamboozled me with their cockamamie attempts in every major museum in the state to "alter the way we experience a particular space." This dude's installation was a wall of violin parts, all painted black and laid out in a linear fashion.

I ran into the dashiki man backstage, so I reintroduced myself. He said his name was Caz. When I asked his last name, he said that he'd had his name professionally changed to be one word, Caz, like Liberace, Cher or Christ. He called it "branding." Although I already had more information than I needed, I asked the name of his installation, and he said it was called *A Rap with No Strings Attached*. He explained its symbolism in a long monologue ending in the phrase "seeing sound in one dimension."

As everyone was packing up and leaving, Caz suggested that, since it was so stultifying backstage, we should go outside on the steps of the south portico to get some fresh air. Laurie was tied up, being interviewed by a black newspaper called the *Buffalo Challenger,* so I went outside with Caz to wait for him.

The gallery was situated on a hill that overlooked Delaware Lake, in Delaware Park, a beautiful 350 acres that felt as majestic as Central Park.

Caz handed me his smelly cigarette and said, "Hey, man, if you really want to get my installation, you need to get high."

I sat on the cool marble floor, leaning against an arch, and fought an inner battle. I knew that drinking had led to my kissing a priest's neck, then staggering down the gorge and almost going into the falls. The memory of that humiliation had put me permanently off alcohol. Who really lived inside me? What if I had this joint and turned into Veronica Nebozenko?

Whenever I even drove by Christ the King Church after the Donny Donnybrook, the words of my father, *Girls that chase boys come to a bad end* and *You looked like the kind of girl I don't want for my daughter,* would echo in my mind. The reverberation was so loud I felt that people must be able to hear it for miles.

One thing I knew for sure. I was on safe ground here in the Albright–Knox Gallery. I couldn't possibly be attracted to this Caz character, and therefore couldn't make an idiot of myself. If I lost all inhibition, there was no drug that could psychically alter me enough to get involved with him.

I choked as I exhaled a lungful of marijuana smoke, tears streaming down my face. I said, "Well, I guess you don't smoke it like a cigarette." After I had a few tokes, I relaxed so much that I felt I had no bones and was held together only by my epidermis. I realized how stressful it had been moving from city to city, standing in front of an audience every night. I'd never caught up on my sleep. All day Laurie and I had walked for miles around the cities and towns, talking and discovering attractions from the Erie Canal to blown-glass factories.

The portico of the gallery was hundreds of feet high and had steps leading down to a manicured rose garden below, where white petals lay spent beneath thorny bushes. Gazing at this, I realized how much I was hanging on to things that should have been long forgotten. Veronica Nebozenko's life was tragic, but I was nothing like her, and kissing the neck of a priest at twelve once or twice after a few drinks, while a mistake, was not who I was. The Donny Donnybrook was my father's problem, not mine. Now I was nineteen and I still hadn't had a truly passionate moment. For Christ's sake, what the hell had I been all riled up about?

I had another drag. The moonlight picked up the sparkly flecks in the huge white marble columns. It was the end of the summer and the trees around Delaware Lake had started, far too early, to show a tinge of orange. In a few days I'd be off to Ohio for my sophomore year. I didn't want to tell anyone, especially my mother, how much I was dreading it.

Caz said, "You into some heavy stuff there, sister? You been quiet a long time."

Sister? "Yeah. I'm just thinking my teenage years are slipping away. Aren't these supposed to be the best years of your life? Yikes."

"Man, you can spend years climbin' the wrong pole, my fox. I took my teenage years and did nothin' but the violin and homework. Went into the Juilliard junior program. Went to the Bronx High School of Science and then Brown. Man, I had a monkey on my back. The second I got to Brown I dropped acid for every day I'd had no life at home. Now that was one mighty acid tab."

I just stared at him, thinking that he didn't look like he'd gone to Brown.

He continued. "I never went to class and flunked out by January. By March I was marchin' in the 'Nam for da Man. I dropped acid in an airstrip in Da Nang and saw my violin in one straight line, each piece workin' on its own. When I got back, I got on the road with my installation to share that whole trip. I suddenly knew we had to break down the traditional dichotomy between life and art. You gots to realize you climb to the top of that pole like I did — you look around and there ain't nothin' happenin' there, man."

"What kind of acid? Isn't that bad for your stomach?" I asked.

"LSD, as in lysergic acid diethylamide."

I had read once in the Sunday *Parade* magazine that Cary Grant saw a psychiatrist and took LSD, which made him hallucinate. I guessed it was the same thing. Not even Sarah had mentioned acid.

Caz was now pacing in front of me like a tiger in his dashiki and sandals. He read my blank expression and began proselytizing, mimicking a black Baptist minister who'd just been gripped by the Lord. "Cathy, Cathy, you have got to know the score. You have been ripped off! You can learn more about your mind in five minutes on acid than you ever thought of learning in some psychology class. You only touchin' the edges with that Psych 101 trash."

I just nodded. For some reason, I now sort of liked Caz. Although, I could also see that he was the worst advertisement for taking acid, whatever that was, that I'd ever seen.

About ten minutes into his rant, I said, "Look, the leaves are reflected in the lake in the moonlight."

Laurie joined us on the portico, with his papers and books already packed in his briefcase, and told us that everyone else had left.

As he was about to light a cigarette, Caz said, "Laurie, my man, share the bounty," and handed Laurie the joint. Laurie took a long drag like he knew exactly what he was doing and held his breath, then let the smoke out. He sat down opposite me and leaned against another column.

"I'm introducing our sweet blonde cracker here to some of the weed from my previous province of Da Nang."

"Her name is Cathy," Laurie said matter-of-factly, but Caz got the message.

"Oh, my man, I am well aware of her name . . . well aware. I have noticed her in all of our humble locales. She is one complicated 'chicken dinner,' to borrow a term from my brother Mez Mezzrow."

Laurie just looked at him. His eyes were bloodshot and he didn't look pleased.

"Laurie, I am not trying to mess with you — no sir. Not for a minute. Just hang loose, my man. You know she straight from suburbia, writes about oppression — I mean, enough to get down. She is happenin'. I mean I knows where she's comin' from."

The joint kept coming around. At one point I held it as one would if pausing with a cigarette, and Caz said to me, "Princess, do not bogart the joint." Then he looked over at Laurie and said, "I mean, she writes this heavy rhet-or-ic and has a spade boyfriend and she is so fucking straight. I mean, you'd have no idea how cool she is by her threads. She got that Suzy Coed camouflage thing happenin'."

Spade boyfriend?

"Are you referring to me?" Laurie said.

"You see any other spade hiding behind some columns? Man, the poets always get the foxes," he said, slapping the sides of his dashiki. "They be quiet, but they know how to make it happen."

Laurie just raised an eyebrow.

This joint had made me quiet. I watched the interchange as though I were watching a play. It was a relief not to have to fill in empty airtime. One thing the dope did was show me, for the first time, that it wasn't always my party. I did not have to host all earthly dialogue.

"You two only have eyes for each other. You got some ease with each other thing goin' on here. You guys got that straight cover thing happenin', for the Man, but ol' Caz is on to the connection vibe."

"Watch it," Laurie said. And his eyes narrowed.

As a joke to break the tension, I said, "You know, once you've seen Syracuse, Rochester and Buffalo with a man, there is no turning back."

"Yeah, man, I been there too — but no one notice me. I'm just some honky, installin' shit. I'm not complaining, just statin' a fact. That's the difference between me and you, Laurie. You just hint at things in your poems and I do the whole thing, inside and out. You know I get as close to reality as I can with my installation. In fact, I get under it. I just took that violin and ironed it out."

The funny thing was, Caz was right. While stoned, I began to appreciate his installation. He was reconstructing a violin — making it take on different, flatter space. Laurie and I went into the gallery then and looked carefully at the splayed violin. Laurie whispered to me on the way in that Caz's mind had been fractured by Vietnam and one too many acid tabs. He said that Caz had once been a smart guy.

"I've known him for a while from the poetry circuit, but the parts of his brain don't work well together any more. The whole is gone. But there are separate parts that are stellar."

"Exactly like the violin parts," I said.

What I didn't say was that Caz had walked in and exhumed two huge elephants from the Delaware Park Lake and laid them dripping at our feet. One was race and the other was relationship. Laurie and I had never once mentioned that he was black and I was white. And although we had spent all of our time together over the past month, neither of us had mentioned a relationship, either. These two topics were unwritten taboos.

While I was stoned, these prohibitions seemed ridiculous. How had we maintained these strange social imperatives in the face of such obvious truths?

Caz came dashing in, yelling, "Here comes the pigs!" as though Eliot Ness were on his heels, when in fact it was a broken-down old janitor who said he was locking everything up. Caz said, "My man, you must get down with us, have a spliff and hear my riff."

I thought the janitor might call the police, but he walked out onto the portico, lit up and was not heard from again for a long time. We found him slumped in a little heap, smiling and singing "Feelin' Groovy," which came over the radio he had put on the public address system while he cleaned.

There was another installation in the room beside Caz's and we had to feel our way over to it in the dark. It was titled *The Mirror Room*, and it was a small structure built out of mirror cubes. Caz yelled from where he was packing up his installation, "Take off your shoes and flick on the light above it." I turned on the one light, removed my shoes and entered through a doorway. When I looked down, I could see myself dozens of times — in front, from the side, from the top and, it seemed, from the depths. As I walked toward one end of the house of mirrors, which was about nine by twelve feet, it was like having to face an army of Cathys (what could be more terrifying?). Caught in the corners, I could see isolated body parts that I had to presume were mine. It was disorienting, seeing myself splintered above and below me.

Laurie hesitated at the door, then took off his high-rise black Converses and entered. It was dim, with only a few rays of light from above. I watched him and could see that when I wasn't looking at him he was looking at me. I saw him from every angle. I couldn't avoid him. Suddenly I had lost my normal compass for what was my own personal space. It was like looking down a well and seeing Laurie standing every five feet down. He kept turning around to say something to me, but I was really in front of him. He would spin around and start laughing, and that made me nervous. The boundaries I'd so carefully set up were gone. I saw myself fall into him, because every time I took a step back I was walking forward. I was suspended in space and sandwiched between layers of Cathys.

Caz called from outside the mirror house, "Is that a heavy acid trip or what?"

The radio on the loudspeaker began to play "Light My Fire" by the Doors. I turned to find the door but couldn't. I kept walking into Laurie.

*"The time to hesitate is through . . ."*

I felt like a bird trapped in a house. I was getting frantic, and began hitting walls and bumping into a mirror-cube table and chair.

Sensing I'd lost my bearings, Laurie held on to me and said, "Just put your feet on mine and we'll find the door."

I stood on his feet and we walked. I felt my arms go up around his neck and his hands fall easily around my waist. I was like one of those life-size rag dolls that has straps attached to her feet. I could actually see my shoulders go down as my back muscles began to relax.

*"No time to wallow in the mire . . ."*

When I looked up, I saw a whole ballroom of Laurie and Cathy.

*"Try now we can only lose . . . And our love become a funeral pyre . . ."*

I reached up and kissed him while still standing on his feet. He lifted me in the air. I knew that now the boundaries were gone; there was no turning back. I had never kissed anyone before, at least not like this. I remember wondering how someone so shy and quiet and reserved had learned to kiss the way he did. I just followed his lead. I'm not sure if I kissed him thousands of times or if I kissed him once and saw it a thousand times.

*"Come on, baby, light my fire . . . Come on, baby, light my fire . . . Try to set the night on fire, yeah . . ."*

I heard Caz shout that he'd roused the night watchman for another toke. However, the guy said he was hours late in locking up and we had to leave. Caz stuck his head in the mirror house and said, "Wow, you are part of the installation. We'll call it *Total Reflection*, or how about *No Way Out*."

"I like *An Army of You*," I said.

As I stepped out of the house of mirrors, I experienced myself as two-dimensional, like a paper doll. I seemed short and stocky, with stubby legs. My feet felt as though they were splayed flat, and I had to walk as though I were wearing large rubber flippers. I was relieved to find that I could once again measure a safe distance from Laurie. The world looked huge and as flat as Kansas, but manageable.

Back in the other room, Caz opened the fringed suede pouch that he wore around his waist, which would have looked normal if he'd been Deerslayer, and said, "Oh yeah, right, I forgot about this message for you, Cathy. Some guy said to give it to you as soon as you finished speaking. Like, what is the fuckin' rush, right, man?" He handed it to me.

I opened the envelope and read the note.

*Cath,*

*We're sorry we didn't make it to your performance thing. I went over to your house and your mom said you were coming home tonight after your reading. She let us drive the 409 down here and leave it for you in the lot. (Like, what are you going to do — take a bus?) I'm going back to Brunner's in Danny's car. Please meet us there when you get off. We will all wait for you — really want to talk to you. Don't worry about the time. We will be there on our regular stools.*

*Steve Bluefeld and the guys*

"Great, Caz. Just great. It's the middle of the night and I have friends who have been waiting for me for hours." As I shook my head in disbelief, I asked, "Can you drive on this stuff?" Judging by my anger toward Caz, I felt myself coming down and my old controlled self making a precipitous return.

"Yeah, you just go slower."

⸺

Laurie and Caz walked me out to my car. When Caz saw the blue convertible, he said, "Man, I thought the Beach Boys were dead. But hey, here she is — the 409 in all her glory. Take a gander at those boss bucket seats. You know what they used to call those?" When I looked like I didn't care, he said, "Birth control seats."

As Laurie and I fastened down the boot, I tried to button down my emotions with each snap. Losing control here would be beyond humiliation. We had been together for almost a month straight. Now we were separating. He and Caz would be getting on a plane in a matter of hours, and I would be driving home. I got in the car and turned the key in the ignition, avoiding eye contact with Laurie and telling myself to block everything out and keep moving. In a few days, I would have the rest of the year in odious Ohio to think about it.

"Cathy, keep hangin'," Caz said as he shook my hand with his yellowed fingers.

Laurie lit two cigarettes and gave me one, and then he walked away. As I slammed the car into drive, he turned around from fifty feet away and waved.

Since I was still a little stoned, I decided to stay on Main Street instead of negotiating the thruway; I would eventually arrive right in the heart of Amherst. Besides, I needed the time to calm down. I knew I had to drive slowly. Because it was Labor Day weekend, the city had emptied out — people were away at cottages and otherwise enjoying the last warm long weekend away before hunkering down for the Buffalo winter. I heard, and then saw, fireworks cascading down, providing shimmering light in the distance.

—

As I headed into Amherst, I passed Brunner's Tavern and suddenly remembered that people were waiting for me there. How could I have forgotten that? The place was still jumping in the wee hours, so I pulled over and combed my hair, looking in the rear-view mirror.

As I walked in, I thought there was something wonderful about having friends since the seventh grade. We had grown up together, been on the ski hill together, gotten stuck in snowstorms and laughed together. No one could ever take away our shared history, and nothing could ever replace it.

When I got to the long U-shaped bar, Doc, the bartender, told me to have a seat. He automatically placed a Tab in front of me. My friends at the bar looked wan, tired, their eyes bloodshot from the hours in a smoke-filled room, and I felt awful for keeping them waiting.

Danny came out of the washroom, and everyone at the bar looked from him to me. He waved and sat down at the end of the bar and a number of guys I knew sat in between us.

Chuck Reilly, a friend from high school who'd returned home from Vietnam on furlough, said, "Let's have a toast to Cathy's tour." He put his arm in the air and it had a large hook on the end where his hand had once been. Something had happened to his eyes, too. He wore big magnifying glasses that made him look like a human grasshopper.

Everyone toasted me, and I should have felt proud and happy, but there was something about Chuck's solemn tone and their dull expressions that made me nervous. I didn't know why.

He continued. "Cathy, you are not the only one who has been on tour. I just got sent home for R and R from Hanoi." He paused. "And I have some bad news. Kip Rogers — he died in Vietnam."

"Died?" I looked at Chuck and then down the bar past Danny

and Shaky to Mr. Blue for confirmation. He nodded. "But, Steve," I choked out, "he just went there to figure out what to do in college."

Steve looked too overwhelmed to speak. Chuck took over for him.

"I know," he said, patting my back. "It's a war. You have no idea what is happening there."

People were trying to toast by hitting the glass that he held in his hook. That hook frightened me. I didn't want to toast.

"I went over to the bakery today and Kip's dad said he supposedly drowned in some reeds. The letter from his troop said he was picked off by the Vietcong guerrillas when he was washing his socks in a stream. But Kip's dad said no one really knows what happened. They are tryin' to send his body home."

"Trying?" I said.

Doc lined up two shots of whisky for everyone at the bar. Doc, always a spokesman, held up his glass, and did a slow 360-degree turn with his drink held high in the air until everyone in the whole bar was silent. Then he said, "To our Kip Rogers. Never once said a bad word about another living soul. May he rest in peace."

We were silent for a long time, and a guy at the end of the bar who'd dated Kip's sister wiped away some tears. Then someone played the jukebox and Bob Dylan's "Blowin' in the Wind" broke the silence.

*How many times must a man look up*
*Before he can see the sky?*
*Yes 'n' how many ears must one man have*
*Before he can hear people cry?*
*Yes 'n' how many deaths will it take till he knows*

*That too many people have died?*
*The answer, my friend, is blowin' in the wind,*
*The answer is blowin' in the wind.*


We sat at the bar, with Doc ministering from behind. We could see one another in the full wall mirror. Doc began to sing in his deep baritone.

We linked arms and joined in at the top of our lungs, and then other people sitting at tables joined in as well, and we all sang and cried until we were hoarse.

## CHAPTER 15

# the avalanche

What causes snow to dislodge and roll down a mountain? Who knows? All I know is you have to listen or you can be buried alive in an avalanche. People who barely get out of these alive say they remember hearing a rumble or seeing a slight movement, but paid it no heed. Then there was a deluge of snow sliding down the hill and before they knew it, they were almost buried alive. I don't know what the first rumble was for me, but by September 1967, the avalanche called "the '60s" was thundering down that mountain; I ran shedding all my pre-avalanche self so I wouldn't be six feet under.

When it was time to pack to return to Ohio for my sophomore year, I looked at my matching golf-club clothes, the hairpieces and shoes that I had spent much of my earnings on, and wondered who the girl was who'd worn them. By then I had switched to hip-hugger bell-bottom jeans, men's long undershirts and desert boots.

My mother, the Carl Linnaeus of fashion taxonomy, had dozens of garment bags full of my coats and matching outfits piled in the hallway to take to the car for my return to school. To me they now looked like costumes from another era. The shoeboxes were piled up in eight stacks of six, with Dymo labels on the side that said things like BROWN KID BOOTS — MID-CALF — FASHION, NOT FOR SNOW — BERGDORF GOODMAN, 1966.

I didn't have the heart to tell my mother that I would never wear any of them again. I fit my entire new wardrobe into a small suitcase that I hid in the spare tire compartment of the 409 so my mother wouldn't see it. When I got to Athens, I took the other clothes and left them in trunks in the underground garage.

My mother, like me, had been highly invested in the pre-avalanche Cathy. She was a perfect dresser until we moved to Buffalo. After her total submersion in Tiny Town, Kennedy's assassination and my father's illness, she pretty well gave up on social-camouflage wear and began wearing polyester leisure suits and Clarks Wallabees. Nor did she replace her coterie of

intellectual friends from Lewiston. I was by now her only invest-
ment in normalcy, and those conformity ensembles were part of
that picture. She and my father were willing to invest much of
their money and time into grooming their "normal" cheerleader
daughter, when in fact my mother didn't buy into that image any
more than I did. But as long as I seemed normal, or even a pale
version of it, she felt she'd done her bit as a mother.

I had learned all kinds of useful information about what normal
was in my courses in freshman year. The concept was overrated.
In statistics, I learned that normal is simply what most people
do, believe or follow. If you meditated in India you were normal,
if you meditated in San Francisco you were a hippie, and if you
meditated in southern Ohio you were nuts. It was now all starting
to fall into place. My mother and I discussed this as we took the
all-day drive back to Ohio that September. I think I was trying to
prepare her for who I was starting to become.

In my sociology class, we'd read the *Kinsey Reports*, the second of which was completed in 1953 while I was growing up
in Lewiston and at a time when my mother thought it was a sin
to wear Bermuda shorts to the post office. The studies showed
that people were regularly having sex outside of marriage. Women
were bopping the mailman and having a field day with the deliv-
eryman from Sears, Roebuck. (My mother said they must have had
better-looking delivery men than the ones she'd had.) More than
50 percent of men had extramarital relationships. Women trailed,
but not by much. People  had homosexual relationships, sado-
masochistic ones and every other permutation and combination
along the sexual spectrum. I told my mother that it was no wonder
so many people hated Freud. He was the one saying we had sexual

instincts and civilization could only take the edge off people's sexual drives. We had defences, like repression and denial, but some of our basic sexual instincts would break through the toughest of defences, even in the most repressed of societies. When I first read Freud in my freshman year, I thought of the 1950s in the drugstore when, on the first of the month, we sold hundreds of *Playboy* magazines to furtive men, and when the people who bought condoms wouldn't make eye contact. While many proclaimed Freud was a nutcase, I knew he was dead on. He was the one who'd blown the whistle on all this behaviour. Kinsey was only the messenger. I thought of Lewiston and its imposing pre-colonial homes and rigid social stratification. I marvelled when I remembered the uproar that resulted when someone got pregnant out of wedlock. Yet, if the statistics are to be believed, almost half of villagers were having some sort of illicit sex and not getting caught. My mother's take on this was that between Freud, Kinsey and me she had no idea who was the nuttiest. She said I was an expert at coming up with crazy ideas and trying to make them sound rational. When I went home at Thanksgiving, however, I noticed Freud's *Civilization and Its Discontents* on the coffee table.

—

Believe it or not, I'd decided to room with Edwina again. Since she rarely spoke and when she did it was to tell me to be quiet, it was like having a single room — and therefore I could study. As I turned down my hallway, carrying my one suitcase, I heard "Ballad of the Green Berets."

What? Even Edwina wouldn't play that. Yet as I proceeded down the hall, I came to the appalling realization that it was coming from my room. I walked into a space that was decorated like

a bedroom in a Shirley Temple movie. The curtains had a bad
pink print that didn't even rise to chintz. A large green ruffle had
been added and a pink sash held them back so the ruffles couldn't
engulf the room. The bedspreads were the same pink flowered
print, with the same manic ruffle that Dumbo might have used on
his bed before he learned to fly. The pink and green theme had
also been added to our desk chairs; there was a cushion on each
chair tied on with pink bows. The same pattern was even glued
onto the cylindrical pencil holder on the desk.

I was speechless as I focused on the girl in front of me, who
was not Edwina. She had curly red hair that she'd somehow
tamed into two braids held together by rubber bands with hearts
on them — the talisman of southern Ohio. She had on what my
mother would have caled a "house dress" and was ironing a stack
of damp rolled-up blouses on a proper ironing board. Our family
had never owned an iron. My mother said anything worth buying
was worth sending to the dry cleaner. She said it was good for the
economy.

"Hey there. My name is Baby," she said. She wore giant furry
slippers that had penguins on them and she waddled over to greet
me. "I just transferred here from Kent State. My boyfriend is up
there. We're pinned. He's in geology and ROTC. I also have a twin
there."

"Where is Edwina?" I asked.

"I don't know. There was a note on the door that said 'Student
Withdrawn,' so the R.A. with the pink bear signs just stuck me in
here." She spoke as though she was thrilled to be my roommate.

On my pillow I noticed a scrap of paper with a ledger of what
I owed for the awful decor — right down to half of the thread.

"I hope you like it," she said, sweeping her hand across the room as though she'd designed a Fifth Avenue penthouse.

At that moment Sarah came in from her room across the hall, looked around and said, "Who the hell decorated this dump? Annie Oakley on speed?" She flopped down on my bed and laid her head on my decor invoice.

"I think it has a certain *je ne sais quoi*," I said, shooting Sarah a warning glance. I had the year ahead with Baby. As my mother used to say, *Why start out on a bad foot?*

Baby went back to ironing as I unpacked.

Sarah said to me, "You look different."

My hair was now past my shoulders, and I'd stopped using rollers or orange juice cans to enhance my coiffure and gone *au naturel.*

"You do 'it' yet?"

"In Buffalo? Get serious."

"Who you waiting for, Mick Jagger? Smoke any dope at least?"

"Once."

"You're supposed to do them both together."

I stopped unpacking and said, "I could definitely see that working."

I couldn't even imagine what Baby thought of this conversation as she ironed her cap sleeves on a midget ironing board that she had placed on the normal-sized one.

"Baby, could you please get that military propaganda off your stereo? I want Cathy to hear this." Sarah pulled out a record with a very strange cover, called *Cheap Thrills.* It had lewd, slightly off-kilter cartoon sketches all over it by a man named Crumb.

As I threw my clothing into drawers, I listened to Janis Joplin wail with a voice that sounded like a freight train with a broken heart: "A Piece of My Heart," "Summertime" and "Ball and Chain." People from down the hall yelled at us to turn it down, but Sarah yelled back, "Relax, Midwest pioneers. You haven't even bought your books yet. Lighten up!"

—

The shadow of Laurie was with me everywhere as I started classes. Finally, I decided to call Leora and go over the whole thing, to try to understand what was going on in my body or my head. What would women do without friends? I guess they would just buy their own straitjacket, wrap themselves up and wait for the ambulance.

I told Leora that I was beside myself. Something had taken over my body and mind. I had constant thoughts of Laurie, and I was unable to concentrate or study. Could that happen with only one kiss? Leora said that in the overall scheme of things one kiss was peanuts. It might mean a lot to me, but to most people it meant, *Thanks for paying for the movie.*

When I told her that it didn't feel that way, she said, "Listen, I'm talking about a symbol, what things mean in society. You're talking about your feelings. Have you ever noticed that what you and I feel is often not exactly on the money?"

Sitting in physics class during the first week of school, I wrote down the meaning of a thermal reaction: "*a reaction in which atomic nuclei fuse into new elements with a large release of heat; especially a reaction that is self-sustaining.*" As I read and reread that statement, it occurred to me that I'd changed into a new element. One kiss from Laurie was all the heat I had needed. Thus far, it had been self-sustaining.

Being alone is just a description of fact, while *loneliness* describes the bleak, gnawing feeling of missing companionship. I was suddenly no longer happy to go to dinner on my own and read Wordsworth or study the bifurcated aorta of the tree frog. Simply having opinions was no longer enough. I wanted to share them with that one person. The problem with falling in love when the recipient of your affections is not there and probably never will be is that you can't imagine the intense feelings will ever end.

I remembered Miss Havisham in *Great Expectations*, who stopped interacting in the world the day she was jilted at the altar. She still had her dusty cake on the table twenty years later and limped around in her torn wedding dress. She never got over love. I hoped that wouldn't happen to me.

I spent an inordinate amount of my free time trying to understand love. Darwin suggested that it is a chemical reaction to draw the sexes together long enough to procreate. That chemical bond gets interpreted as love. Freud said love is the myth used by civilization to allow us to procreate and to stay tied to another in a monogamous relationship. He said that if men were mating all the time, as their instinct dictated, they would not have the sustained energy to build a civilization. Thus, the terms *instinct, love, monogamy* and *civilization* are linked together.

I read all of the greats on the enigma of love. Was an instinct a biological drive or a psychological need, and what was the difference? Was love an instinct unto itself or was it a necessary paving of the way for reproduction, which according to Darwin was one of our two instincts? Was love a fantasy? Did women in civilized society need to believe in love in order to allow themselves to have sex? Back in that basement in grade seven did Veronica

Nebozenko fantasize that Skip Stephens loved her? What was the relationship between love and sex? I bombarded Sarah, who was the most experienced person I knew, with questions such as, Why would a human being pick one other human being and say life could only be shared with him? After all, this represents a loss of free will. Why would his mere smile be heavenly, and the loss of him heartbreaking?

She would finally shout, "Who gives a shit?"

I was undeterred, and one day, as Sarah and I lay on the matching Dumbo ruffled beds and Baby sat at her desk I said, "There must be a chemical release that bonds people together — like a psychological rubber cement or, in the case of some people, Krazy Glue. You have to be glued together long enough to trust each other to mate."

"Look," Sarah said, "I figured this out years ago on my sister's wedding day when the groom tried to back out, but my father told him he was just having cold feet and basically pushed him down the aisle. Girls have all the eggs they will ever have when they are born. They have to be picky choosing who they mate with. Men make sperm every day. The guy has to court the girl and talk her into sex. She has to feel love, or at least feel like she isn't a one-night stand. As far as I see it, courtship lasts about six weeks to six months. By the time you act on it and waddle down the aisle, you look at the person on your arm, and you say, *Who the hell is that and why is he hanging on my arm?* The courtship stage is over right about the time of the marriage, and the man hasn't got a clue how he got caught and reeled in."

This had a depressing ring of truth to it.

She went on. "Courtship, which is a maximum period of one

year, is the time when the man tries to make you happy. Then it's your job to make him happy for the rest of your long life." On that note, she sat up for emphasis and butted out her Tareyton in an already full ashtray.

Baby said, "Gee, that sounds like a lot of work." Then she added hopefully, "Maybe it doesn't feel like work if you love him."

"Washing socks is washing socks," Sarah said. "What I do is get out of a relationship when the courtship days are over. I've been moving on like that since I was in junior high. Take what you can and run."

Sarah was always good at the précis. "God, Cathy — have you never heard of a summer romance? Jesus, do I have to sing every cheesy lyric to you?"

I decided I had to follow Sarah's advice, which was to "face it when things are history." I'd learned a thing or two about love. Laurie was gone and it was time to chalk one up to experience. I was determined to keep busy. At home, whenever I complained, my mother said there were people less fortunate than me. When I complained to Mother Agnese, she said I should be on my knees, thanking God for two arms and two legs. And my father said, "No one who is busy ever has time to complain."

I studied hard and also got a job in the biology lab on the weekends, injecting white rats with thyroxine, a hormone that was hypothesized to induce schizophrenia. My little rats jumped with joy when I entered the room. At least someone was happy to see me at Ohio University — or maybe their behaviour was just early onset schizophrenia.

One day in October, when the leaves were at their most glorious, I got a postcard in my mailbox with no return address. It had a picture of Edith Piaf. She was singing her heart out on the street for a group of bystanders. I flipped it over and read, "*Bodacious* is an interesting word — far more interesting than *audacious.*"

I stood there dumbfounded. How did he know where I lived? The postcard had my name and address on it, complete with the right dormitory and room number. I ran to my dictionary to look up *bodacious*. Sarah, who came into my room just then, said, "It means 'great body.' Break it down to the Latin roots. *Body, ish.*" Doubting that, I continued paging through until I found it. The definition said, "remarkable, bold, prodigious."

The next day another postcard came, this one with a picture of "Our Gang," from the 1930s comedies with child stars who always dressed as adults. One of the little girls was blonde, and the boy was black and wore a bowler hat. The card read, "It's hard, too hard, to forget someone so bodacious."

As I walked by Sarah's room, looking at my card, she was standing at her door and said, "Mail?" She grabbed it out of my hand. "This wouldn't be from the spade you were tooling around New York with now, would it?"

I gave her the how-did-you-know look, to which she replied, "Jenny Goldman saw you at the matinee of *Cabaret*. She said you looked through her like she was a footlight."

"I never saw her."

"She said you and the spade were in some trance of your own — chatting away like there was no tomorrow." She read the postcard and then said, "Don't try and hide things from me. I'm way more bodacious than you."

Baby was lying on her ruffled bed, reading *The History of Western Civilization*, highlighter in hand. She asked, "What's a spade?"

"A trowel you use to dig up things that are better left buried," I said, shooting Sarah a glance.

I didn't need Baby in on all of my life. As my mother used to say, *Not everyone has to know everything about you*. Whenever I went to a birthday party, she would hand me the present and say two things: "Remember, don't be bossy, and the less said about our life, the better."

The next Thursday I received a postcard of the Flatiron Building in the New York fog. As usual, it had no signature and no return address. On the flip side it said, "Can humans gambol in Washington Square?"

Baby saw the postcard on my desk and said, "Whoever wrote that misspelled *gamble*."

The word was *gambol*. I recited to her what I'd read in the dictionary: "A playful skipping or frolicking about."

A few weeks later, on a Saturday morning, I received a postcard that had a picture of Miró's *Relationship*. On the back it said, "I took a gamble on a gambol." This time there was no postmark or stamp of any kind.

I went on to the cafeteria for breakfast and sat down at a table for two, placing my books on the other chair so some idiot wouldn't join me. As I took out my philosophy notes, someone set down two coffees.

"Double cream, no sugar, right?"

I looked up. There stood Laurie. His hair had grown a bit. He was wearing an untucked blue oxford-cloth shirt, jeans and a pair of strange cork sandals that I found out later were called Birkenstocks.

"Hi," I said, as though he lived in the dorm next door. Suddenly I was attacked with my first and only fit of shyness. I had nothing to say. If only I'd known he was coming. I had a huge botany project due. I had to collect cataphyll leaves. Although I had dreamed of this moment, I was actually frightened of having a relationship with Laurie. As long as he was only in my mind, I could control all that happened. What was I supposed to say? *How was your trip?* So I didn't say anything.

Then I felt angry. Where had he come from? And it was ludicrous for him to declare himself in the cafeteria, with twelve hundred pairs of eyes on the two of us. The football team dinner table simply stared. They knew he wasn't from here. You could hear a pin drop.

Without a word Laurie sat down.

We sat in silence, and eventually everyone went back to eating and chatting. I drank my coffee in just two gulps and he got me another. I put away William James's *The Meaning of Truth*. I couldn't believe we had all day to ourselves to do whatever we wanted.

After a while I said, "Where did you come from?"

"Ohio State. I'm a student there."

"How come you never told me that?" I asked.

"You never asked," he said.

"How far away is it?"

"In Columbus — about an hour and a half away."

"Are you staying overnight?"

"I'm staying for the weekend."

"Where are you . . ." I stammered, "s-s-sleeping?"

"Guest rooms at the O.U. Athletic Complex."

"Who said you could do that?"

"I know some people over here."

"Well . . ."

I was about to ask something else, but he smiled and said, "Let's not waste any more time with interrogation. You've asked more than I've answered in ten years."

He laid his hand over mine where it rested on the table. I smiled and didn't ask anything else — suddenly I didn't need to.

That was the beginning of my first real relationship.

———

Baby was fairly surprising in some ways. Once, when Laurie was visiting, we were having lunch in the cafeteria and Baby came over, put down her tray and sat down. No one ever joined us at lunch.

"Hi, Laurie," she said. "I read some of your poetry book that Cathy had on the dresser. I really didn't understand it, but I feel I know you better."

Baby was from a poor family of fifth-generation farmers in the Hocking Valley, and was the first in her family to go to college. She was a co-op student who had a job in the cafeteria and another one at her family home on the weekends. She studied like mad and never went out, but occasionally visited her boyfriend, Robbie, who studied earth sciences.

Laurie said I was way too hard on Baby. She reminded him of Ma Joad from *The Grapes of Wrath*. He said it was important to know some "real people."

At Christmas, Baby was on the committee to decorate a tree in our lounge. She spent ages making all of the decorations by hand. Laurie loved her homemade spun-sugar ornaments and how they sparkled when hung above the tree lights. There were presents under the tree, which I assumed were empty boxes wrapped up to make the lounge look Dickensian. I hadn't thought of getting anyone a Christmas present.

At the dorm party hardly anyone brought boyfriends, but Laurie was there for the weekend. He was sitting with Sarah when the resident head said, "Cathy and Laurie, there are some presents for you here under the tree."

They were gift baskets, and the baskets themselves were works of art, handwoven out of red dogwood. Inside were homemade fudge and two woven placemats with what looked like a matching tiny hand-made sock in the same material. (I was told it was an egg cozy.) There were preserves and peaches in brandy with a gorgeous bow, and a matching pair of homespun wool socks. My card said:

*Dear Cathy,*

*Merry Christmas. You have been the most interesting friend I've ever had and probably will have. I will never forget you. Cathy, you have made college everything I imagined it would be when I used to dream of getting here.*

*Love,*
*Baby*

Laurie's card read:

*Laurie, you are a really different kind of man — different from any I've ever met. If I ever had a son I'd like him to be taught English by you. Thanks for all the new words.*

*Love,*
*Baby*

Baby would draw maps of interesting rural places to see in southern Ohio. She told me that we were near the Hocking Hills, some caves and eighteen covered bridges. Laurie and I would take off on weekends in Laurie's yellow VW Bug and go to places like Stroud Run National Park. It was the first time I'd taken long walks in the winter. We would both bring books and read to each other. We had always read something during the week that we wanted to share with each other. Laurie and I had no group of friends, because he was black and I was white. In some ways that was isolating, but at the same time it gave us a special closeness. We only had each other, so we built our own world and happily lived in it.

Laurie came down most weekends and together we got involved in civil rights demonstrations and worked for the National Association for the Advancement of Colored People. We spent hours on voter registration and became "specialists" in how to disseminate information across the state. We both enjoyed writing, so we created brochures on what needed to be done and how to get groups of people to divide up and cover certain territories. In fact, I was doing for civil rights in southern Ohio and West Virginia what my mother had done for Kennedy.

Laurie and I always agreed on what needed to be done and how to do it, and we worked well together. We actually had a lot in common. We were both well organized. We were only children from families who had owned their own businesses. Laurie's parents ran a paint and wallpaper company with more employees than we had ever had at the drugstore. His mother, like mine, had been a teacher, but had left to run the financial arm of their business.

The difference between us was that his parents never had him work in their business, which, given that I'd helped in my father's drugstore from a young age, struck me as odd. Another difference was that his parents had bought and renovated several homes as a sideline in the city of Cleveland, where they lived, while my parents had suffered real estate disaster.

—

That winter Sarah introduced me to some theatre types whom she'd known from her chic New York City private high school. They came down from Manhattan for the weekend and we all went to a local, mediocre production of *Oklahoma!* I had directed plays in high school, so I spouted off my ideas on how it should have been staged.

That spring they wanted to mount some goofy rock musical they had seen at a hole-in-the-wall theatre in New York. They wanted to produce it on the central green at Ohio University and then take it on the road. They asked me to be in it for some reason I could never fathom, since I couldn't sing. They said I had "stage sense." When I asked my mother what that meant, she said, "You're a ham — what do you think it means?" Once I heard some of the songs plunked out on the piano, the lyrics grabbed me and

I agreed to take part. The play was called *Hair* (I told them the first thing they would have to do was change the name).

One of the good things about southern Ohio was that spring came surprisingly early, especially for someone from Buffalo. By early March we had jettisoned our winter coats, the damp earth already had fields of waving Virginia bluebells, and cherry blossoms lined the Hocking River.

The production was done as planned, outside in early March on the large central green, and much to our amazement hundreds of people came. Laurie came down to see me in the production and lay on the grass in jeans and a T-shirt, flashing that smile that showed his beautiful teeth — something he didn't often do.

When we sang the title number "Hair," everyone watching let down their hair too and joined in. It really defined the mood of the time. People were just beginning to grasp that hair was a part of our identity, so why straighten it or curl it or do anything but display it. Black kids who had started out their first year with straight or short hair were by now sprouting afros, white guys were letting their hair grow long, and girls were no longer using curlers or orange juice cans to straighten their hair, but were just letting their hair "do its thing."

Blacks, whites, rich kids from Shaker Heights in Cleveland and coal miners' children from Appalachia — we all observed the dawning of the Age of Aquarius. Someone passed joints around, and together under the linden trees at Scott Quadrangle we wholeheartedly believed that love would indeed "steer the stars."

After the musical we decided to celebrate and go to the Biggie Burger in town and pretend we were at Birdland in New York City. Laurie said, "Thank God we have imaginations."

As we sat reading the menu and discussing the musical and how well Hamlet's soliloquy had worked as a song, a middle-aged man with a southern Ohio accent came over to our booth with his young blond preteen son. The boy was carrying a pad and pencil and he shyly asked if he was bothering us. I said no, and then he asked for Laurie's autograph. Laurie had just had his third volume of poetry published by a good-but-obscure poetry press, but this father and son didn't look like poetry aficionados.

Laurie acted as though this had happened to him many times before, and he was gracious, asking the kid's name, and what position he played, as he autographed the notepad. They shook hands and the father and son left.

I was bewildered by the exchange. Typical of Laurie, he said nothing about it.

I said, "I had no idea you were such a famous poet."

"I'm not a famous anything," he said, and kept eating.

I'd seen people look at him and point him out. I'd assumed that this was because I was white and he was black. People mostly focused on *him*, but then, he was handsome, so that didn't seem crazy to me either.

"What am I missing? Laurie, what's up?" I was getting a bit tired of our rarefied Robert Browning–Elizabeth Barrett existence.

We'd never had an argument, or even "words," as my mother would have said, so he looked surprised by my tone.

He said, "I guess I'm one of the stars of the football team for Ohio State. We are supposedly going to the Rose Bowl this year, and I am getting a lot of press."

"You're not a football kind of guy," I said, and in my surprise didn't hide my derision.

"I'm fast and accurate and I do what I have to do if someone's in the way."

It was out of character for him to speak that way.

"Do you like it?"

"It's all right. Takes a lot of time."

"Why do it?"

"Money," he said.

"Scholarship?"

"Full, and they pay me in the summer as long as I go to football camp and stay in shape, and it gives me time to do my writing."

"Do they know about your writing?"

"As much as you know about the football."

"So I could come to Ohio State and see you play football?"

"No."

"Why?"

"Our relationship is not . . . that."

For an articulate person he was being pretty inarticulate. He really didn't seem to want to talk about it, but after a few moments he managed to say, "Being a football star is not being a person. All kinds of other people attach to you because you make them look better, more important. You aren't one of those. I know that. I'd like to keep our relationship away from all of that. Read Ralph Ellison's *Invisible Man*."

This was the first time he had made reference to his colour.

"Football is just a legal cockfight. If they pay me enough I'll do it, but I'm not pinning my identity on it. Words and you are my world. I don't want it sullied. Girls come on to me because I'm a football star and I'm supposed to fill some black fantasy for them. I'm not interested in it. I've had to endure coaches who get prostitutes as a reward for the end of training camp. I don't want to be a character from *Dutchman*."

—

That spring I found out I was at the top of my class and was invited to join a group called the Ohio Fellows. It was a special gifted stream begun by the president of Ohio University, who'd come from Harvard. He wanted to identify people who could go on into leadership and other academic positions, and give them the best education possible. Out of sixty-thousand students, only twenty-nine were selected. Ohio had a great deal of football money and the president dropped a bundle into the Ohio Fellows program. He brought in talented professors from all over the world. We met in an old mansion. The student–professor ratio was ten to one.

I had been moving in a more intellectual direction for the last year, and now this program was taking all of my energy. I was focusing on scholarship. I thought carefully about what I said in class, and I never went to class without having done the reading, for fear I would look foolish. Since there were scholars in the class, we began to have serious conversations that sent me scurrying back to original sources. My values had changed, and I was transforming from a social maven to an academic one.

I had promised my father, before he lost his mind, that no matter what I would finish college with a professional degree. He said he had two reasons for demanding this: one, he had lived through the Depression, and teachers and nurses always had jobs; two, I had to be able to care for myself because I "was not the marrying kind." My grandmother once said I was "as likely to marry as Calamity Jane."

I couldn't be a nurse. I would have to touch people and care

305

for them, and besides, I was too pale to wear white. I decided on teaching. My mother had been a math teacher, though she taught for only one day. She chose what she referred to as "a graceful retirement."

I had to get an education degree because I'd promised to become a teacher. Yet I had no intention of ever teaching, especially young children, since I believed that maternal instinct ran in families. I decided to combine what my father wanted and what I wanted, which necessitated doing a double major and getting two degrees, a Bachelor of Education and a Bachelor of Arts.

—

Taking the two majors added extra courses and extra studying, and once I really got behind in assignments. Professor Fowler, a remarkable scholar from Oxford, taught our Ohio Fellows Milton poetry course and had assigned an essay on Milton's *Paradise Lost*. I had great respect for him and didn't want to hand in some sophomoric tripe.

I went to Sarah and said that I needed to stay up for one, maybe two nights. I asked if she had any No-Doz tablets, which were basically little blue packets of concentrated caffeine. They could help you pull an all-nighter when you couldn't drink any more coffee for fear of permanently branding your stomach lining. I told her I was way past the point when I could use secondary sources, so the essay had to be full of two things — Milton and me. Professor Fowler had handed out a sheet of topics; I chose "Justice in *Paradise Lost*."

I showed Sarah my copy of the text, and after paging through the thick book of the seventeenth-century poem, she said with clinical detachment, "Adam and Eve's disobedience and fall from grace is too big a job for No-Doz. You need a specialist. You're going to have to go to Melinda Swinton and her gang."

Melinda Swinton was a mousy girl from Cleveland. Four girls had been put together randomly in a corner quad, and Melinda Swinton's quad was an unfortunate combination of four quiet, insecure girls who were on work–study programs in merchandising — whatever that was. Somehow this foursome of amorphous humans joined forces and together they acted as one psychopathic individual. They chose to make their mark by being just plain bad. Melinda made extra money by selling clothes, which she stacked to the ceiling, that she'd stolen from May Company, a department store in Cleveland where she worked in the summers. Melinda justified this caper by saying, "Well, I *am* in fashion merchandising."

In our freshman year the resident director confined them to their rooms for a specified number of weekends for stealing cookies from the cafeteria where they worked and then selling them late at night as snacks. The Swinton Quad paid back the resident director by cutting pubic hair and sticking it to her doorknob with Vaseline. They thought no one would know this pubic vendetta had been engineered by them; but who other than the Swinton Quad was quite so deranged?

But on Sarah's advice I slunk off to Melinda's room. When I knocked on the door, she hollered from within, "Enter, peasant." Reluctant to touch the doorknob, I waited for her to open the door.

"Uh, Melinda," I said when she appeared, "I heard you have a pill that could keep me awake for two days."

"What do you have to do?"

"A paper on *Paradise Lost*."

"Aha. That would require the large green pill." She ordered her frumpy triumvirate to get down a shoebox, which was piled up with dozens of other shoeboxes, all apparently filled with different pills.

"Five dollars," she announced casually.

"That's a hell of a lot of money for one pill," I said. Melinda remained silent, so I asked, "Where did you get it and what's in it?"

"I have a contact in Accessories at the May Company." She said it as though her source were a doctor from the Mayo Clinic.

I hesitated, worried that the pill might make me crazy — or crazier.

She said, "Take it or leave it."

There was a lineup behind me to buy God knows what, so I ponyed up and left.

Fortunately, Baby was away at Kent State, so I was alone. I took the pill, locked myself in my room with a pile of food, drinks and cigarettes, and started reading the first of the twelve books of *Paradise Lost*. The pill didn't seem to be working. In fact, I was getting tired on Book One. I didn't know why I'd wasted five whole dollars on something that was probably a rip-off. But if I complained, who knew what I'd get on my doorknob?

Slowly, over the next few hours, I became engaged in Milton's argument. The Bible came thundering back to me. I remembered Satan's fall from grace and Adam and Eve's expulsion from Eden with the intensity of the child who believed what the nuns had drilled into her head: we had to pay for original sin. It was not Adam's and Eve's sin, but ours as well, for placing knowledge, curiosity, concupiscence or anything else above faith.

Usually a slow reader, I read all twelve books aloud in what felt like a couple of hours, and occasionally I found myself jumping on my bed. I felt beguiled by Satan as he said it was "better to reign in Hell, than serve in Heav'n." I began running around my room, reciting passages, and I broke two pens by pressing too hard on my paper. I gave up on note-taking and began acting out the plot of Adam's fall from grace.

The whole story came alive in my mind. The flora of Eden was palpable. I saw my convex image in the red of the taut and shiny apple skin. I, like Satan, was burning in the amber light. Then I came upon it. The flaw in the justice system. The serpent.

God was so careful to give everyone their just reward or punishment, except for the serpent. I became outraged. I couldn't believe what Milton had gotten away with. I sat down and began answering in kind, but from the point of view of the serpent. In fact, I tried to match his verse, and, after reading twelve books of his poetry aloud until I was hoarse, I had established the rhythm and could have scanned the poetry in my sleep.

God had done the classic "shoot the messenger." What free choice did the serpent have? All the serpent was doing was walking along upright, blending into his environment and minding his own business, and God randomly had Satan enter his body. That is not free will. That is predetermination! Then God unfairly punishes the serpent by forcing him to slither along the ground forever after.

I called the essay "Book Thirteen." All of my rage at Catholic school and my memorization of the Bible and my anger at questioning its injustices and having to "ask God's forgiveness" in front of the third grade class for being a "doubting Thomas" flowed like hot lava back into my heart.

After using up several pens' worth of ink, I was finished. I looked at the clock. It had only been nine hours. That didn't seem possible.

I raced down the hall and gave my screed to the coed who typed my papers. (My mother had told me never to learn to type or to cook, or I'd do both unwillingly someday.) Then I returned and cleaned my room for the first time in my entire university career. I washed my floor by hand with an old nightgown because I was too frenzied to wait for the communal mop. I labelled all of my drawers with some of my old nail polish, called Coral Gables. I later had to use nail polish remover on the wood to rub out the three-inch label that read FOUNDATION GARMENTS. The closet said FROCKS.

I realized sometime later that, in fact, I'd worked on the paper for thirty-three hours. I had missed an entire day.

Professor Fowler called me about a week after the paper had been handed in. He asked me rather solemnly from behind his desk whether I'd written it. I assumed from his grave manner that he had received a yellow slip from Health Services. If I said I hadn't written it, it would be plagiarism. If I acknowledged I had, I would be admitting to lunacy. I finally admitted that I had written it in an "overtired state."

Professor Fowler just looked at me and blinked, so I continued. "You know . . . when you can't get to sleep and you get jittery?"

He put up his hand to stop my excuses and told me he thought the paper was "dazzling." He then asked if I wanted him to pull a few strings to get me into Oxford. He thought sending the paper to well-placed colleagues would be enough.

"What about college board scores and my GPA?"

"The British don't go in for that sort of numerology," he said with disdain, as though being at the top of the American SAT was equivalent to being slow in England.

I asked about money, but he just swept his hand in the air as though the British never discuss anything so grubby. I asked him if I could think about it for a day or two, and he said fine.

As I walked back from the Ohio Fellows mansion, I was dazed. My mother had always said I was smart and "an individual" and that someday someone would recognize it. She'd said all I had to do was wait. She was right yet again. Her undying belief in me, through the expulsion, the calls from the school office and the sometimes desultory grades over the years, brought tears to my eyes.

I hated Ohio University, but going to Oxford would mean leaving Laurie. We had been together a long time now. The magic, and the tragedy, of first love is how ignorant you are that it will ever end. No one uses the phrase "first love" until they are on to their "second love." If I went to England, I would not be back for years.

I never informed Laurie about the offer; he was kind and he would have told me to go, realizing it was a once-in-a-lifetime opportunity. I wanted to tell my mother, to brighten her life, but she would want me to go and be terribly disappointed if I decided not to avail myself of such an opportunity. My father would once have been proud of me, but it was too late for him to understand it.

I called Leora and poured my heart out. She said she knew how I felt and that Laurie, a man she now knew, was one in a million. If it was true love, she said, he would wait. I asked if she would go if she were me. She said that one thing she did know was that if there were no emotional entanglements involved, she would be on the first plane.

After forty-eight hours of gruelling introspection, I told Professor Fowler, a man whose regard meant a lot to me, that I had a sick father and needed to go home at regular intervals to help my mother with the burden of taking care of him. I therefore could not accept his offer.

I think we both knew that there was more involved than a sick father. But Professor Fowler, being British, never changed his expression or tried to change my mind. He simply said, "Very well then, but the offer remains open."

I wondered how many other girls had given up opportunities in the name of love. Probably more than there were serpents in the world.

CHAPTER 16

# love it or leave it

Laurie and I were on our way back to my dorm one warm April evening in 1968 at around ten o'clock. He had just finished a paper on Rilke and I had just finished mine on Wallace Stevens. He was telling me that Rilke described happiness as "that over-hasty profit of loss impending."

We cut through the green until we came to the main intersection of the one-block business district. We saw a few dozen black students sitting in the middle of the intersection, blocking traffic. White students stood on the sidewalks, looking on like stunned snowy owls. The roads were jammed, so people were getting out of their cars in what seemed like slow motion and standing on the street, mumbling to one another and shaking their heads. The man who owned the photography studio near the corner came out and stood on the stoop of his establishment. I asked what was wrong.

"Martin Luther King was assassinated."

Laurie and I looked at each other in bewilderment and then alarm. After a few seconds I said, "By whom?"

"I'm not sure. They said on the news it was some white guy or white people in Memphis. I don't think they have all the details yet."

We went to join the others in the middle of the intersection. Eventually, the entire street was full of people, both black and white, just sitting silently, looking at the ground. Someone in the bookstore on the corner hooked up a loudspeaker outside, and we heard Bobby Kennedy announcing the assassination to a crowd. He said King had been killed by a white man, just as his brother John Kennedy had been killed by a white man. He asked all Americans to find it in their hearts to move forward. He said that our country had had difficult times in the past and would have difficult times in the future, but that the majority of blacks and whites wanted to live together in peace and to have justice for all.

Later, as Laurie walked me back to my dorm, we talked about what King's death meant for the civil rights movement. After having worked on the inside at the Southern Christian Leadership Conference, we both knew in our hearts that now, with King gone, the association would flounder. There was no one with charisma to take his place. And, in fact, King's death would spark rioting and looting across American cities.

—

I returned home that spring after my second year of college to help my mother and get a summer job. My father was about the same, slightly more frail but still able to walk and talk. He had forgotten what some words meant, but he could still read. My mother had labelled everything in the house with his prized Dymo machine. The house looked like a kindergarten. The front door had a red label that said FRONT DOOR. I thought my mother deserved a medal for what she had to deal with every day. When I told her she didn't look stressed, she said it was no worse than dealing with me when I'd been home.

I had by now moved on from reading nineteenth-century novels and made my mother read *The Autobiography of Malcolm X* and Black Panther Eldridge Cleaver's *Soul on Ice* with me. (My father thought soul on ice was a cocktail.)

I was offered a job with a new department developed by the city called Upward Bound, a local initiative to get youth into university who didn't have the grades but had "life experience." I was never sure, but I think it was funded through welfare. I was connected to the University of Buffalo and I was to be a liaison officer between the university and black youth. Although it was still pre–affirmative action days, the university, as an experiment, had set aside some spots for black youth and had lowered the admissions bar, and through Upward Bound I was to help find the right candidates. I was surprised that I had been offered this job, until I found out that my youth employment program last summer had made a bigger splash than Mr. Shoomack had let on.

Laurie would be coming to Buffalo for the summer after his football camp in Ohio and would live with his aunt. We had never introduced each other to our families. We figured we had enough problems without that. Laurie said, "Why court trouble?" And I had a father who was calling black people "Rochesters." (For some reason, he remembered Jack Benny's black sidekick on *The Jack Benny Show.*)

Outside of my job and Laurie's training, Laurie and I would volunteer together on what was to become the Storefront College, which was loosely affiliated with the University of Buffalo. It was organized by student radicals and Marxists and professors who wanted to contribute to civil rights. It was a college set up in a storefront near the university through which professors would teach courses for free to whoever wanted to take them. There were no admission requirements.

Laurie suggested that I contact his cousin Splits to organize some English professors for the Storefront and to get the black students association involved. Splits's and Laurie's mothers were sisters, and the cousins had spent summers together. Splits, unlike Laurie, was not raised in a middle-class home with a father. The father had abandoned him and his six brothers and sisters when he was small.

He was called Splits because he had a large scar starting at his hairline that went from the centre of his forehead and ended at the bridge of his nose, visually splitting his face in half. He told several versions of how he got his scar. One was that he was fishing as a child and his big fish got away, and he banged his head on a rock in frustration; another was that he was in a fight over his stolen bike; and a third was that he'd had a fall during an epileptic seizure and gashed his head in the pet food aisle of a supermarket. My father would have called Splits "full of malarkey," while Laurie referred to him as "a mythologizer." Laurie said that if you split his tales open, there was always a kernel of poetic truth. Although Splits was large and his scar made him look imposing, he had a winning smile that he often used to his own advantage.

Splits was a University of Buffalo student, but I had met him over a year ago in Ohio, where he spent time visiting Laurie and his aunt and uncle. I had gotten to know him quite well because Laurie had, on occasion, brought him down to Athens to work on our voter registration committee. He could win over a room with his rhetoric, but I had had a few altercations with him in the past because, while he was good at carrying placards and always showed up for the TV coverage and demonstrations, he wasn't willing to do the gruelling grassroots work that carried a movement forward. When I told Laurie that Splits was a grandstander, he said that he knew that and had been listening to Splits all of his life. But he pointed out that Splits had a way with people and that all movements need a spokesman.

I had several meetings with Splits about the Storefront University. Together we talked with professors who were willing to get involved. Splits had his finger on the pulse of what liberal Americans were feeling; he had enough energy to fill a room; and despite his over-the-top rhetoric and antics, he knew how to motivate people. He seemed to know everyone. He could gather hundreds of people in a short period of time for a protest, and he had his own couch in the Student Union and was always rapping with admirers who milled around him.

At meetings with the Storefront founders, Splits would say, "The people who need to learn most are locked out of this institution on elitist grounds. You speak the King's or the Queen's English. You white people decided yours was better and black dialect didn't count. Where you dudes gettin' off with that?"

Splits would pace at meetings, gesticulating wildly. "What the hell are you readin' Marx on oppression for?" he'd say. "He's one dead Russian. I can teach that course, my man. I live it!"

—

By early June I hadn't seen Laurie for a month, which had been our longest separation, but he'd written to me every day. We had agreed to meet on the university's library steps, where we had met many times in the past. My heart started to hammer the second I saw him coming from the parking lot. I asked if everything was all right and he nodded.

When we got over to the library steps and I had a closer look at him in the light, I noticed he was wearing his hair in more of an afro than before. He wore his usual jeans and jean jacket, and on the jacket pocket was a large black and white button that said SNCC.

"SNCC?" I said.

"Student Non-violent Coordinating Committee. I've been following this Stokely Carmichael for a while. He wants me to write for his organization. I think his time has come," he said.

"How is he different from Martin Luther King?"

"One is alive and one is dead, for starters."

I had read about Stokely and knew that he thought passive

resistance was passé. Stokely probably believed, if not in violence, then in retaliation. I feared he would cause the moderate blacks to drop out of the movement. America could crush any uprising from radical blacks as easily as I could crush a gnat. I sensed the death knell of what we had worked so hard for over the last year and a half.

"Stokely thinks that America was keeping King on a puppet string for one long freedom ride and then pulled him off that horse when he got goin' too fast."

I picked up when he said *goin' too fast* that he was using black dialect for the first time.

"What or whom do you mean by 'America'?" I asked.

"We have no idea who killed King, or for what reasons. Even King's family thinks it was the FBI or the CIA. King was becoming a threat. Too many people were behind him."

"What do you think?" I asked.

"How can I know the truth? We'll never know."

I realized on that summer night that Laurie hadn't mentioned any new words. He was becoming less intellectualized — which was now called "sitting on your ass" — and more politicized, which was what the late 1960s would be all about.

——

A few days later we went to a talk by Angela Davis, a black Marxist Ph.D. candidate. She was accompanied by Marcuse, her famous Marxist thesis adviser from Berkeley. Both Laurie and I had read Marcuse's book *One-Dimensional Man* in our "isms" course (social-ism, capitalism, communism, et cetera). In fact, Laurie had given it to me for my birthday. Angela stood before us in her huge afro and told us that racism was only a symptom of capitalism.

Laurie and I stayed up all night on the steps of the library, talking about *One-Dimensional Man* and Angela Davis's presentation. By the time we saw the sun come up over the University of Buffalo's library tower, we were hoarse from discussion.

That summer we went to see the movie *The Battle of Algiers* together and were moved to tears by the Algerian battle and by the women who made the strange, unearthly cries of support. I introduced Laurie to Bergman movies that Leora's parents had introduced me to while I was in high school, and together we went to weekly film festivals at the university. And we laid our plans for change that we thought would shake the world.

There is nothing more gratifying than having a kindred spirit and working toward a goal. It was a time before we had to worry about our own future, so we could focus on worrying about the rest of the world. We could afford the luxury of asking, "How can we make the world a better place?" We weren't yet old enough or wise enough to realize how hard it was to change anything — let alone ourselves.

—–

Leora was spending another summer studying neurophysiology at the University of Chicago. She could only come home for a few weeks because she had to monitor her stuttering lab rats. She was already on her fourth generation. When she called, she never said "hello" but did a fantastic imitation of a rat stuttering.

We agreed that we were far more suited to the theoretical than the practical. We happily spent hours on the phone discussing the theory of stuttering and the theory of dyslexia. But neither of us ever mentioned the humans who suffered from them. Through my conversations with Leora, I became more interested in the brain and the sciences than I ever had been before. Scary as it seemed to me, I was turning into my father.

Leora wrote and said Laurie and I should stay with her for the Democratic Party National Convention, which would be held in August, just minutes from the university. She said there was a large Students for a Democratic Society (SDS) presence on campus and she knew there would be demonstrations. Everyone was gearing up for these. Laurie agreed because he wanted to check out a friend that Splits had met in California named Bobby Seale, a co-founder of the Black Panther Party, as well as participate in the Poor People's March. It worked out perfectly because the convention would be in late summer, and I could work until then and get in lots of overtime.

———

Laurie and I buzzed along the thruway on our way to Chicago in the 409. On the back window I'd stuck a peace-sign sticker. My father thought it was a symbol for "Keep Off the Grass." We drove all day, eventually stopping at a god-forsaken spot somewhere between Erie, Pennsylvania, and Steuben, Illinois, just to stretch our legs. We went into a tiny truck stop where the men smelled like diesel fuel.

Once we sat down, Laurie said, "Those drivers saw us drive in and they checked out the 409. I saw them standing around outside, looking at the rear window where you have the peace sticker."

Having eaten in thousands of diners in my short lifetime, I replied, "So? Men in small towns stand around for ages outside of diners and look at each other's cars and have cigarettes. It's called 'chewing the fat.'" I continued reading the menu, my attention caught by the "whistle pig," a hot dog with bacon and cheese. It was depicted as a pig wrapped in an orange blanket with musical notes coming out of its puckered lips. My father always said, "Whenever you're travelling, order the local delicacy," so I decided to try the whistle pig.

When I glanced up from my menu, Laurie still looked concerned. Trying to reassure him, I said, "Who cares what they think?" It was unlike Laurie to be anything but calm, but he looked far more vigilant than usual, his eyes darting like those of a junkyard dog ready to pounce.

"We may face a quandary."

"New word — *quandary*. I got it on the first try," I said, looking back at the menu.

The waiter, who was presumably the owner and cook as well, had a Midwestern flatness in his voice as he asked, seemingly for the benefit of the "regulars" at the counter chewing toothpicks, "Where you folks blow in from?"

"Buffalo," I said.

"Where you off to?"

"Chicago."

The waiter said that they were expecting fireworks out there. I said I had no idea what Mayor Daley was talking about, because all the demonstrations were going to be peaceful and all anyone wanted was to make sure that we had a viable candidate to run for the party. I had been to a lot of demonstrations by now, and there were always police present, which was fine with me, but the whole point was only to demonstrate.

Laurie didn't look up from the menu during this conversation. All he said was "I'll have a Western."

The waiter said, loud enough for people at all five tables to hear, "I thought maybe you was runnin' away from home with that big convertible . . ." He hesitated, looking at Laurie, " . . . an' all."

"No" was all I could think to say to such an odd comment.

Later I thought that I should have told him to mind his own business. It hadn't occurred to me that he was suggesting I was doing something illicit. I had eaten in diners throughout my childhood with Roy, and he was black, albeit known around the vicinity, so it didn't occur to me that Laurie and I were causing a stir.

After we ate, we strolled out to the three-car parking lot. There were neat yellow lines painted on the pavement — as though three cars could get disorderly. A red pickup truck had blocked us in our parking spot while we'd been in the restaurant. We were about to get in when Laurie caught my eye over the top of the car and shot me a subtle but unmistakable look of warning. The rear window on the pickup had a sticker that read AMERICA, LOVE IT OR LEAVE IT. Had America become so divided that a peace sign could be a red flag? Earlier I had thought Laurie was being paranoid, but even I was beginning to feel the hostility in the air. Laurie had picked up on it long before I did. Clearly he'd had to develop far more sensitive antennae. We were on these people's turf, and now we were outnumbered and trapped here.

As we opened our doors, one of the men said, "Yaw know that's one great ol' buggy."

Another said, "Your daddy's?"

"Yup," I said.

"We just jawin' here and thinkin' maybe he don't like what you're doin.'"

"Travelling to Chicago? I don't think my father is opposed to travel. He would, however, find it strange that some men would block my car to inform me of his imagined likes and dislikes."

The men looked confused. Finally, one said, "You callin' me a liar?"

"No, I'm calling you a roadblock."

He stood with his hands folded over his chest and sort of puffed himself out like pastry rising. The red plaid on his shirt became convex and his buttons threatened to pop. He was a big guy, but it was mostly fat. The other two were scrawny.

His buddy said, "A roadblock ain't nothin' bad. Just makes you stop and think is all."

Plaid went over to the truck that was parked next to us, opened the passenger door and bent over to get something from under the seat. That's when Laurie jumped him and started tearing into him. Within seconds he had laid him out on the ground between yellow lines like a plaid parked car. Laurie just looked at the other two, and they leapt into the pickup and took off, leaving their fat friend lying there.

We got into the 409 and peeled out.

As I drove along even faster than my usual speed, Laurie panted, "Drive slowly, because they're going to have been on their CBs, calling every racist cop in the county."

An hour ago I would have said, *I doubt it,* but now I felt as though I'd landed in a foreign country and didn't know the rules.

Less than fifteen minutes later, trucks were passing us, cutting us off and then slowing down. The word was out. Fine. Laurie could fight; I could drive. Those truck drivers had no idea; I'd been driving since I was nine. I just put the pedal to the floor and cleaned those spark plugs.

Laurie said quietly, "You know those truckers are goading you to drive over the speed limit. They want the police to have something to lay on you."

Next thing we knew we heard a siren and saw lights. I looked in the rear-view mirror and spotted a police car that was having trouble keeping up with us. I pulled to a stop at the roadside.

"You goin' to a fire, young lady?" he asked as he took my licence. "I clocked you at 128 miles per hour, Miss McClure." Still looking at my licence photo, he added, "You better wipe that shit-eating grin off your face."

Then, for some reason, he demanded to see Laurie's licence. He took one look at it and said, "Lawrence Coal!" as though he had just met the Pope. "Why sure! No wonder you levelled that guy with one punch. He's in the hospital as we speak." Then he started laughing.

"You don't want to go around pissing off Lawrence Coal, the greatest tight end alive today. What you did against Duke was amazing. I had money on that one and you came through for me. Now, you say hi to Woody. Is he one hell of a coach or what?"

"Sure is." Laurie nodded.

The cop began blathering on about various games, and Laurie was able to speak about football minutiae, which surprised me since I'd never heard him mention one word about the sport. I was not from a family of spectator sports fans. I hadn't realized that sitting on your behind, watching someone throwing a ball that looked like a giant peanut around a field, could produce such strong feelings.

After about fifteen minutes he said, "Well, I don't want to hold you up — where you off to?"

"Chicago," Laurie said.

"Careful you don't get into trouble up there," he said as he returned my licence. "I hear they're gearing up for a major tussle. Got enough tear gas to stop a herd of elephants."

And he waved us on.

CHAPTER 17

# the white rabbit meets
# the blue elephants

We drove into the centre of Chicago, and I felt elated to be in

a city with a heartbeat after having spent my last few years in

Athens, Ohio, which was basically on life support. When Laurie

and I headed up the major artery of Michigan Avenue and crossed

the Chicago River, we both remembered the Carl Sandburg poem

"Chicago," which we'd learned in high school. We chanted the stanza together:

*Hog Butcher for the World,*
*Tool Maker, Stacker of Wheat,*
*Player with Railroads and the Nation's Freight Handler;*
*Stormy, husky, brawling,*
*City of the Big Shoulders.*

That entire summer, the upcoming Chicago Democratic National Convention had been making headlines and building momentum. By the time we arrived, the atmosphere was electric. The Democratic Party was in disarray and needed to choose a candidate to run against Richard Nixon in the November election. Johnson had announced he would not run again. Robert Kennedy, the party hopeful, had been gunned down in June. The party was weakening in its support for the Vietnam War, but its position was not consistent. There were two possible candidates: Hubert Humphrey, who was not openly against the war, and Eugene McCarthy, who was against the war but didn't have a powerful enough caucus.

Vietnam protestors were planning a peaceful protest and had been arriving steadily from all over the continent. The Yippies, as members of the Youth International Party were known, including Jerry Rubin and Abbie Hoffman, were offering street theatre accompanied by a threat to put LSD in the Chicago water supply. The SDS and all of its less radical sympathizers were also on board. As well, Ralph Abernathy's Poor People's "mule train" — protesters leading mule-drawn covered wagons — modelled on the protest that had been conceived by Martin Luther King and that resulted in the "Resurrection City" shanty town and protest in Washington, D.C., in May, was to parade through Chicago.

Mayor Richard Daley, a fat party boss who ran Chicago for years on a strict law and order platform, was preparing for the worst. He had amassed a huge task force and given them riot training, and had backup from the National Guard. He was already famous for having said "Shoot to kill" on television that spring during the riots following King's assassination.

Laurie and I were both working for Abernathy's Poor People's March. The problem was that King was now dead and the campaign had not had enough publicity. Unfortunately, Abernathy had about as much charisma as the mule he rode in on. Plus, the planners of the demonstration had thought more about the politics than the logistics. They failed to establish a detailed plan for how the mules, collected from all over the area, were going to get to downtown Chicago. We got calls saying some of the animals were grazing near a thruway outside Gary, Indiana.

—

The University of Chicago was in the middle of all the protesting, and only a few minutes' walk from Democratic Party headquarters at the Conrad Hilton. As we pulled into the parking lot of Leora's dorm, I felt unexpectedly nervous. It took me a few minutes to realize what was causing my panic.

Leora's college roommate, Beverly Griesdorf, had also gone to our high school, but she had been more Leora's friend than mine. She was creative and wrote plays for the class, as did I, and we clashed. In grade twelve, each class put on a play to launch our March of Dimes campaign. It was at the height of the Batman craze, and I wrote, directed and starred in a skit in which I played the Riddler. The idea was that the audience would ask questions and try to stump me; if they succeeded, our class donated money, and if I knew the answer, the other classes had to donate. If I didn't know the answer, I made up something funny on the spot. Improvisation has always been my best medium.

Bev came to the microphone and asked, "What president has also been mistaken for a golf ball?" I was president of the ski club, and I had been called a golf ball by some of the meaner boys, due to my pockmarked skin. I was mortified. All I had to do was say something witty and it would be over. I knew that, but I couldn't speak. The seconds ticked away. Finally Kip, who was playing Robin, came forward and said, "Aha, the Riddler is stumped. Everyone in her homeroom has to donate a quarter each. Now let us move from this sand trap and return to the green."

When I told Laurie about that experience, he said that Bev probably had no idea it had been one of my worst moments. He said, "When you look and sound invincible, the problem is people think that you are invulnerable."

But I had never gotten over the incident, and now, three years later, I had to face Beverly.

Walking with me toward the dorm, Laurie said, "Your friendship with Leora is so poignant. I wish there was someone that I had been friends with for so many years that went in the same direction as me."

"What about Splits?"

"We do go back a long way, but I'm not so sure we've taken the some route."

It had been almost a year since Laurie and I had been out to see Leora, and I was overwhelmed and moved to tears when I saw her. Leora had a circle of friends, mostly New Yorkers, whom I had met on previous visits and had found to be fun.

One of her friends was a high-powered politico, a member of SDS named Myra. Soon after we arrived, she began talking to Laurie about how she was from a "working-class family," and how they were "comrades in the struggle." She monopolized him, and I noticed her touching his shoulder as she spoke.

After a while he came over and sat next to me. Myra followed and said she was going out to buy some beer and asked him to come along to help her carry it.

He said, "Cathy and I can do it. We'll be back soon."

Outside, in the car, I didn't say anything.

"That really took a wrong turn," said Laurie. "I was just talking to her on a political level and it turned a bit weird."

"I think she likes you or something."

"She doesn't like me. She just wants a black boyfriend because it's coming into vogue for SDSers to be with someone oppressed. I refuse to be used by her. I'm not interested in her black man fantasies."

I wondered what he meant by "black man fantasies." Reading my confused expression, he smiled and put his arm around me as I drove, saying, "You know a lot about a lot of stuff, but very little about some things everyone else knows a lot about." He added, "Hey, it's one of the things I've always liked about you."

— — —

Over the next few days we had a great time partying with Leora, Beverly and their friends and talking about demonstration strategies. Bev and I got along well and I realized that my attempts at humour in high school had probably hurt far more people's feelings than hers ever had. Plus, it was great to spend time around people with whom I had a shared history. I had no brothers and sisters, so sharing past memories gave me a sense of belonging. We went to all kinds of ethnic restaurants that didn't exist in Ohio or Buffalo. I had Lebanese food for the first time, and for free — one of Beverly's classmate's fathers owned the restaurant.

I stayed with Leora and Bev at their dorm, and Laurie stayed with some guys in the North End, where he was doing some hands-on organizing of the mule train. (He tied three mules in the basement of Leora's dorm, and since they had no food, we bought them Rice Krispies and named the animals Snap, Crackle and Pop.) I went over in the mornings to help by making signs and leaflets. There were all kinds of logistics to check on, like road permits.

After that was organized, Leora's friend Len said that the only way to make the convention "more real" was to take some acid. Len said it would really engrave this historical moment in our consciousness. I had no intention of taking it, especially because I didn't feel totally comfortable around Beverly or this new interloper, Myra. Laurie agreed with me, saying if you felt leery about someone you were with, any mind-expanding drug could result in a bad trip. Acid breaks down your defences and enhances your senses. I figured defences were invented for a reason.

Laurie said he thought he'd pop a tab himself, though, since he felt good about the people he was with, even if he didn't know everyone as well as he knew Leora. He then said for the first time, not in a romantic way but as a point of fact, "If you're with someone you love and who loves you, then you're safe."

"Right," I croaked.

Considering how loquacious I was on other topics, it was strange that when it came to discussing love or romance, I found it hard to say one word. Laurie didn't seem to mind my romantic parsimony. After all this time, I guess he understood me. Neither of us liked public displays of affection. Both of us felt uncomfortable when Leora's friends acted mushy toward one another. I had never had sex with Laurie, although we had had many wonderful passionate moments and I couldn't think of anyone I could love more or be more physically attracted to. The truth was, I was frightened of physical intimacy. A part of my mind was unwilling to give up decades of previous training. I could still hear my father's words ringing from the belfry of Christ the King Church — YOU'RE NOT THE DAUGHTER I WANT. I had talked to Laurie about this, and he said that we had our whole lives to have sex and that I shouldn't worry about it. He never pressured me, or made sex an issue.

My fears about having sex were exacerbated by a bizarre incident that had occurred in the early months of my relationship with Laurie. I had missed my period for a couple of months and told Sarah about it. The first thing she asked was if I was pregnant. I told her it would have been an immaculate conception. She told me that when I was forty I would kick myself in the head if I didn't have sex with Laurie.

She then referred me to a Dr. Konnig who had an office above a dime store in town. He was an old German man with a heavy accent and his wife was his nurse/receptionist/cashier. He sold his own medicine in small, dark, identical bottles that lined the wall. Sarah said he gave out birth control pills like M&Ms, helped girls "in a jam" and kept things "off the record." When I got to his tiny downtrodden office, he gave me a pelvic exam and announced that I was pregnant. I was so shocked that I could hardly say a word. I never told him that I hadn't had sex. I just paid and staggered back to my dorm room, sure that this was the way that God was punishing me for all the awful things I'd done, particularly how mean I'd been to my dad. What better retribution was there than making someone who had not had sex pregnant? Who would ever believe me? The words of Mother Agnese came back to me — "God works in strange ways."

I called Laurie and told him; he was unfazed. He said the doctor was wrong and people who don't take off their clothes can't get pregnant. I said, *But he examined me.* He suggested I get a pregnancy test at a drugstore just to reassure myself. The results took over a week and were, of course, negative. It was the longest week of my life. I never got over the shock of that event and developed an irrational terror of pregnancy. I have no idea how Laurie could have been so patient and kind — he never yelled at me or said I was crazy during that long week of waiting.

The other reason I didn't want to take hallucinogens, which everyone seemed to be trying at the time, was that I felt I already *had* "the volume" turned up on my senses. I could remember certain points in my life vividly because my antennae were always raised to their full extension. I could still remember the peonies on the altar blossoming when I was in grade four, and running to Mother Agnese to ask her to stop teaching because a miracle was happening. I had always seen and felt too much. The last thing I needed was more volume.

And underneath all this, some part of me didn't want to do

drugs because I worried that I might be crazy. In grade three I'd stabbed a school bully, Anthony McDougal, and I'd been shipped off to a psychiatrist to unearth the reason for my not-so-latent aggression. My parents never made a big deal about my "psychiatric disorder." My father never mentioned it. My mother said I was unique, not crazy, and surely any doctor worth his salt would agree. Roy said that people who were crazy didn't work, because they didn't know the day of the week; since I had a job, I couldn't be crazy. Yet even with all the support I received, I feared that I might have a screw loose.

What if the acid shook up my brain, and the crazy part that now lay dormant, folded neatly in a crevice of my grey matter, were to rise to the surface when heated, like scum on chicken soup, and take over? That was not a chance I was willing to take at that moment in Chicago, or ever. No matter how much the 1960s raged, no matter how much I longed to be part of it, and no matter how much Ken Kesey or Allen Ginsberg told me I was seeing and experiencing only one one-hundredth of possible experience, I was content with the little corner of the cosmos that I had unravelled. Grace Slick's white rabbit had red eyes that scared me.

When I confessed all this to Laurie, he said, "You are not crazy. Since I met you, you have never done anything even mildly erratic. You have an A average, do your work, don't drink, smoke dope once a year and work for the political good."

I wondered who he was talking about.

Everyone except me popped their pre-Convention tablet and then we had a pizza in the dorm lounge. About a half-hour later, I started noticing some strange behaviour. Myra said her pizza slice was three storeys high and the pepperoni was up on the roof deck.

Bev described hers as a bloodbath, and threw it into the dorm suggestion box. Then Bev went over to a pencil sharpener that was nailed to the front desk in the lounge and began sharpening a pencil. She kept winding the handle frantically until the whole pencil had worn down. The student who was paid to man the desk finally said, "Uh, I think it's sharp enough."

I went over to the desk because I could see that Bev's wild turning of the handle was winding her up too. She was perspiring. And she was bothering the desk clerk. I suggested she relax.

She mumbled, "If I can get this pencil to straighten out — you know, get flat — then I think I can straighten out the world's big problems. I think the trouble is that the sharpener is attached to the counter," and she tried to yank it out.

Having always had a flair for the obvious, I said, "Beverly, it isn't going to get flat. It will just get shorter."

She began crying. "That's the problem, isn't it? It can't get straightened out. It can never be straight. It just gets diminished!"

Laurie and Leora held on to Bev as we started out for Lincoln Park for the demonstration. We never got there, though, because on the way Bev tried to jump off the Michigan Street Bridge and Laurie caught her just before she went over. A little later, shaking and screaming, Beverly tried to jump off the loop, the elevated streetcar, ranting that she needed to be flattened.

—

On the second night of the demonstrations, everyone in Leora's group had to stay behind to tend to Bev, who they thought was having a really prolonged "bad trip." Laurie and I went to hear Bobby Seale speak at Lincoln Park.

Surrounded by rows of cops and the National Guard, Bobby

reminded us to defend ourselves with any means possible if we were attacked by the police. I thought he was being hyperbolic. What policeman was going to hit us? And for what? Standing in Lincoln Park on a hot summer night?

After the talk we decided to go down to Grant Park and see what was happening with the mules and the Poor People's March. We'd heard that Rennie Davis, the SDS spokesman, was going to speak there.

On our way down we saw protestors stampeding toward us, screaming that police had charged and Davis had been beaten unconscious. There was nowhere to go. Suddenly everywhere we looked we saw policemen. There was a steady line walking toward us, swinging billy clubs rhythmically like Officer Krupke did in *West Side Story*. It was hard to grasp that this was for real and not a movie set. It looked like the city was under siege. We were terrified. The police in their uniforms, snapping their clubs against their hands, looked like a herd of blue elephants marching our way. When we turned to go the other direction, we were met by a fleet of army jeeps with barbed wire over their front grilles like fierce mouths full of braces.

We wound up in front of the Conrad Hilton Hotel. I figured Mayor Daley wouldn't dare to carry on these tactics in front of the TV cameras. Yet again I was wrong. Laurie and I were leaning on the bar lounge window outside the Hilton, listening to protesters chant *"Dump the Hump,"* when police started coming toward us, tanks blocking all of the side streets. The officers pushed the crowd back by swinging their billy clubs in unison, and the press of bodies broke the Hilton's window. It didn't shatter, but kind of popped out and then crumbled to the ground, and protesters started flying through it into the Hilton lounge. Some were jammed on top of others. The police were getting closer, so the rest of us had no choice but to jump through the jagged glass into the lounge as well. We crashed in on bewildered hotel guests who were immobilized, still clinging to the pink umbrellas in their mai tais. Somehow I lost Laurie in the mayhem. Then I began choking, tears running down my face from the tear gas tossed into the hotel bar. I felt like I had been underwater too long and couldn't get up for air. Stink bombs were thrown as well, which made me feel nauseated; the air I was gasping for was making me sick.

Earlier in the day, when we had checked out the scene on the TV in the lounge of Leora's dormitory, it hadn't looked like this. We had seen crowds of college students in the park, singing "We Shall Overcome." The police had thrown mace, and as people scattered, the students threw it back. I realized how different a picture on the small screen was from the real thing: choking on tear gas and stink bombs. I couldn't catch my breath and my lungs were burning like I was a fire-eater.

More and more demonstrators were cramming into the lounge, and I was shoved up against the bar. The police followed us in and kept forcing people back, but there was nowhere to go. Leaning on my high jumping expertise of yesteryear, I leapt over the bar and hid behind it. Those in the first line, closest to the police, got clubbed. I could hear the thwack of the batons making contact with their skulls.

When I peeked above the bar for a second to see if I could locate Laurie, I saw a guy who'd been clubbed who was holding his head. He looked like a tourist from Idaho, there for a Shriners convention. I ducked down even farther, almost putting my face in a bowl of lemon wedges.

Some time later, when the whapping sounds were less frequent and fading, like popcorn almost popped, I rose up from behind the bar, thinking I was safe. Most of the room had cleared, other than the wounded who were lying there bruised and bleeding. One girl, who looked terribly Seven Sisters in her blonde braid and faded wraparound skirt, was sitting on the plush carpet, dabbing at the cuts on the face of a very skinny boy in a fake camouflage jacket. He had a swollen eye and had clearly lost bladder control.

A policeman yelled at her, "Move it."

She shouted back in a trembling high-pitched voice, "All we wanted was a voice. A choice. Hubert Humphrey is not a choice. Both candidates are for the war!" She started whimpering, but managed to choke out, "This is not democracy."

He looked at her with disgust and said, "Your father should have spanked you when you were five."

That comment enraged me. Despite the ache in my throat from the tear gas, I yelled, "When we want your advice on child-rearing, we'll ask!"

He came over to the bar and leaned on it, one inch from my face, little drops of spit flying onto my tie-dye tank top as he said, "Listen, you little brat, you wouldn't know shit if you were a fly. Have you ever had a job? You listen to your Commie professors and think you know what's goin' on in the world. You think it's so bad here in America? Get the fuck out. Move to Vietnam and sweat, or maybe you want to ride on a tank in Czechoslovakia."

"I'm glad this is being filmed, because no one would believe it, least of all Thomas Jefferson."

"I'm doin' my job. What's yours? Bein' a student? Well, go home and study."

"What is your job? Beating unarmed kids with clubs?" I said.

"You actually think you're a 'kid'? Well. That's the problem. You're supposed to be an adult."

I didn't know at the time that "the silent majority," as that huge voting block was later labelled, did not agree with the students or the liberal press. With most of America watching this mayhem on television, the majority were outraged — but their outrage was directed at us, the protestors.

—

Laurie was waiting for me outside the hotel, and looked relieved to see me unhurt. He had his shirt off and tied around his mouth and nose to ward off the stink. He threw his arms around me and said he'd been looking for me.

On the way home, I could only whisper. I guess I'd yelled at that cop louder than I realized, or else the tear gas had constricted my vocal chords. As we made our way up Michigan Avenue, an organizer with a bullhorn walked up and down, trying to rally the crowd by singing, "This Land Is Your Land," but no one joined in.

I saw the mules lined up for the poverty march as we trudged back to the dorm, but no one was paying attention to them. The protestors were nursing their wounds, only some inflicted by the police (although there were 668 arrested and 110 admitted to hospital), the rest from being trampled by crowds in the chaos. The streets were littered with bandanas, scarves, bloody T-shirts and stray sandals.

The mules watched us, tattered and defeated, limping home.

CHAPTER 18

# the hour of the wolf

Leora, Laurie and I assumed positive changes would happen as a result of the convention — and we were so totally wrong as to be completely off the map. As Leora said, "Our skewed perception of the world never fails us." We thought that we had done a great thing for the nation in Chicago, because everyone in TV land had

had a chance to see what Mayor Daley's and Richard Nixon's "law and order" platform really looked like. But it seemed Daley, and Nixon, who was gearing up for a landslide victory based on "law and order," knew far more about what Americans wanted than we did.

—

We were wrong about Bev as well. We assumed that she was a normal college student who had taken one tab of acid and would soon return to normal. She never did. The diagnosis started out as transitory drug reaction. Over the years it changed to drug-induced schizophrenia. Bev was still in the hospital nine years later. When I went to visit her, she said, "I've lost the plot." She looked at me and mumbled, "Take my advice: don't roll the dice too many times."

Only a few weeks after the convention, I was back in Ohio. Laurie was down for the weekend and had brought Splits with him. Splits took more time off from college than anyone I'd ever met. He was still hanging on at the University of Buffalo, though, so I assumed he must have been passing.

I had been doing nothing but my school work and my political work. I had tons of energy and believed wholeheartedly in equal rights; I felt privileged to be at this point in American history when I could make a difference. On weekends Laurie and I travelled all around in his little VW Bug, registering blacks in West Virginia, preparing them for the November election.

Last year when something had been accomplished in the movement, we would all cheer. If things didn't go well, we would hold strategy meetings into the night and try a new approach. This fall felt different. For one thing, most of the white students who had been welcomed in the SCLC when King ran it had now left the movement entirely or had joined the more conservative NAACP. Most radicalized black students scoffed at the NAACP, feeling it spoke more to their parents than to them.

Many black students had come back to school with bushy afros, and the fashion trend was decidedly dashiki. When we worked on voter registration, I didn't feel we were all working together. Blacks called one another "sister" and "brother" and slapped palms, but no one slapped mine any more. The SCLC, which we had all believed in last year now had no real leader, and campus radicals thought the organization was moving too slowly and was not nearly radical enough. They felt the group died with King. Most of the blacks I knew were now members of the Student Non-Violent Coordinating Committee, led by the charismatic Stokely Carmichael. The SNCC had become increasingly radical in the past year. It was now more in line with the philosophy of the Black Panthers, which was to end racial imperialism with whatever it took.

That weekend Laurie said we had to go to a basketball game against Bowling Green. He and Splits knew some of the players and had agreed to go to see them. There were thousands of people in the auditorium, and when the national anthem was played, each of the black players on the team, the majority, raised one arm straight up in the air and wore one black glove as a sign that they supported "black power." To my surprise, Laurie stood up and did the same, as did most blacks in the audience. Laurie looked straight ahead, never glancing my way. Things were moving too fast for me. I wanted to support him and the movement in general, but I felt uncomfortable doing so during the national anthem.

Also, I wasn't black. But I had been working toward solidarity, so it only made sense that I should support it. So I too stood and saluted with the black power sign.

—

The following evening I was working on a project for voter registration and Splits was sitting backwards on a chair, chatting up some girls, telling them he knew Angela Davis. I had had enough of his antics in the summer over the Upward Bound program and I was not going to get bogged down in his braggadocio now, when we had so much real work to do before the election in November.

Laurie and I had done months of hard work in the spring, interviewing all the likely candidates for voter registration in the area, and the ones worth a second visit were marked as red dots on the map on my desk.

"Why the hell do you get to tell me who's the most likely candidate?" Splits asked.

"Well, Splits, you can sort out your own list. But that would require about 120 hours of work, driving around Wheeling, West Virginia, the hill towns, and writing down the names of those who showed interest in voting. Unfortunately, you only came to some of the planning meetings and you've done no work in the field."

"You sayin' I'm some lazy nigger? I don't need to do no field-work. I *am* the field!"

"I'm saying Laurie and I have canvassed the area and have an idea where to put our energy. If you've done the same, lay it out right here," I said, pointing to my chart covered with red dots. I had cornered him. He had nothing to show us.

Suddenly Splits swung his arm across my desk. Everything flew. "Don't go around tellin' me what to do or who I am."

Laurie spoke calmly. "Splits, I suggest you pick up the things you threw."

Splits didn't move.

Laurie let out a long sigh, as though he didn't want to get involved in Splits's antics, then he moved his desk chair back and its legs scraped along the linoleum. "Splits, don't make me come over there."

Splits didn't move. It was a stalemate.

Laurie stood up and said, "Cathy is not crawling around the floor cleaning up after your rile-up."

"Cathy been on the floor followin' you for all this time, man."

The whole office stopped working. I waited in the resounding silence for someone to say that I had been in this office far longer than Splits.

No one spoke for a full minute. I could hear the oscillating fan turn this way and that.

Just then, a pretty black woman named Andrea, whom I had often seen around the office but had never talked to directly, came in from the hall. She had a heavy New York accent, wore hoop earrings and a bright yellow dashiki, and had a swagger that let everyone know she was way beyond Ohio. She had tried to engage Laurie on many occasions. I had seen him laugh at her jokes but not respond to her flirtation.

Andrea had heard the fracas and she chose her moment well. "We don't need no white woman here. She already walked in and took one man who could have led this movement. She got him led around by the dick. You tell me what army has the enemy within their ranks."

Laurie, who had already started to advance toward Splits, turned

345

to Andrea and said softly but resolutely, as though thirty people were not in the room listening, with more scurrying down the hall to see what was happening, "You're out of line, Andrea. Drop it."

"I ain't droppin' nothin', man. You the one droppin' every black woman in the gutter. You think Splits don't tell me you gots yourself a wife and kids at home. You come down here and skulk around with some white meat and call it workin' for the brotherhood. You got some strange ideas, man. You workin' somethin' but it ain't for the brotherhood."

There was silence in the room. No one moved. They all looked at me. You could hear the Gestetner spewing out its purple-inked propaganda. I waited for the denial that never came from Laurie.

Finally I turned to him and looked into his face. His eyes were lowered to the ground. It was enough to tell me what I needed to know.

I turned around and walked out. I tried to put one foot in front of the other, but I felt like my muscles had a life of their own. My legs were shaking and going off to the side — sort of flying up as though I had lost all voluntary motion. As I crossed the bridge over the Hocking River, I passed one normal-looking couple after another holding hands and smiling at each other. They looked like figures in the Norman Rockwell prints my dad had mounted in the drugstore. I had no thoughts other than that it was imperative I not cry. For some unknown reason, the song "Oklahoma!" came to me, so as I stumbled to the dorm I sang it under my breath to block out all thoughts.

Fortunately, my room was empty. I sat on the bed and tried to light a cigarette, but my hand was shaking so much I could hardly get the match to touch the end of the butt. When I did light it and took a few drags, hot ashes fell on my hip hugger bell-bottoms and singed them. The Doors played on the stereo across the hall, the lyrics wafting into my room:

*When you're strange, faces come out of the rain.*
*When you're strange, no one remembers your name . . .*

I listened to footsteps in the hall. There was part of me that expected *someone* from the movement to come find me after all the hours, the years, of working together. Not that I thought it would be Laurie Coal. He'd know better. I looked out my window at a wasps' nest perched snugly below the eaves. I thought of how much the shape of the nest resembled a human heart, with its bifurcated valves. You could mistake it for a heart but for its potentially painful sting.

When I finished my cigarette, I lit another. I was feeling less numb. Little things began to add up. It's amazing what can rip through a person's mind in a nanosecond. Now I knew why Laurie had taken so long to move on our relationship; why he never wanted to come to my house or have me to his; why he never wanted any public displays of affection; why he had never pressured me about sex. Perhaps that way he could say he wasn't having an affair. Now I understood why he never wanted me to go to his football games. And no wonder he hated questions.

Why had I never suspected it? It was completely beyond my ken. I thought of my father, who would never have left his child or lied about having a wife. It was inconceivable. I thought people that did that were deadbeats, and would have believed that I'd recognize one immediately.

I felt profound humiliation. I had invested so much of myself in him. I had been ostracized in a racist hick town on the West Virginia border for my entire college career — all for him.

As I sat smoking, I thought about my life and how pathetically out of it I was. *What had I been thinking?* There was a pattern here. Each decade, it seemed, I had the need to make an idiot of myself. In the fifties, I was infatuated with a priest who wined and dined me and then had sex with my friend. My delusion of the sixties was Laurie. I had thought we were soulmates who wrote poetry and shared new words. Funny we never shared the words *mistress, dumb honky* or *white trash.*

What was the appropriate word for him? *Casanova* was the only negative sexual word for men, and it wasn't all that negative. *Philanderer* applied, but didn't totally cover it. *Liar* was the one that applied. Plain and simple — Laurie Coal was a liar. Realizing this made my heart pound. Both people I'd been in love with, or had thought I loved, I hadn't really known. I'd made them up to be what I wanted them to be. They were just extensions of how I needed to see myself at the time.

I was even stranger than the stranger described in the Doors' song. Why had other girls liked normal boys who were who they said they were? I had picked a black male poet who was married — with children, no less. Nobody my age was married. I had never, for one moment, considered that he might be.

And who had known? Had everyone? The black and white worlds were almost totally separate, so some black students probably knew but I doubted that any white ones did.

What would my mother say if she knew the whole story of what had happened? She would simply say, *Hold your head up. You couldn't have known. You can only be responsible for yourself. It's over now, so move on.* I looked in the mirror at my tear-stained face and remembered a scene from my childhood. When I was working the cash at the drugstore, I gave a large credit to a man who said he needed the medicine for his children. I found out later that he was an addict who'd stiffed me. The police came in looking for him, and the cosmetician told them that I had been stupid enough to fall for his con. With everyone in the store gathered around, my father told me that it's always better to trust people and be proved wrong than to be hard-hearted. He said, "Life will have some tough lessons for the kind-hearted, but it's worth getting knocked around a bit."

That night, when I found out about Laurie's marriage, I didn't let myself face the fact that I'd lost the first and only man I'd ever loved. I was too overwhelmed with shame to mourn. I woke up at three in the morning — during what Ingmar Bergman called "the hour of the wolf." It's the time of night when you can't shake your nightmares and they intrude into reality. Fears and feelings you've blocked during the day stealthily sneak up on you. I got up, switched on the turntable and played whatever was on. It was Dylan's "Just Like a Woman."

*But what's worse is this pain in here*
*I can't stay in here, ain't it clear that —*

I laid my head on my flowered pillow and sobbed and sobbed so hard the bed shook.

*But you break just like a little girl . . .*

CHAPTER 19

# hooke's law

A few months after I found out the truth about Laurie, I was home for Thanksgiving vacation. When my father heard it was Thanksgiving, he suggested we invite the Pilgrims for a home-cooked meal. In our house, the idea of a home-cooked meal was more delusional than that of visiting Pilgrims. My mother expressed my sentiments exactly when she said, "What on earth are we supposed to do with this holiday?"

Whenever I was home for short vacations, I called up Hengerer's department store and worked in whatever department needed someone. This Thanksgiving was spent in Foundations. If you want to know who is having an affair in your vicinity, get a job selling lingerie. When men buy undergarments, they are never doing so for their wives. Even I figured out that when husbands buy two sets and have them sent to different addresses, all is not monogamous.

But I never blinked an eye when these men perused the teddies. Once you look in the mirror, it is hard to feel moral outrage at those around you. I just wrote down the two addresses, popped the guy's small metal Hengerer's charge card into the huge machine, crunched it and made a triple imprint.

I'd hardened, just as in geology particles pile up and then solidify when certain temperatures and pressures are applied and eventually become sedimentary rock. Laurie Coal had turned up my temperature and then crushed me under his lies. I, like other sedimentary rock, was imbedded with fossils. If someone ever analyzed my formation, they would find fossil remains of Laurie coal and political activism.

I hadn't seen Laurie again and had completely cut my ties to the civil rights movement. I even cancelled all of my father's current events magazines. I took solace in reading fiction.

Laurie had written me a number of letters. The envelopes were thick. I scrawled across the name, *No longer at this address*. It was in a way true; I was not the same Cathy McClure who had been at that address. She had turned into a rock.

One crisp morning the day before Thanksgiving — one of those days right after all the leaves fall and there is still no snow and the world looks embarrassingly bare — I was watching my father while my mother was at master's bridge. While getting ready for my stint in Foundations, I heard a knock at the door. I ran to answer it so my father wouldn't mess things up. Sometimes he gave the paperboy a paper, forgetting it went the other way around.

There stood two Brylcreemed men in dark suits. I assumed at first that they were Jehovah's Witnesses, but one said, "We're from the FBI and would like to see Catherine A. McClure."

I asked to see their proof of identity and they seemed quite annoyed when I took a long time checking their photos.

They shook hands with my father, probably noting his radiated head and the Dymo'd furniture, and were quite respectful when he asked what corner of the earth they hailed from. When they said they were from the FBI, my father didn't miss a beat and said, "Oh, do you know J. Edgar Hoover? He's our vacuum."

They said they had some business with me.

"Well, offer the men a Coke, Cathy," Dad said in his old voice. He would be civil right up to the end.

I said, "Dad, I'm going to close the door, because this has to do with some people I worked with at the welfare office."

"Yes, confidential material," one of the officers said in agreement.

We sat down at the kitchen table with our Cokes. I was surprised they took one at 9:30 a.m. They must have had mothers like mine. They got out a huge file, with my name on it in thick black letters. I couldn't believe it. Then I thought of everything I'd ever done wrong. You can come up with quite a list when you've been to Catholic school and can count your sins. Having the FBI come to my door felt a bit like meeting God at the Pearly Gates. They both have a file on you, it isn't all good, they know how to use it and you're powerless.

They had a strange recording system that took the technical FBI officer ages to set up. It wasn't exactly a tape recorder; it resembled a small record player. They said they were going to record my responses. The record was a kelly green disc that looked like a child's 45 rpm. I was to speak into a microphone. What if I was framed or inadvertently framed myself?

The other FBI man, the interrogator apparently, said, "We will ask you questions and you respond with the shortest but most complete statement of truth."

I was so flipped out I didn't even think of getting a lawyer. I was also thrown off by my father being in the next room.

The interrogator said into the microphone, "Officer 2890 interviewing Catherine A. McClure, November 27, 1968. Officer 4591 is in attendance."

I just listened as though I were not really the person they were speaking about. I held the microphone.

"Did you know Cornell Phipps?"

"No." Please let this be a case of mistaken identity.

"Did you know a Cornell Phipps, also known as Splits?"

*Oh God, no.* The trick was to sound calm. "Yes."

"How many times did you meet with him?"

"I met him about ten times, maybe twenty."

"Were you ever alone with him?"

"No. Well, maybe. I really don't remember."

"Did you ever purchase any illegal substance from him?"

"No."

"Do you have any idea who would want to harm him?"

I thought for a second and realized that when you got right down to it, I couldn't stand him. Also, just before I'd left the room the last time I saw him, Laurie had threatened him: *Don't make me come over there, Splits.*

I said, "No."

"You hesitated. If you want to alter that statement, you may do so now. Otherwise, it is on the record," the FBI interrogator said.

"Splits was annoying — a blowhard. He could be quite witty, but he was ultimately a lot of hot air. But that doesn't mean someone would want to 'harm him.' I believe *harm* is the word you used."

"He was found murdered behind the Student Union Building at the University of Buffalo three weeks ago."

I didn't say anything. I heard the little record spinning slowly in the machine as new grooves were made in the kelly green plastic.

"Did you know of his murder?"

"No. I haven't seen him in a month or two."

"Did you know Lawrence Coal?"

*Oh my God, no. This can't be happening.* My heart was pounding so fast and my every breath stabbed my ribs. I was having trouble speaking.

"Yes."

"What was your relationship to him?"

"We worked together in the SCLC and then SNCC."

"He has hundreds, maybe thousands of letters from you."

To my horror they opened a grey satchel and dumped a huge bag of my letters on the table. Each one was in a plastic bag that was sealed shut like high-fidelity records are sealed when you buy them at the store.

The FBI agent said into the microphone, "Exhibiting letters from Catherine A. McClure to Lawrence Coal to the interviewee."

I was beginning to feel awful stomach cramps, like I had food poisoning. I waited for him to say more.

"When did your working relationship end, or has it?"

"It ended the first week of September."

"Please for the record state the year."

"1968."

"Why did it end?"

"It ended . . ." I hesitated, but realized they probably knew everything so it was best to come clean, "when I found out he was married."

He nodded as though he'd heard that sort of tripe before.

"What was his relationship with Cornell Phipps, alias Splits?"

"I think they were first cousins."

"Could you expand on that?"

"Laurie's mother and Splits's mother were sisters. One lived in Ohio and one in Buffalo."

"Were Coal and Phipps close?"

"They've been close since childhood and spent summers with each other. I got the impression that Laurie was loyal to him and took his ranting with a grain of salt and seemed to allow him excesses since they went back a long way and were related."

"What excesses?"

"He would exaggerate and would spout rhetoric that was not productive to the movement. To be fair, he could also be really funny, almost a stand-up comic."

"What movement?"

"Civil rights."

"Don't you mean black power?"

"It didn't exactly mean that when we started out in the movement together. It was beginning to mean that when I got out of the movement."

"Are you an advocate of black power?"

"I believe that blacks need more political clout to help them achieve equal rights."

He reached into a three-ring binder that must have had about six inches of paper and several file tabs. It appeared to be a photo album with text that explained each picture. Some phrases were covered with white stickers. The stickers all had Classified stamped on them. He flipped to a page and showed me the photograph.

"Please say into the microphone who is in this picture and what is happening in it."

"I am at a basketball game at Ohio University, sitting in the stands next to Laurie Coal." I paused, but then decided to explain completely. "Some people, including Laurie and me, are standing, giving the black power sign in the stands during the national anthem."

"Isn't that the sign of black power?"

"Yes. That's what I just said."

"Ever heard of Stokely Carmichael?"

"Yes."

"Do you know what he stands for?"

"Yes. Black power."

"Do you know how he plans to gain black power?"

"By peaceful means, hopefully, but I guess by violent means if peaceful means are denied."

"You guess? Please clarify."

The technical FBI man interrupted and said, "Sixty-three more seconds."

Suddenly the interrogator changed his line of questioning. "What was Cornell Phipps's, alias Splits's, means of income?"

"I have no idea."

"What was Lawrence Coal's means of income?"

I felt my face heat up. I stuttered, "I d-don't know."

"You don't know? He had a car, gas, money to travel, wine and dine you, and you never saw him work? You have no idea what he did?"

"I knew he went to college and had a football scholarship. He wrote poetry books. That's all I know, or knew."

"How did he support a wife and two children?"

"I don't know."

"After writing hundreds of letters to each other, you never asked what he did to make money?"

"No."

"Did you know that Cornell Phipps was a drug dealer at the University of Buffalo and supplied drugs to other universities across the country?"

"No."

"He sold drugs to students and whoever else wanted to buy them. His job was to sit in the Student Union and sell dope — to wander around the campus and masquerade as a student and sell marijuana and hard drugs like heroin."

"Until someone killed him?" I asked.

Ignoring my question, he flipped to another photo. "Can you

identify these two men?" It was a picture of Splits laughing in a bar.

"That is Splits."

Then he showed me a picture of Laurie in the football field, wearing a black glove and raising his hand in the black power sign from the forty-yard line. He wore his usual serious expression.

I only glanced at the picture, which turned into a blurry impressionist painting as tears clouded my vision. I looked down at the Formica table and managed to choke out, "Lawrence Coal."

The small shiny green record was finished and it made a *bing* sound.

"Should I start another?" the technician asked the interrogator.

He thought for a second and then said, "No, turn it off."

The officer glanced down at the picture of Laurie doing the black power salute and then looked at me and said, "That kind of photo takes you right off the list for the Heisman Trophy. Too bad. He was a man with so much potential in so many areas." He shook his head. "Made some bad choices."

The features on his florid face softened, "Miss McClure, you are a good student, an A student. Your professors think very highly of you. You don't want your record ruined. I read those letters. Some were quite beautiful — mostly about ideas. The letters betray nothing about the drug activities."

I didn't say a word.

While the technician of the duo packed up the equipment, the man who had interrogated me said, "I have a daughter too. You know, nineteen or twenty seems old — but I know how young it can be."

When my mother got home, my father remembered, for some reason, that the officers had been there and said, "We had a pleasant visit from the FBI today."

I wondered why Dad recalled some things and not others. When I researched brain injury, I found that shocking or traumatic events are held in several areas of the brain and take up lots of memory space. The evolutionary reason for this is to prevent dangerous things from being forgotten. I guessed having the FBI at your door qualified as shocking, if not traumatic. Fortunately, the previous week, apparently trying to express that a woman had come collecting for the Catholic Charities, he'd said that Mary Magdalene had been at the door.

So on hearing the FBI had been around, my mother responded, "Well, that's interesting. I'm glad I was playing bridge."

"I wonder why they were here?" my father said.

"Maybe they saw Cathy's copy of *Soul on Ice*," she said, picking up the paperback off the coffee table. "Eldridge Cleaver claimed the FBI was after him." She sat down and opened a *National Geographic*.

He spun around to address me where I sat in the corner. "Is your soul on ice?"

He probably thought it explained why I'd made him a ward of the state and taken away his car keys. He'd called me cold-hearted at the time.

My father, quite agitated, started pacing in the living room. He sensed something was wrong, but he was confused as to what.

"No," he said, "it wasn't about the soul. They mentioned a murder. I was in the garage and heard snippets when I opened the kitchen door to let Willie in."

"A murder? Oh well, one less Christmas gift to buy." She continued paging through the magazine.

"They made a recording of Cathy, actually a 45 record. I saw it through the kitchen window."

"Wow, your big break, Cath. A new version of 'All Shook Up' by Cathy and the FBIs," my mother said.

"Well, we were pretty shook up, weren't we, Cath?" he said.

"Yup," I said, and my mother and I exchanged the "let's let sleeping dogs lie" glances we adopted when we feared my father might, as my mother would say, "get going."

Later that day, June Redkin, a neighbour who was solicitous about my father's illness (fortunately, she had no idea that my father had nearly killed her with the wrong medication) dropped by and asked who had been over in the morning. I believe she was worried it was the undertaker. When you think about it, other than the FBI and undertakers, who wears dark suits and travels in unmarked black cars?

My mother said, "Oh, that was the FBI, investigating a murder. While they were here, they cut a 45 rpm of Cathy singing 'All Shook Up,' so be sure to pay attention to the Top Ten."

Mrs. Redkin gave a conspiratorial nod and went home.

—

When the FBI comes to your door, you know it's time for plan B. If you have no plan B, you are in hot water.

How had this happened? I sat up in the attic of my garage, hoping . . . but Roy never appeared. Even *he* had moved on. I sat clutching my BUTT OUT ashtray for over an hour, just looking at my father's edging machine and his snowblower. They were covered with cobwebs.

I tried to ask myself the tough questions. Like: Had I made up Laurie to be what I needed?

The whole thing was so confusing, to say nothing of terrifying. I felt I was trembling on the inside while my outside stayed still. I had begun to lose weight. I had always been thin, but in the last two months I'd lost about twenty pounds. I simply could not eat. I always felt full.

The combination of Beverly's mental illness, the FBI at my door, the murder of Splits, the SNCC rejection of me and, most of all, Laurie's betrayal unnerved me. The profound humiliation of knowing that others knew about Laurie while I remained in the dark was too much for me. I had to go back to Ohio University, but now I could understand how Hester Prynne felt in *The Scarlet Letter* when she stood in the stockade, wearing the giant red *A* for *Adultery*.

All of these events contributed to what I termed an inner quaking. What I really feared was that I was going mad. I looked up *mental illness* in every psychology book in the library, and all of them said that a history of poor decision-making preceded an actual breakdown. My heart pounded as I read that, for I had left a clearly marked trail of bad decisions.

Even when I read physics to get away from my fears, I was reminded of my fragile mental state. I read Hooke's Law, or the law of elasticity, which states that the extension of a spring is in direct proportion to the load added to it as long as this load does not exceed the elastic limit. I felt this equation perfectly described my mental state. I was holding up to the strain, but my hold was indeed precarious. Just a bit more stress and my spring would be sprung. I would be a Slinky permanently stretched out of shape.

Leora too had been in bad shape after Beverly's breakdown. She'd been extremely loyal to Beverly and had felt traumatized over having shared a drug experience with a friend who never came back to the normal fold. Whenever Leora would visit her, Bev would say, "But we both took the same acid tab. We split it. Why did I lose my mind?"

Leora took a semester off from school and went to France for a break. Her parents never suggested that she work, believing she needed to save her strength for school work. The day she got home for Thanksgiving, I dashed over to see her. While she was unpacking, I locked her bedroom door, turned on the radio so no one would hear, and confided the whole sordid tale of Laurie's marriage and how I found out about it.

She said, "God, what does he do — change into a husband and father in a phone booth?"

"No, he's just a liar."

She was unfailingly charitable to others and never focused on anyone's shortcomings. If she'd been Catholic, Mother Agnese would have called her a saint. After my rant, Leora looked pensive as she folded her purple Peter Max T-shirt.

Then she said, "Maybe he just fell in love with you and then became too frightened of losing you to say he was married."

I looked dubious and said, "Yeah, he made sure everything worked out perfectly for him."

"Love can lock you in a box and leave you no exit sometimes. I mean, why else would he come to see you so many weekends in Ohio and spend every summer here and write you all those letters?"

I still wasn't convinced. "I guess it was more fun to have an affair than to look after your children."

"Affair? It wasn't for sex. You never had sex with him, right? Or did I miss something in Europe? Maybe the wife was a high school sweetheart, got pregnant, and he married her to save her the shame. Then he was stuck."

"Why can't you believe he was just a liar? Have you ever heard the word *liar*?"

"No one ever knows the truth about love or another human being. Every version of reality lends its heart to someone."

I wasn't ready to give up my dark interpretation of Laurie's behaviour. Leora's version would have allowed the pain that I had filed somewhere to flood forward and overwhelm me.

When I told her about the whole FBI "Minutemen" number, she flopped down on her bed, aghast. "Yikes! You had your dad in one room and the FBI in another?"

I assumed she'd tell me not to worry and that it was all over now. Instead, she said, "I have to have a Tab and some Sara Lee cheesecake."

We sat in her stylish living room as we wolfed down our cake. I can still hear the silence as the moments ticked by with only the intermittent hissing of the humidifier spraying in the greenhouse. I was surprised that Leora had not yet said anything reassuring about what had happened. I had waited for her to come home from Europe to tell me things would be fine. She'd always done that before.

When she spoke, my heart sank.

She said, "This is serious. The odds are that some weird things will happen in life, but this is greater than the odds."

I owned up to feeling like I might be going over the edge. I was on the precipice and could feel the wind coming from behind me. The weight loss, the inability to concentrate, the wolf that woke me at three in the morning and howled that I was going insane — it was all terrifying me. I had no way to judge people. So many around me had lied, been murdered or gone mad. Why? Was it a sign that I was next? I was having trouble focusing on what Leora was saying and caught only the last little bit.

"The FBI is not the black lawn jockeys, or the big doughnut caper. No one has the FBI on their tail unless there is bad shit involved."

We didn't usually use words like *bad shit*.

Tears stung my eyes. "Well, the FBI is not exactly for political change, you know."

"Cathy, it doesn't matter what the FBI stands for politically! Splits is as dead as a doornail. He wasn't killed because the FBI was worried about him taking over the government. He was not a political threat. So why was he killed? What were they involved in? If Laurie could lie about being married, what else did he lie about? How did he make a living? The FBI must have been stunned that you hadn't even thought of it."

"I don't think dumb honkies stun them, judging from what I've seen."

Rarely a dominant person, Leora took hold of my shoulders then and said, "You *have* to get rid of everything that had to do with Laurie. If you are ever called as a witness, you don't want that stuff subpoenaed."

I looked at her blankly.

She said, "I'm serious."

Leora took charge and made me go home right away to get all

of Laurie's letters to me and all of the pictures and memorabilia I'd collected during our relationship. I piled the legal boxes full of letters in the car and drove back to Leora's house. We went out to her backyard and burned them in the fireplace in the pool cabana. It took a grinding few hours to get rid of it all. Then we buried the ashes under the cabana. We told her parents we were doing a "sweat facial" — whatever that was.

After we dealt with what Leora termed the "secret service schmozzle," we went to Gleason's Restaurant. We were too keyed up to go in, so we went to the car-hop service in the back. The waitress skated out in her short red skirt and red striped shirt with the little Gleason's logo: a man carrying a tray piled high with burgers, his feet speeding in cartoon circles underneath him. The waitresses were all blonde with teased hair, the Hooters of yesteryear.

As the waitress fastened our tray to the window of Leora's father's maroon Mustang, Leora turned to me and said, "The FBI still have all of your letters to Laurie and their own set of pictures. You should think about getting out of the country for at least a year."

"Please spare me," I said, looking at the Hi-burger I couldn't eat.

"Hear me out on this. The FBI has to squelch this black power thing. It's gotten too big. That's their job. They will not hesitate to bulldoze you. Your gullibility is not their problem. Now do I have your attention?"

I nodded, numb with fear.

"Remember last year, or was it the year before, you wrote that paper on Mickey Mouse, Milne, Milton or whomever, and your professor loved it?"

"Milton."

"Didn't he say you could transfer to Oxford? And that he had contacts there? You hardly entertained the idea because you wanted to stay in Ohio because Laurie was there."

"Oh yeah, I remember. What a bad decision that was." Then I thought for a second. "But England. It's full of the English."

"At least they speak the language, and you'll get away from the FBI. I hate to tell you this, but they could come back. There may be a trial. There will have to be witnesses and evidence."

"With my luck the M-5 will hunt me down."

"The M-5 is a highway. You mean the MI5."

We started laughing and then the mention of Oxford reminded us of the Milton-on-the-green-pill story, which made us laugh harder. It had happened only a year ago. I felt like it had occurred when I was so much younger — back when I thought I had the world by the tail and was convinced I knew how society could be made better.

—

A month later I got on a plane and waved to my parents on the runway. I looked out my little window, which framed them in a cramped proscenium. There stood my brave mother holding my father's hand.

I had been reluctant to go away with my father so sick, but recently his tumour seemed stable. He was stuck in "no man's land," as his doctor put it. He'd lost some frontal lobe, some memory, some intellectual functioning, but his autonomic system hadn't yet been hit. And even with all the chemo and radiation he'd had, he never complained.

Nor did my mother, and she'd had the worst of the situation by far. Dad would constantly forget what was happening. She had to care for him all day long, never knowing what he would do next. Yet she insisted that I go to England and said she would call me if, and when, he declined. She said that if he were in his right mind he would want me to go too. "He won't miss you. He'll just think you're gone for a minute."

I wanted to cry out, *But what about you, Mother?* What about the sweet, kind, wonderful woman who said she loved her husband "as much as Myrna Loy loved William Powell in *The Thin Man*"?

As I waved, tears welled in my eyes and I wished I could trade places with her. *She* was the one who had always wanted to travel. She'd spent a lifetime reading *National Geographic* and writing notecards on various destinations. Our whole basement was full of her travel maps, TripTiks highlighted in emerald green with untaken journeys. My father hadn't wanted to travel; he said who knew how many parasites people brought back from exotic places like England. She would smile and agree that travel could be risky, just as he would smile when she told him that she could never cook. They accommodated each other without complaint.

My mother had sacrificed her real self, all to appear like a normal woman, which in the 1950s was a married woman with children. It wasn't that she didn't love my father or me. You can love someone and not like the job description. (She loved math, but not teaching it.) You can love your family but not like the role of wife or mother. She would always be one of those women who produced no fanfare. Yet, like so many mothers in history, she made the impossibly difficult job of being a mother appear easy. She never made a ripple in the history of mankind, but she made an incalculable difference in my life.

Through ridiculous high school hijinks, the black lawn jockeys, my refusal to do school work, the calls from the guidance centre, the fire at the doughnut shop, she was always behind me, never wavering in her belief in me. She managed to have such an impact on me that two words, *I'm surprised,* made me modify my indolent behaviour at the welfare office within twenty-four hours. I knew what *I'm surprised* meant. When I didn't work hard at a job I was getting paid for, I was not living up to her expectations of the person she knew me to be. There were no lectures or punishments; there was no removal of privileges. I pulled up my socks because I never, ever wanted to hurt or disappointment her.

When my life became darker, I didn't involve her. She had enough to deal with. Yet even when I felt I was blindly heading down that dark tunnel of political chicanery, infidelity, drugs and murder, she was always leading me to the light. When I was humiliated by Laurie, I heard an inner voice that was hers telling me that I was only acting on what I knew. Believing what others tell you is not a crime. There was no point in self-recrimination. It was best to dust yourself off and head into a new day. The voice inside you is your parents' and you are lucky if it is a supportive one.

I don't know how we grow up, but we do. We lose so much along the way, but the upside is we manage to pick up some tricks to avoid complete meltdowns. A few betrayals and our naïveté is painfully scaled away, and gradually we manage to acquire a certain amount of wisdom. No one is born wise. You have to get burned before you're wary of others. Loss of innocence is really only a realization that the world has set traps. Life is like one of those old *Sheena, Queen of the Jungle* movies that I loved on Saturday morning TV when I was a kid. One minute you're exploring the jungle, and the next you're caught in a tiger trap and hanging from a rope at the top of a tree.

We learn to step gingerly.

—

As time passed I realized that Laurie wasn't just a liar. And I wasn't just gullible. We were two people who cared for each other in fraught circumstances. There was no point in looking for "the culprit" or wasting time on blame. Nevertheless, it took several years before I'd grown up enough to figure that out.

Forty years later, in an effort to find out what became of Laurie, I searched everywhere for his whereabouts. I couldn't find evidence that he'd graduated, nor did he appear in any pro-football roster. He was not on the Internet. He was no longer being published in any poetry magazines. I suspected he might have gone to law school but could not find him in any state bar. After a year of dead ends, I called a guy I knew from high school who was a private detective in Kansas City. He said the first thing you do when looking for a young black male is to check the death records. It didn't take long for me to find Laurie's.

He had been found dead at the age of thirty-six, having fallen in his driveway. He apparently hit his head and suffered a subdural hemorrhage. The death was declared accidental, according to the autopsy report. He was divorced at the time, lived alone and suffered from alcoholism. He weighed 136 pounds. He wasn't found until two days after his fall.

—

First loves come and go. We've all had them. The real tragedy of my life wasn't Laurie's betrayal, I would realize only later. It was that I had been trapped in teenage rage at the same time that my father was losing his mind, and that I would never be able to make amends. As usual, I would rely on Roy's judgment. In my memory I would have to cherish the best times of my relationship with my father, and know that those were our true feelings. The rest, as Roy once said, "was just interference."

CHAPTER 20

# a real pip

My mother called me in February, the second month I was at

Oxford, to say that my father was starting to breathe with a hor-

ribly loud rattle. She said it sounded as though he'd swallowed a

maraca. I called Dr. Zukas, who said my father was now breathing

in a pattern called Cheyne-Stokes, which occurs when someone is dying. The doctor assumed that the tumour had hit his autonomic nervous centre and that he "could no longer sustain life without assistance." The doctor thought he had only a matter of hours.

When I arrived home from England thirty-six hours later, I went right from the airport to his hospital room, to find that his breathing was indeed louder than a frightened rattlesnake's.

My mother, who appeared to be calm, said, "Do you believe how loud that is?" as though the noise was that of an annoying lawn mower and not the husband she had always adored. "I have asked for Father McMahon to come down and give him last rites."

I had been entranced by all kinds of death scenes in my compulsive reading of Victorian literature. I was old enough to know that this was the last chance to say goodbye, and I was hoping to wipe the slate clean with a heartfelt sign-off.

I had always hated public displays of sentiment. I would cringe when Johnny Carson kissed his guests hello on *The Tonight Show.* If someone was moving away, I would make up excuses not to go to their farewell party, for fear that I would have to embrace the person and say that they'd meant something to me. My mother said that when I went to kindergarten, all the tykes would hug their mothers goodbye; to her embarrassment, I would only shake hands.

I waited until my mother was in the hall talking to the priest. I went to my dad's bed in intensive care and took his black and blue hand, which had been pricked with so many IV needles the veins were riddled with bruises. He looked at me over the top of his green oxygen mask with his piercing blue eyes. His once muscular tennis arm, which in his college years had made him Buffalo's tennis champion, now looked like a strip of yellow blanket trim lying on the bed.

As he nodded between gasps, I squeezed his hand. "Dad, there is so much I have never said." I was so nervous expressing these words of closeness that I could feel rings of perspiration developing under my arms.

He rasped through staggering breaths, "If . . . anyone . . . has . . . said . . . enough . . . it . . . is . . . you."

"Seriously, Dad, we have to talk. I've never told you I loved you — ever."

He let out a long rattle. His old voice returned and he barked, "I am fighting for my life here. I'm busy. I don't have time to do things your way. My job is to stay alive. Besides, if it's death, it's mine — not yours." He started fluttering his hands.

The nurse stepped up. Patients flutter their hands when they want to be alone, she told me. "He's agitated. I think you should go now so we can settle him down."

He didn't die that time. In fact, he would drift in and out of Cheyne-Stokes several times, and even return home.

—

On the way back from the hospital that evening, as we pulled into Arby's takeout, I told my mother what he'd said. She parked the car and looked over at me. She explained again that at some level he still knew that I was behind taking his car keys and his money. Consciously he didn't remember it, but she thought it had registered. She added, "But I'm glad he has the chance to be the boss of his own death. That's all he has left."

"You're right — it is his death."

While my mother and I ate our shaved roast beef sandwiches, she said, "Death scenes are overrated. They are just a moment in time. You have spent more time together than any father and daughter. You worked side by side in the store for years. He knows you love him. Who cares what is said? People can say anything. It's just words."

As usual, my mother's words were simple, soothing and true.

＿＿

When we got home, I went up to the attic in the garage. I didn't expect Roy to come — I knew I was too old for that. I wanted to sit alone in the cold for a while and have a cigarette.

I sat there rocking in the wicker porch rocker, holding the BUTT OUT ashtray and thinking how life was short and so tawdry. First you go to crappy school, and then you get married and have kids and everything else that entails; you get a crappy job, a crappier house, have your kid treat you like crap, your wife feels like crap but tries unsuccessfully to cover it up as she lies on the crappy couch. You smoke two packs of crappy cigarettes a day and then you die many years before your crappy retirement.

When was the good part for my dad? For sure it was before I ever came along. The part he relived right after he got his tumour was his glory college days. I thought he also enjoyed his time as a pharmacist when Roy was still there. But memory is a funny thing — maybe because I was happy then, I thought he was as well.

I had an unsettling epiphany. The best part of my life might be right now — the years I was living. All this time I had been waiting for life to start. I thought of the girl in Thornton Wilder's play *Our Town,* which we had performed in high school. She died and then observed the living while in her grave. When she saw life from the hereafter, she realized that the best parts of her life were the small moments of her childhood and teenage years. There were no huge moments.

Looking out the window at the prism of ice, it came to me that if I was going to have a future, I sure as hell better start working on it now.

—

Three months later, in the spring, I came home once more from Oxford when my father was rehospitalized with Cheyne-Stokes. Physical changes were predictable, and although they dismayed my mother, I wasn't as fazed by them. When I was a kid, I'd delivered medicine for years to the chronically ill and dying, so I was used to the sight of physical deterioration. But my father's mental changes were unnerving. Later I understood why the unconscious was discovered by doctors studying people with degenerating frontal lobes: when those lobes are gone, the layers of civilization are peeled away and the instincts push forward.

My dad had been a "gentleman" in the 1950s and "uptight" in the 1960s and would have been "straight" in the 1970s, "buttoned down" in the 1980s and "a suit" in the 1990s. He was one of those men who shined his shoes every night and kept his feelings in check. The emotions that came out were as polished as his shoes. He never said anything untoward. Even when the employees at work would comment on a prostitute, or, as my father referred to them, "a woman of the night," who came into the store for antibiotics, he never treated them differently from the way he treated his other customers. He was polite, while Irene, the cosmetician, was frosty. Although he never criticized Roy and the others who flirted and kidded around, Dad never joined in. His behaviour, while fun and outgoing, was always very proper. He was the only child of a strict math-teacher mother who had high expectations for him morally, religiously and educationally, and he continued to live by these standards long after she'd died. He had built up a storehouse of perfect responses and always knew the right thing to say in any situation.

The tumour had slowly stripped those niceties away, until he said exactly what he felt, which must have been a release for him.

Once, my mother and I were sitting in his hospital room when a nurse walked in.

My father said, "Well, well, Dorothy Koza, how *do you do*?"

The nurse looked at him at first without understanding, and then said, "Oh, I'm fine," and set his white paper cup of chemo-therapy cocktail on the bedside table.

"Dorothy, you don't look a day older."

"I'm Lucinda, the RN on this floor."

"Doesn't she look exactly like Dorothy Koza, Janet?"

"No," my mother said.

"They both sashay the same way when they walk. Maybe they're sisters."

"I do have five sisters. Is Dorothy black?"

"No."

"Well, I am," Lucinda said.

My father didn't see this as a deterrent, and said, "Janet, doesn't she fill a room just like Dorothy — the way no one else ever could?"

"Yes, Lucinda is very beautiful and so was Dorothy Koza," my mother said. "She was homecoming queen and you were king. I remember I read about it in the university newspaper. You looked really handsome in that picture. I cut it out and kept it in my cal-culus book as a bookmark for a whole year."

My father smiled at Lucinda and said, "If I were on the committee, I'd make you homecoming queen."

"That sure would be nice," she said, reading his chart.

He reached out and touched her hand as she increased his IV drip rate. He said in a conspiratorial voice, "Let me see what I can do."

It wasn't so much what he said, but the flirtatious tone that was startling — coming from him.

When the three of us were alone again, my mother and I looked at each other as if to say, *Oh my God — now this?*

He must have sensed the tension in the room, because he stared at us and said, "What's wrong?"

"Nothing," my mother said, smiling stiffly.

"Did I say something wrong?"

"No. I'm just surprised you remember Dorothy Koza so vividly."

"Dorothy was a real party girl." He smiled a broad smile I hadn't seen in years. "I can see a trip to Crystal Beach — kissing on the Caterpillar ride. I can still smell that canvas cover. Why, I can't remember such a good time!"

"Sounds like fun" was all my mother managed to choke out.

I felt her pain so acutely that I couldn't help asking, "I'll bet you had fun with your wife, Janet Mahar?"

He smiled lovingly at my mother as though he hadn't seen her in many years and said, "We sure did. Remember the night before we thought I was going to war — what we did? Wow, after that I was glad I didn't get called so we could keep it up." Then he laughed and reached for her hand.

She smiled back, almost shyly, and took his hand. She rubbed her other hand over his head.

"It was sad when the baby died, wasn't it?" he said, gazing into my mom's eyes.

Baby? What baby?

"You recovered, Jim. I never really got my strength back."

"We never mentioned it," he said.

"No."

"He was just going to stand up."

"He'd already pulled himself up."

"He liked it when I played milkman with him on my back."

"Tommy loved that."

My mother laughed at the memory. I had never seen such unreserved joy on her face.

I slipped out of the room.

———

Sometimes family taboos are established without words ever being used. You can sense what is off limits. I knew that I could never ask my mother what had happened to the baby — the brother — that I hadn't known existed.

I discovered later, from my own research, that when they were newlyweds my parents lived in a small apartment in Buffalo. My father was just starting out in his first job at the Upjohn Drug Company. They had a baby boy twelve months after their marriage and they named him Thomas Robert McClure. He died thirteen months later. The death certificate read, "Unknown causes."

One month after the death, they moved to Lewiston and started a new life. They did not have another child for fifteen years.

Why had I not known this? It explained so much that had happened: why Mom didn't invest in being a traditional mother; why she was often reluctant to enter the world and fully participate in it. She didn't want to enter the fray again. She couldn't risk another loss. She would always love me, but she kept her distance. It explained my father's behaviour as well. He was always guarding her, protecting her from pain. And I had picked up on the unwritten rule of our home: that my mother must never be hurt. She was fragile. It was our job to protect her, and we both did it with ferocity.

Forty years later, when I asked people in Lewiston, no one knew about the baby. I could only find one of my mother's single college friends from Buffalo, Edith, who had ever seen the baby. She said that one morning my mother walked into his nursery and found him dead in his crib. No one ever knew how he died. My father called Edith and told her the baby was dead; he asked if she would kindly not visit for several months, and when she did if she would please not mention the child.

—

After my sojourn in England, I was home at the end of 1969, preparing to student teach in Cleveland. I was dreading it, but I had promised my father I would get a teaching degree, so I had little choice. In a few days I would head into Cleveland to an inner-city area called Hough that was experiencing rioting and fires. All teachers had to have police escorts from the parking lot to the school.

I was about to spend my last night at Brunner's Tavern with my friends before shipping out for what would be a rough mission. I was wearing a pair of pants I'd brought home from England that were much like the ones I'd seen Jimi Hendrix wear at a concert in London. They were a facsimile of the American flag. I'd found them in a head shop on Carnaby Street and had spent a lot of my hard-earned money on them.

I walked through the living room on my way out, braless, with Band-Aids to cover my nipples, wearing a tie-dyed T-shirt and the new American flag pants.

My father's brain was unpredictable. He had lost most contact with reality, but occasionally, when something was important to him, he could spring to life and take me by surprise.

He looked up from his paper, eyed my outfit and said, "What are those?"

I turned in a circle and he got a full gander of my ensemble. My mother was sitting on the couch, reading *Ordeal by Innocence,* an old Agatha Christie, and didn't look up.

Dad's old voice returned, the authoritative one that rarely surfaced, but when it did, people listened. "No one who lives under my roof will desecrate the American flag. Remove those pants at once and never wear them again."

My mother looked up then. He had uttered a coherent sentence, and he was even in the right time frame. He hadn't done this in a long time.

"Relax," I said as I moved toward the door, assuming he would soon forget what he'd said and begin reading the newspaper again. He always read the same page.

He sprang up and barred the front door, so I headed for the back. Despite his frail body, he caught up with me.

He raised his voice and said, "The American flag is not a rag or a joke. It is a symbol of true democracy. No one who lives on my dime will desecrate it. The game stops here, young lady."

He looked steely-eyed and angry. In fact, his expression was one I'd seen just once before, at the time of the Donny Donnybrook.

He said, "I may not hold keys to my car, but I am not Benedict Arnold."

I went to my room, took off the pants, put on jeans and re-emerged. I passed him in the living room going out, but he kept his nose in the paper.

When I got home that morning at one-thirty, he was still up in the same chair, reading the same page of the paper. In my room I found the American flag pants cut into three-by-five-inch patches of material and placed neatly in a pile on my bed.

I yelled, from behind my closed and locked door, "If you believe in democracy so much, why have you violated my right to wear what I want?"

"Tough tacos," he said, and went back to not really reading the paper.

Tough tacos? I had never heard of a taco. Where had that come from?

He said no more about it, but for two days he called me Dolly Madison, as though it were my real name.

—

When I returned home from student teaching six months later, I visited him in the hospital, where he now spent most of his time, and I was distraught by his decline. He was covered with a blanket and all I could see was his head. He was so emaciated that I could make out his jaw and his facial bones. His skin was so thin I could see the tiny capillaries all over his face and denuded head. He looked like he was wearing a hairnet of blue thread.

I said, "So, hi, big guy. How're you doing?"

"Fine, and you?"

"Good." To make conversation I thought I'd bring up high

jumping because it had occurred at a time of our lives when we were still close. "I attempted to do some high jumping in England just for fun, but I never got up to my old height."

"My daughter was a high jumper. She did so well as a kid — even went to the state championships."

The man in the bed next to him looked over at me and shook his head in sympathy, knowing how I must be feeling. I gave him a sign that it was okay, and that he should not correct my dad. What was the point? It would only hurt him.

Dad didn't know who I was. I'd been erased, consumed by cancerous cells. He had some memories of me as a little girl, but he didn't recognize me as an adult.

Inside I didn't feel like an adult. I felt lost. I was still a kid who needed her dad. I thought of all the times we had gone to work together as the dawn broke over the falls. All the breakfasts we'd shared. He'd called me his "right hand man." I wanted to go over to the bed and shake him and cry on his shoulder and say, *Dad, it's me — Peaches, the daughter you love. Remember me. Please.*

I turned my back to him and went to stare out the window at the ghetto below. Burned mattresses lay by the curbs of rooming houses. At the corner I saw a street sign that said PEACH STREET. I felt tears threatening, but willed them not to spill down my cheeks. I dried my eyes and swallowed hard so as not to cry, then turned around.

He smiled at me and said, "Where do you hail from?"

I hesitated, and then said, "Oxford."

"Long way from home."

"Very long." To keep from sobbing, I gulped again and said, "So tell me about your daughter, the high jumper."

"Well, let's see. She's bossy, that's for sure."

My heart sank. The man who shared his room looked over with sympathy in his eyes. My dad's face swam in front of me as my eyes filled. "There must have been something good about her."

"She was a real pip," he chuckled. Then he said, "I'm tired. I'm going to Kalamazoo," closed his eyes and fell asleep.

A pip? What the hell was a *pip?*

When I got home, I looked the word up in the dictionary. It said, "Pip — also called pipperoo. Informal. Someone or something wonderful: 'Last night's party was a pip.'"

Another meaning was "facetious." Another was "feeling of irritation or annoyance."

In the library I found a historical dictionary of American slang, which said that in the 1920s, *pip* meant something excellent, outstanding. Example: "Gwendolyn always pays the bill; she's a pip." In the 1950s it meant a difficult person. Example: "Hilda is quite a pip; she likes to do things her way."

He had chosen a perfectly enigmatic term. I guess we all know that our parents love us, but not many of us know what they actually think of us.

—

Many years later, after my father's death, an old friend of his came up to me after I'd given a talk in California on Darwin's theory in *The Descent of Man.* This man had studied pharmacy with my father at the University of Buffalo, and had gone on to medical school and moved to San Francisco. That night we went out for a drink.

He told me he hadn't seen my father in years but had heard he died young. He said, "I remember how he could dance. He could do the swing and was one of the best white men I've ever seen do the Lindy. When we were about twenty-five or twenty-six, we used to dance till the sun came up. He could really cut a rug. Why, I even remember the number he was dancing to when he won the big contest the night the Glenn Miller band was in town." He chuckled and sang:

*Oh what a gal, a real pipperoo;*
*I'll make my bid*
*For the freckle face kid,*
*I'm hurrin' to,*
*I'm goin' to Michigan to see the*
*Sweetest gal in Kalamazoo–zoo–zoo–zoo, zoo Kalamazoo!*

When my father was diagnosed, he still had his long-term memory, but as the cancer grew it chomped through his short-term memory bite by bite. And when it had fully devoured that, it began gnawing into his past. In his last years, he could only remember the first twenty years of his life. Toward the end, he couldn't remember anything, and in his final year he forgot how to walk.

Six years after his diagnosis, the doctors said they had no idea how he had lived so long. One radiologist showed me his X-rays and said he must be "living on fumes," because there were so few brain cells left. He said to me, "I would have given him six months. Will to live can never be measured in an X-ray or through a biopsy."

One day, when my mother and I were sitting in my father's hospital room, the chief of the department came in with a group of resident oncologists. The doctor stood at the foot of my father's bed, exhibiting my father's chart, and softly said to the residents, "Whenever you give a life expectancy to a family, remember that there are tough hombres who defy the bell curve. Although this man's brain was an empty honeycomb last year, while in year five with his tumour, he could still walk and talk — until about two months ago, when he slowed down. He must be in pain, yet he has never admitted it when asked and he has never taken any morphine when it was offered."

He stepped up to my father's bed and, bending down to his ear, asked in a loud, cheerful voice for the sake of the residents, "Mr. McClure, you are holding on for a long time."

My father nodded and tried to smile.

"Who are you holding on for?"

My father said, "Janet."

The doctor looked at the residents and said, "Janet is his wife, sitting there in the corner." He looked touched and said to my mother, "Quite a love story."

— —

Eight months later I came home from Canada, where I was now a graduate student at the University of Toronto. It was the end of the sixth year of my father's tumour and he was on a respirator. He had no bodily functions left and received nourishment through an IV drip. He could no longer even breathe on his own. He had shingles, thrush, an impacted bowel, a kidney infection and bed sores, but still he refused to die. My mother had a note on the chart that said, "Do not resuscitate."

The doctor said that they'd been waiting for me to arrive to decide what to do. A devout Catholic, my mother believed that it was God's decision and not ours to make, though she hoped God would take him soon to end his misery. The doctor had never had anyone live so long with a similar tumour, he said. Since my father couldn't talk, we had no idea if he was in pain.

I said we should take him off life support. My mother wanted nothing to do with it. I said I would take full responsibility for the action. I said, "If God meets us at the Pearly Gates, I will raise my hand and yell out, *I ended my father's life — not my mother!*"

She said, "I hope he knows your voice."

—

The next morning my mother said she was staying home to think and I should go to the hospital on my own and do whatever I thought best. She did not want to discuss it further.

My unconscious father was unplugged in my presence and died fifteen minutes later, and then I called my mother.

While I waited for her to arrive, I saw his body slowly expel the air that had been forced into him. As his chest sank and his mouth went slack, he almost appeared to be smiling. I thought he looked as contented as he had behind the prescription counter at McClure's Drugs back in the 1950s, when I would load the candy counter and he would glance up from mixing some unguent, grin and say, *Great work, Peaches.*

## ACKNOWLEDGMENTS

First I would like to thank all the people in the book who allowed themselves to be made into characters in these pages based on my idiosyncratic imagination. It was extremely kind of them and I am particularly indebted to Louise Greenberg and her parents. Once a best friend, always a best friend.

My parents, Janet and Jim McClure, deserve a special mention. I don't know if acknowledgments are for the dead as well as the living, but if they're listening in heaven, which is undoubtedly where they reside, I want to do something I never did when we three inhabited the earth — say thank you for being the best parents a child could ever imagine. None of the adventures in this book could have transpired if they hadn't encouraged their strange only child to be herself at all costs.

Thanks to my close friends Jon Redfern, Linda Kahn and Janet Somerville, who read various drafts of the manuscript. They helped me mould and shape the book for untold hours. You have them to thank for cutting it nearly in half. Otherwise, you could be reading *War and Peace Goes to Buffalo*. If it weren't for Anna Koven telling me that I could become a writer at the advanced age of fifty, I'd still be toiling as a psychologist. Thanks go to Damiano Pietropaolo for help with the Italian translation and my late father-in-law, Chaim Gildiner, for help with the Yiddish. Thanks to Anita Lauer for creative input and Lisa Fraser for ongoing great work on my website and newsletter. I'd also like to thank Sue Avner for all the detective work. And finally, thanks to my agent, Dean Cooke, for his guidance.

Louise Dennys at Knopf Canada has supervised a great team of experts. Allyson Latta is an amazing copyeditor. She could find a missing tooth filling in *Where's Waldo*. Also I would like to express my gratitude to my editor, Angelika Glover. Now with a bit of distance I am able to see that although she wasn't even born in the sixties, her unerring editorial skills triumphed. She also deserves a Nobel Peace Prize for getting through an entire edit without one altercation. They said it couldn't be done. If you have ever wondered about what has happened to the work ethic, you have never met Angelika. And even though Adria Iwasutiak also wasn't born in the sixties, she knows how to rock and roll.

For this new edition of *After the Falls* I would like to thank my old friend Jack David, the co-publisher of ECW Press. Jack keeps popping up in my life when I most need him and offers his quiet, kind, always sage advice. Jack, let's hope we live long enough to see a three-volume boxed set together. Kudos to Tania Craan and Rachel Ironstone, who tweaked the cover to highlight the civil rights theme. And finally, Crissy Calhoun, thanks for the proofread.

I would like to thank my three sons, Jamey, David and Sam, for hearing me out. Finally, I would like to thank my husband, Michael Gildiner, for supporting me during this venture and assuring me daily that there are more than a few people who indeed remember the likes of *Mr. Magoo* and *Ramar of the Jungle* and other icons from the fifties and sixties.

Grateful acknowledgment is made to the following sources for permission to reprint from previously published material.

## Get the eBook FREE!

At ECW Press, we want you to enjoy this book in whatever format you like, whenever you like. Leave your print book at home and take the eBook to go! Purchase the print edition and receive the eBook free. Just send an email to ebook@ecwpress.com and include:
- the book title
- the name of the store where you purchased it
- your receipt number
- your preference of file type: PDF or ePub?

A real person will respond to your email with your eBook attached. Thank you for supporting an independently owned Canadian publisher with your purchase!